THE POTENTIAL OF
MODERN DISCOURSE

Advances in Semiotics

Thomas A. Sebeok, General Editor

THE POTENTIAL OF MODERN DISCOURSE

Musil, Peirce, and Perturbation

MARIKE FINLAY

INDIANA UNIVERSITY PRESS

Bloomington and Indianapolis

Manufactured in the United States of America

Library of Congress Cataloging-in-Publication Data

Finlay, Marike.
The potential of nodern discourse: Musil, Peirce, and
perturbation / Marike Finlay.
p.   cm. — (Advances in semiotics)
Includes bibliographical references.
ISBN 0-253-32279-0
1. Discourse analysis.   2. Knowledge, Theory of.   3. Semiotics.
I. Title.   II. Series.
P302.F54   1990
302.2—dc20   89-45413
                                                            CIP

1 2 3 4 5 94 93 92 91 90

For my teachers:
Vivian Schulman, Claude Treil, Gary Retzleff,
Matei Calinescu, Wladimir Krysinski, Timothy Reiss,
Walter Moser, Michel Foucault, Louis Marin,
François Lyotard,
Michel Serres, Jürgen Habermas
It is hard to tell where their ideas end and mine begin.

To be Socratic is to feign ignorance. To be modern is to be ignorant. (Musil, "Sketch of a Writer")

The full meaning of the adage *Humanum est errare*, they have never waked up to. In those sciences of measurement that are least subject to error—meteorology, geology, and metrical astronomy—no man of self-respect ever now states his result, without affixing to it its *probable error*: and if this practice is not followed in other sciences it is because in those the probable errors are too vast to be estimated. (Peirce, "On Four Incapacities")

. . . every research process moves in such a circle between theory formation and a precise specification of the object domain. (Habermas, *Communication and the Evolution of Society*)

Alice thought she had never seen such a curious croquet-ground in her life: it was all ridges and furrows: the croquet balls were live hedgehogs, and the mallets live flamingoes, and the soldiers had to double themselves up to stand on their hands and feet, to make the arches.

The chief difficulty Alice found at first was in managing her flamingo: she succeeded in getting its body tucked away, comfortably enough, under her arm, with its legs hanging down, but generally, just as she had got its neck nicely straightened out, and was going to give the hedgehog a blow with its head, it *would* twist itself round, and look up in her face, with such a puzzled expression that she could not help bursting out laughing and, when she had got its head down, and was going to begin again it was very provoking to find that the hedgehog had unrolled itself, and was in the act of crawling away; besides all this, there was generally a ridge or a furrow in the way wherever she wanted to send the hedgehog to, and, as the doubled-up soldiers were always getting up and walking off to other parts of the ground, Alice soon came to the conclusion that it was a very difficult game indeed.

The players all played at once, without waiting for turns, quarrelling all the while, and fighting for the hedgehogs; and in a very short time the Queen was in a furious passion, and went stamping about, and shouting, "Off with her head" about once a minute. (Lewis Carrol, *Alice's Adventures in Wonderland*)

CONTENTS

CONCLUSION: Praxis
Abduction in Human Interest

THE POTENTIAL OF
MODERN DISCOURSE

INTRODUCTION
EPISTEMIC CROQUET

> "The problems appear unmodern. The prob-
> lems of the present day are unmodern!"
> (DMoE, 1938)

0.0 The Potential of Modern Discourse

Does modern discourse have within it the potential to address present-day unmodern problems or must it give way to some post-modern alternative? *The Potential of Modern Discourse* begins with the hypothesis which it subsequently seeks to substantiate that the modern project is not yet finished with. In the light of the current "querrelle entre les Anciens et les Modernes," read between the moderns and the postmoderns, this is a risky point of departure. Writing by way of refutation of François Lyotard's *La Condition post-moderne*, Jürgen Habermas paraphrases the postmodern claim that we have witnessed the end of the great narratives of history, indeed the end of the ontology of this subject, and the possibility of meaning and of history altogether.

> "Postmodernism definitely presents itself as *Antimodernity*." This state-
> ment describes an emotional current of our times which has penetrated all
> spheres of intellectual life. It has placed on the agenda theories of post-
> enlightenment, postmodernity, even of post-history.[1]

Modernist formalism has often been accused of divorcing ethics from discourses of aesthetics and now postmodernism,[2] that is, a certain current of it, theorizes and practices the end of linking discourses of knowledge with ethics of legitimation of practice, indeed the only "ethical" discourse being the one which plays on the surfaces of the signifiers or traces of language. In this study we wish to hold firmly onto the modern project of undoing the split between ethics and discourse, aesthetic or scientific. In this sense the very transdisciplinarity of this work which makes major leaps from the novel through political theory and philosophy of language to physics is making the statement that discourse is not ontologically distinct from ethics and politics.[3]

1

All are textual forms of world transforming and world constituting practices. If Michel Serres' *Northwest Passage*, and Prigogine and Stengers' *Nouvelle Alliance*[4] are considered to be postmodern incidences of the transgression of disciplinary boundaries, we can only remind the reader that such tendencies existed "in potentia" in the Romantics. Musil was soldier, physicist, and novelist, and Peirce posited semiotics as an interdisciplinary approach to all studies.

The Potential of Modern Discourse is most certainly "post-structuralist"; however, it would not be accurate to label it "deconstructionist" or "postmodern" in that, while cognizant of and constantly referring to the war on totality, a nihilism of values, the glorification of disorganization and random mapping, it does not content itself with pure stochastics, the dispersion of the subject, and the end of ordering history altogether. It seeks to surpass the failings of classical representational discourse but to maintain the modernist project of constituting an ethical discourse without regressing to the position of a master narrative such as that of the privileged position of the occidental, white, male Christian industrialist, e.g., Musil's character Arnheim.

Rather than reacting against the classical theory which transcendentally guarantees that the map equals the territory, by producing a purely random mapping, we are attempting here to explore the potential of modern discourse to produce what Jameson, in the vein of Bateson, would call a "different cognitive mapping." This is a project to explore the potential to rework the rules (habits or procedures) by which subjects gain a sense of place in the global system of history.

0.1 Epistemic croquet

The object that Alice is trying to hit is living and dynamic. The instrument with which Alice is trying to hit the object is also alive. The environment in which Alice is playing her game is fluctuating and changing. And of course, so is Alice herself, as well as the other players who interact in a sometimes conflictual way. The aim of the game, to connect up the object, the instrument, the environment, and the players, with a certain order, is thwarted at every instant by a random change in one or more of the variable elements of the game. And, finally, the stakes of the game are high indeed. When one fails to give at least the impression of succeeding, the bad queen, or those who claim power, threaten to implement strategic action. The croquet game in Wonderland is a most fitting analogy for the problems of knowledge and representation facing modern science and discourse, including our own meta-discourse.

Trying to write about Robert Musil and C. S. Peirce is very similar to Alice's croquet game. There are probably as many Peirces as there are Peircean texts, and Robert Musil's *Der Mann ohne Eigenschaften*[5]—*The Man without Qualities*—quite simply never came to an end. Thus, rather than attempting to construct a closed system which would explain either author, or to interpret the meaning of their work once and for all, we have chosen to seek and place into relief a certain epistemological richness in the very difficulty that these texts present to the theorist of discourse. In other words, we have chosen to espouse fully the movement and the interactions of epistemic croquet in our own critical discourse. Rather than seeking the singular correct reading of Peirce, or which of Peirce's texts are the "real" Peirce etc.,[6] rather than putting a closure on the narrative in *Der Mann ohne Eigenschaften* that Musil said could never be narrated, we will attempt to make these writers play croquet with each other, we will place them into dialectical interaction, and this within the context of the much vaster game of the discourse of knowledge at the time in which they were writing.

One of the main and we hope original contributions of this work is the attempt actually to *apply* a particular reading of Peirce's triadic semiotics to a text in order to determine if it can possibly function in practice and not merely as semiotic theory. Thus, we elaborate at length upon Musil's own theory of discourse, while attempting to illustrate that Musilian narrative and Peircean semiotics are paradigmatic of the transformations of the epistemic climate of the times and that such an alternative semiotic theory would be required to talk about other textual practices of the age. Our aim here, then, is to construct theoretically an alternative theory of discourse which would account for certain scientific and literary tendencies at the turn of the century, and, furthermore, to begin to render such an alternative theory operative for the analysis of discourse, however embryonic that attempt may be.

Musil's narrative practice in *Der Mann ohne Eigenschaften* inserts a certain radicalization and expansion of contextuality in discourse, an epistemologically explicit surpassing and criticism of past scientific and interpretative discourses: a search for a replacement of them. In C. S. Peirce's triadic semiosis we can find a practice animated by a similar motive. Through the definition of the sign as continuous interaction, indetermination, and contextualization, a criticism and surpassing of established discursive practices is posited. At issue in both Musil's narrative and Peirce's pragmatics is a radical contextualization of the *episteme*: a radical redefinition, common perhaps to the whole of discourse in the time and space of what is now chronologically referred to as "modernity," a period ranging roughly from the late 1800s to the mid-1900s, although we must recognize immediately the problems of periodization.

We will explore the contextualization of discursive formations by Musil and Peirce—and, in particular, the relevance of Peircean pragmatics to the understanding of Musil—and seek to relate our inquiry to the role of discourse in the work of Werner Heisenberg, Michel Foucault, and Jürgen Habermas in an effort to see if it is possible to constitute what one could call a "modern episteme." The primary textual "object" of our exploration will be Musil's novel *Der Mann ohne Eigenshaften*.

While Nietzsche's linkage of the will to knowledge to the will to power and its developments by Foucault interest us in our work on classical discourse, in this study we are more interested for purposes of studying Musil and Peirce in Foucault's insistence on the materiality of discourse and on discourse as practice and procedure, which owes less of a debt to Nietzsche and more of one to the pragmatic philosophers of language such as Peirce and Wittgenstein. Much traditional writing on Musil has stressed the influence of Nietzsche. However, while Musil does address issues raised by Nietzsche, notably in his treatment of the character Clarisse, we will argue throughout this work that the epistemology espoused by Musil is far more akin to the pragmatics of a Wittgenstein and a Peirce than to the "Gay Science" of a Nietzsche.

The strategy of writing of this book is meant to be a re-presentation of the epistemology elaborated in the content of the book. We jump back and forth from Musil to Peirce to Heisenberg by way of the gesture of temporarily isolating synchronic cross-sections of the sign-field and then open onto other such synchronic cross-sections in the writing of the inheritors of the potential of modern discourse such as Habermas, Foucault, and Bateson.

At first glance, especially at the table of contents, this work may appear to be a series of distinct units of thought by a variety of writers from a host of disciplines. We would ask the reader to bear with us in a writing and reading exercise which sets out to reenact the very epistemological position developed in our work's thematics.

To show our orchestrating hand from the beginning, we might state, somewhat paradoxically, that our research and writing strategy depended on allowing a less than "engineered" consensus to emerge from among a host of discourses that were grappling with the crises of positivist knowledge and authoritarian politics around the turn of the century. We also refer to a second set of texts of more recent, if not contemporary, writing in an effort to show that the "fortune" of this earlier emergent procedure among its heirs such as Foucault, Habermas, and Bateson has been one of consolidating the consensus of a community of investigators, which for Peirce will be seen to be the legitimation of truth and validity that replaces any correspondence theory of truth. The substance of this consensus is that modern discourse does have some potential after all to resolve the crises of classical representational discourse in the light of the demands made by twentieth-century society upon discourses of knowledge.

Nor do we deal exclusively with authors in this work, something which would be awkward in the light of the modern problematization of the classical tenet of the author as subject and source of discourses. For this reason we make no attempt to enter into a discussion of whether *Der Mann ohne Eigenschaften* is autobiographical. We are interested in fields of sign-production which exhibit certain habits or regularities of discursive practice. Two of these fields of habit we refer to with respect to Musil as "irony" and "essayism," practices of discourse which go beyond classical discourse. We have chosen to emphasize irony and essayism as the traits of modern discourse with the most potential by way of an implicit rejection of the more typical Nietzschean reading of Musil and the solution to the crisis of representation.

The radical practice and comprehension of irony in this novel require some other means than a syntactico-semantic, referential metalanguage to account for it. *Der Mann ohne Eigenschaften* seeks, in all avenues of discursive practice—scientific, social, political, erotic, economic, artistic, and narrative—an alternative discourse of knowing and of acting, as well as an alternative kind of narration. *Musil's narration develops into an attempt to create or to produce a discourse which would avoid the pitfalls and the assumptions of classical discourse.*

In Part One we suggest that there exists a *consensus* among various theorists of all types and disciplines of discourse, ranging from philosophers of language to philosophers of physics, concerning the inadequacy of existing "scientific" discourses. What is more, most of these epistemological thinkers have also suggested various ways (not all of them fully explicit or feasibly operative) of overcoming the limitations of classical discourse in order to fulfill its scientific and social functions. Indeed, most of them suggest that the functions of discourse themselves must change. We plan to show that the critique of discourse in Musil's narrative and Peirce's triadic semiotics overlap with and add to the theory of knowledge of the Copenhagen interpretation of quantum mechanics by Werner Heisenberg.

In Part Two, we begin to *practice* a possible alternative applied critical discourse based on the theories of discourse of the "modern episteme." We make an attempt to apply it to the discourse of Musil's novel, *Der Mann ohne Eigenschaften*. Our very method here is already Peircean in that it seeks a consensus as some sort of collectivist and constructivist foundation of the validity of science in order to replace any notion of a transcendentally guaranteed absolute truth. We also seek to practice a type of "Interaction" of discourses, rather than remaining attached to a single, fixed perspective which lays claim to absolute truth for itself. This makes the alternative discourse what we could call a "co-constructivist" discourse of knowledge.

0.2 The classical episteme: A review of the discursive procedures

Any work which proposes to discuss modern discourse cannot, of course, neglect some treatment of premodern or classical discourse as a backdrop of past critical theorizing from which to assess modern discourse. *The Potential of Modern Discourse* follows from where our previous works, *The Romantic Irony of Semiotics: Friedrich Schlegel and the Crisis of Representation* and *Powermatics: A Discursive Critique of New Communications Technology* left off. These earlier studies have dealt with the tenets, limitations, and crises of classical discourse at great length, while *The Potential of Modern Discourse* sets out less to review classical discoveries and more to salvage certain modern tendencies as viable transformations of, and alternatives to, classical discourse. In the study on Romantic Irony we reviewed classical theories of aesthetics and rhetoric showing how they conform to what Foucault called the representational episteme. In *Powermatics* we demonstrated with the aid of a discursive analysis how contemporary discourses on and practices of new communications technology conform to the age-old procedures of classical representational discourse as opposed to being at all revolutionary, as is often claimed.

Briefly, then, we may review those tenets of classical discourse without replaying the entire exercise of their discernment in a corpus of texts. The postulates which make up this earlier episteme, as stated by Foucault in *L'Ordre du discours* and in *L'Archéeologie du savoir* will serve to illustrate the task at hand for any would-be successor to this episteme:

(1) The doctrine Foucault refers to as the "Thème de l'expérience originaire" is a belief that facts precede discourse just as our experience of facts precedes our conscious grasp of them: "This asserts, in the case of experience that even before it could be grasped in the form of *a cogito*, prior significations, in some ways already spoken, were circulating in the world, scattering it all about us, and from the outset made possible a sort of primitive recognition. [. . .] Things murmur meanings our language has merely to extract."[7]

(2) Second, there is the referential theme of "universelle médiation," which assumes that discourse is the transparent mediator between logos and object or concept, giving an immediate synthesis or mediation of, on the one hand, consciousness or knowing subject and, on the other hand, object or concept of knowledge. Signs are supposed to refer adequately and transparently to external or internal reality, thereby constituting the postulate essential to representation, *referentiality*, and the belief that syntax reveals the order of the world while semantics is its referent.[8]

(3) The theme of the "sujet fondateur" assumes that the isolated human subject is the sole source and author of discourse, and is its point of origin, unmodified or unperturbed by any other source or place of mediation. This postulate of this theme gives the subject the authority to know perfectly, and to say objectively, its object.[9]

(4) The complete objectivity of truth and meaning (whereby the active or relativizing role of the subject's consciousness and discourse supposedly filters all objects of knowledge transparently), suggests that there is no subjectivity of knowledge, no permutation on the part of the source of discourse which says its knowledge of the object.

(5) A corollary of this last postulate is that a fixed, objective, absolute knowledge is possible, and what is more may be possessed by a single knowing subject to the exclusion of all other subjects. For example, Des-

cartes' "Method" is first an individual's private method, which all others should adopt.

(6) If postulates (1) through (5) are accepted, then the possibility of scientific truth, be it the science of physics or the science of philosophy and interpretation, is unquestionably secure.

(7) Where science is secure, so too are its models and its capacity for true model formation, i.e., models which refer to the reality of the object under study. These postulates of the security of reference (i.e., science and its models) are necessary, for example, in order for rhetoric and semiotics to pose the syntactico-semantic models of irony.

(8) Finally, where discourse exists in the unquestioned possibility of saying that which is "true," absolute, fixed, objective, knowledge there exists a corollary of the investment of power in the one who says "true": "a technical utility whose end is the amelioration of human life and a special power to one who can produce this utility."[10] In classical discourse the modality of "knowing" is accompanied by that of "power."

However, even in these earlier works we have not simply left classical discourse intact; rather, we have illustrated the theoretical and practical crises of such a discourse of knowledge. The infinite self-reflexivities of Schlegel's ironic discourse were seen to radically contextualize classical discourse, both in theory and in practice in that it resists representational critical models such as those of Saussurean structuralist semiotics. Furthermore, we have argued that the classical discursive procedures underpinning technological and political discourse can no longer function practically without occulting a host of contradictions and undemocratic interests. These two critiques, then, have necessitated a quest for an alternative, postrepresentational, modern discourse in order to solve the epistemological, ontological, ethical, and political crises of classical discourses of knowledge and power. This is the foremost task which this work sets out to begin to accomplish.

We introduce this problematic in this present work by showing how Musil's Ph.D. dissertation on Mach and his reflections in *Young Toerless* on the problematic of Kantian synthetic knowledge in a modern world without a divine transcendental set the stage for the necessity of a more pragmatic theory and practice of discourses of knowledge and legitimation.

0.3 Constituting the modern epistemic context

Modernity's paradoxes of modern physics, of "exact and human," of "theory and praxis," of "story to be narrated" and "inability to narrate," will be seen to highlight modern discourse as a dominant episteme where procedures of uncertainty and relativity prevail. Modern discourse will be seen both to negate and deviate from classical, referential, absolute, and powerful discourse. The discourses of Peirce and Musil, we will wish to argue, place the postulates of classical discourse into question by opposing referential, absolute knowledge with such notions as the "plurality of realities" (Musil) "triadicity" (Peirce), and "uncertainty" or "complementarity" and "perturbation" in experimental procedure (Heisenberg). The extreme realism of the "thème de l'expérience originaire" will be shown to be countered with a view of the "Man without Qualities" who is nothing more than a discontinuous collection of discourses. This notion is reconfirmed by Peirce when he states that everything, even man, is a sign, and much later echoed by such "postmoderns" as Foucault, who states that the subject is no more than a "field" of discourses, or an authorial "function."[11]

To the classical notion of the possibility of absolute knowledge, Musil will be seen to oppose the notion of "Teilloesung" ("partial solution") which parallels Peirce's notion of habit and field taken as only a temporarily isolatable context of study within an infinitely expanding signfield. We will also discuss Heisenberg's development of a similar solution to the plurality of realities via his concept of "potentia," which we will show to be epistemologically coherent with the Peircean notion of habit. What Peirce refers to as the "infinite production of signs" and Heisenberg as the "continuum" of the energy field will be seen to be quite comparable to Musil's discursive practices of "Essayismus" ("Experiment").

We will explore Peirce's, Habermas', and Bateson's notions of "Interaction" and Heisenberg's notion of "public objectivity," precursors to Bakhtin's now popular notion of "dialogism," to see if they provide concepts for Musil's search for a practice of an ideal dialogue ("Heiliges Gespraech"). In addition, the concept of discourse as "Interaction" will begin to explain how Musil contextually relativizes various classical absolutist discourses, that is to say, how he sets them into a mutually relativizing dialogue. Finally, after the failure of the utopian experiment which takes the form of an incestuous dyadic discourse of solipsism between Ulrich and Agathe, Musil, in the "Nachlass," poses the necessity of social reintegration, a notion which reiterates the Peircean definition of truth in terms of the consensus of the community. This modern project was later to be taken up by Habermas in his "modern" search for postulates of communication which would establish consensus as a democratic basis for legitimation in the community.

0.4 The practice of interactional triadic semiosis

Musil, like Peirce in the triadic contextualization of his own writing, not only talks about or theorizes, but, more importantly, *practices* discourse as irony, experiment, essayism, partial solution, interaction, dialogism, relativity, and finally as continuous production of discourse. All of these discursive procedures will be viewed as an attempt to derive an alternative discourse of knowledge as a basis for social practice.

Not only does he make irony and essayism main threads of the elaboration of an alternative discourse, but certain practical political dilemmas subtend the whole work. These are the crucial questions to be addressed by any discourse of knowledge which posits itself as legitimating praxis. One such issue to surface time and again is that of the relationship between discursive constitutions of reason, madness, and criminality in the work of Musil, Bateson, and Foucault. Another constantly subjacent theme is that of war or the relationship of relinquishing a discourse of certainty to the likelihood of entering into strategic action. We have not chosen these themes; rather, they have imposed themselves on any discussion of the potential of modern discourse to suffice as a guiding discourse in the late twentieth century.

In order to show that Musil goes beyond the classical, referential type of discourse in practice, it will be necessary to make an attempt to render some of these notions operational for a critique of *Der Mann ohne Eigenschaften*. The attempt can, however, only be embryonic, if only for the reason, as will be seen, that it would require a whole community of investigators to study the complexities of the whole sign-field. No single authorial subject could englobe the complexity of the multitudinous, interacting fields throughout time.

0.5 The utopian potential of modern discourse

Musil describes his hero, Ulrich, as confronting the question of how an intelligent being can live in modernity, a quest that is carried on through two world wars. Thereby he reaffirms the modern project of finding a discourse with which to guide and legitimate praxis. As seen earlier, one of Habermas' main criticisms of the postmodern worldview is that it preaches the end of history in the sense of some form of directed teleological attempt to alter the world in time and space.

Postmodernism has placed on the agenda theories of post-enlightenment, postmodernism, even of post-history.[12] A modern discourse with potential would have to demonstrate that it is impossible to discard history and that it can come to terms with history. One of the major criticisms of the pragmatics of Peirce and Wittgenstein is that it ignored history in the sense of concrete materially situated agents deciding about values and acting in time and space. Whereas, from the very beginning the issue of modern discourse and its "postmodern" potential centers around the problematic of "morality" in Musil as well as in relation to the critiques of pragmatics for neglecting morality. We are thinking here of the common criticisms of Wittgenstein's *Philosophical Investigations* for dealing with "beetles in a box" rather than concrete materialist contextual issues of ethics in the lifeworld. Peirce, also, has often been criticized for an absence of social morality in his pragmatic thought, an attack that we will seek to reply to by pulling out of pragmatics an implied ethics in the sections of the book dealing with "utopia" and "induction."

While Peirce and Wittgenstein did not often write specifically about materialistically framed issues of the subject in history, this is not to contend that a more pragmatic approach to discourses of knowledge and the power-knowledge relationship is necessarily ahistorical. We will attempt to uncover an implied politics in Peirce's work. However, in order further to make the point that a pragmatic philosophy of language grounded in communicative interaction is not ahistorical we will make constant reference to the work of Bakhtin. It is our none-too-original contention that Bakhtin, in his *Marxism and Philosophy of Language*, elaborates a pragmatic theory of discourse as an interactive production of meaning within concrete social contexts which shift and which are themselves altered by discursive production. In other words, we will wish to argue that a pragmatic theory of discourse is by no means at counter purposes with a materialist theory of history; this may explain how Musil could simultaneously be so concerned about history while theorizing and practicing a radically contextualized production of meaning.

Musil's modern discourse must be situated within the sociohistorical context of his contemporary period of crisis, where, in view of modernization, technocratization, dehumanization, urbanization, and warmongering aggression (all thematized in *Der Mann ohne Eigenschaften*) the question of discourse's relation to social praxis and to utopian possibility imposes itself. Musil's so-called constructive irony sought to construct a new social ethics of praxis.

To achieve this discourse Musil begins by functioning within its limitations and acknowledges its own irreducibility to a classical paradigm. The ignorance associated with Socratic irony returns in modern discourse as uncertainty and indeterminacy. The discourse of knowledge comes to include the will to knowledge, a triadic discursive horizon in which the subject appears as constituting knowledge, a relation which is a mode of the Peircean sign-function. What is the relationship of this new discourse to the classical episteme? What more does this new discourse require than ironic unknowing, its sincere or feigned ignorance practiced in irony from the time of Socrates onward? In other words, does not the *method* of grasping the epistemological problems of classical discourse, namely irony's heuristics, also become the *possible procedure of discourse* which surpasses these limitations? Modern discursive practice (as conceived and practiced by Musil, and as implicitly or explicitly developed by the pragmatic theorists of discourse, Peirce, Habermas, and Foucault) may be the solution to the short-comings of classical discourse. The problematic of the relation of modern discourse and discursive criticism to history as social praxis aimed at change is an imperative consideration of any pragmatics of socio-discursive analysis. For example, contemporary with Musil's works are Mauthner's pragmatic concerns for an action-oriented language practice and for a view of language as practice. "What really matters, what really has meaning, is not the image a word or sentence conjures up, but the *action* that it suggests or commands, warns from, or prohibits."[13]

This pragmatic turn will also be seen to have occurred first of all in much of the philosophy of language of the times and to have thrived since then. Wittgenstein in his *Philosophical Investigations,* and later Austin in *How to Do Things with Words,* are two other theorists of language who emphasize language as practice according to conventional rules which establish interrelationships between speakers as well as between them and the world they set out to know. Janik and Toulmin's *Wittgenstein's Vienna* has done a far better job at illustrating this than we could ever hope to. While we have referred to Wittgenstein as yet another case of the shift from the analytical referential to the pragmatic, we must also refer the reader to Janik and Toulmin's discussion of this preoccupation with the "fact/value" issue. This raises the whole question of values and their legitimation of practice in history. We will see that this pragmatic turn was taken up by contemporary social and political theory, more specifically in the work of Juergen Habermas and Michel Foucault, both of whom sought to analyze power relations as a function of pragmatic discursive relationships and rules.

0.6 In search of a consensus among "discontinuous systems": Transdisciplinarity

Just as Foucault must justify juxtaposing biology, economics, and grammar in his *Archeology of Knowledge,* some explanation is due for our choice of theorists of discourse; namely, philosophers of language such as Peirce and Foucault, physicists such as Mach and Heisenberg, social theorists and epistemologists such as Habermas and Apel, all of whom we use to "contextualize" Musil's theory and practice of discourse.

The epistemological dilemmas which we see these theorists groping with are much the same as those which Toulmin and Janik and Schorske find to situate the epoch to which Musil belonged. What they refer to respectively as *"Wittgenstein's Vienna"* and *"Fin de siècle Vienne"* gave rise to Wittgenstein's speech pragmatics, of the *Philosophical Investigations* which went beyond even his own analytical, referential, formal, or transcendental logic of the *Tractatus* (although, as Janik and Toulmin argue, the seeds of this movement were already in the *Tractatus*). In this epoch we find not only the physics of Mach, on whom Musil wrote his doctoral dissertation, and who is known as the precursor of relativity physics, but also the psychoanalysis of Freud, the great destroyer of the myth of the "objective" cogito. Here we find not only Mauthner, one of the first pragmatists of discourse, but also Karl Kraus, a politically relativizing satirist; not only Schoenberg, who placed the laws of harmonic music into question, but also anti- or arepresentationalist painters such as Klimt and Kokoschka.

What is more, Janik and Toulmin's as well as Schorske's books situate their critique of decadent, bankrupt procedures of reasoning and their search for a new discourse, within the center of non-discursive practices leading to political, economic, and sociopsychological crises. Events of these crises include the economic collapse of 1873, the defeat of Austria-Hungary by Prussia at Sadow, the escalation toward World War I, the exposure of "moral degeneracy" among what had appeared to be "respectable" politicians and noblemen, the great number of suicides among the prominent young intellectuals of Viennese society, the inability to come to grips with technological modernization, and the dwindling of both the power and the democratic procedures of Franz-Joseph's empire.[14]

Our preoccupation here with the relation of Musil's epistemology to modern science was provoked in part by none other than Musil's own constant thematization of this problematic of scientific discourse under the heading "exactness and soul" ("Genauigkeit und Seele") as well as by the fact that Musil was himself a scientist earlier in his career. Having written his doctoral dissertation on Ernst Mach,[15] he criticized his positivism yet flirted with some of Mach's more relativist moments. In addition, throughout *Der Mann ohne Eigenschaften*, Musil demonstrates his awareness of the paradoxes of classical knowledge when confronted with modern problems such as criminal ethics or the inadequacy of Boltzmann's calculus of probabilities to solve the crisis of referentiality. For example, at the very beginning of the novel there is a passage mocking the certainty of modern-day "Kakanian" citizens that accidents (involving mutilation and death) are accounted for statistically and need no longer concern us, once they are transformed by the exact sciences: "According to American statistics," the gentleman observed, "there are over a hundred and ninety thousand people killed on the roads annually over there, and four hundred and fifty thousand injured" (M.w.Q. 1:6; DMoE, 11).

We will round out this discussion of modern discourse and an alternative to classical science with reference to Juergen Habermas' attempt to construct a social theory based on a modern project of communication as universal pragmatics. It is this, our concern with moral issues, which necessitates the extensive treatment of Habermas' communicational ethics grounded in a universal pragmatics. As K. O. Apel was first to point out, Habermas has attempted to bridge a concern for a Peircean pragmatics of discourse with the moral dilemmas of modernity without transcendentals, thereby making of pragmatics the new *summum bonum*.

Habermas is crucial to our conclusions because it is his work on the speech ethics of pragmatic claims to validity which attempts to solve the dilemma of reconciling a theory of discourse with *existential* problems of morality. Habermas' own doctoral dissertation dealt extensively with the American pragmatists, including Peirce. Also, in his book *Knowledge and Human Interests*, he devotes a good deal of consideration to both Peirce and Mach. Habermas, then, takes up the challenge, which we have described to be elaborated by Peirce and Musil, that of resolving the problem of ethics in a theory of discourse as social communicative practice. He does so partially, we will argue, in a very Peircean and agonistically Musilian manner, i.e., by retaining pragmatics while seeking a "quasi-universal" ground for an emancipatory, humanly interested one, couched implicitly—counterfactually—in every speech act, however distorted it be in practice. Habermas' critique of communication is the culmination of this search for an "ethical" modern alternative to classical discourse. Habermas will be seen to attempt to uncover the implicit emancipatory interest in this discursive pragmatics.

It is perhaps Patrick Heelan, in his excellent study of Heisenberg's philosophy of physics, who most succinctly expresses the pertinence of the epistemological arguments and findings of modern scientific discourse to the social sciences and humanities:

> Logically implied in Heisenberg's view of the measuring process is the position that the behaviour and pattern of objects in human empirical consciousness are also subject to quantum mechanical laws. Acts are specified by their objects. If then the object of empirical consciousness is *identical* with reality, and if reality is subject to the quantum theory, then the behaviour and pattern of objects in human empirical consciousness is also subject to quantum mechanical laws. The quantum theory then takes on the character of a universal explanation for physical and mental events.[16]

To provide some intellectual historical background, modern discourse will be situated here within the consensus of a certain axis of development which counters the classical language philosophy based on the formation of universal, absolutely fixed, syntactico-semantic categories. This latter axis might be seen to begin in modern times with the interpretation which Bertrand Russell gave to the *Tractatus*, and which led to developments in analytical language philosophy based on syntax and its referentiality. The counter axis, still often struggling for respectability in positivist, analytical circles of language philosophy, is the interpretation which Janik and Toulmin give to the *Tractatus*. They find there exists no break between Wittgenstein's first work and its sequel, twenty years later, *Philosophical Investigations*. This latter work is based on finding laws of language-use which change with each context and hence lay no claim to transcendental, absolute universality.

There is one striking absence in the group of thinkers to whom we refer in this reconstruction of the transformation of an episteme, namely Sigmund Freud, also a prominent figure in Wittgenstein's Vienna. This is no reflection upon the importance that Freud occupies in this transformation of the episteme. Indeed, as Habermas has so well argued in his three chapters on Freud in *Knowledge and Human Interests*, Freud's interactive self-reflective hermeneutics, as well as the revolutionary concept of transference-*countertransference,* are a radical deviation from the dominant classical scientific paradigm of the age. Indeed, one might make the argument that the notion of transference-*countertransference* around a patient's text is a precursor to Peircean triadicity and to Heisenberg's concept of the perturbation effect. We have omitted Freud here more due to the extant body of research on his epistemological innovativeness than due to any wish to diminish his centrality. He is but one, however crucial, of many writers and scientists who were transforming the episteme at the time yet with whom we have not had the space or the expertise to deal. We are, however, in a sequel to this work dealing extensively with Freud in an attempt to read the ontological sphere of interiority back into pragmatics.[17]

Finally, this book makes the argument that modern discourse, including Musil's irony, is a discourse-practice, a pragmatic series of games, which cannot be resumed under any absolute laws of syntax or semantics. Furthermore, modern discursive practice must be "explained" by means of a new, modern critical discourse. Hence our task in Part Two of developing an alternative critical discourse that can be applied to a modern narrative text.

0.7 The modern potential of "constructive irony"

Often in Musil we find many of the procedures of modern discourse associated with what Musil calls irony, more specifically "constructive irony." It would be wrong to assume that irony has not changed since Socrates. The following perusal of some of the general thoughts of Musil about irony will indicate that he develops a new, modern, epistemological, constructive, utopian irony, while at the same time acknowledging his sources in Socrates, Schlegel, and Pirandello.

First of all, a consensus of Musil criticism generally agrees that Musil's *Der Mann ohne Eigenschaften* is predominantly ironical. Musil constantly notes in his *Tagebuecher* and in the "Nachlass" that irony is a necessary element in his narrative:

> . . . irony is the style of writing I am best suited for.

> If I describe my life as an exemplary life of these times which I want to pass on to later generations, then everything becomes tempered with irony, and the objections I have raised simply fall away. (Tgb., 891)

> To be ironic. Poet/politics. This is also the attitude to take. (Tgb., 934)

In the following list of various types or manifestations of irony in *Der Mann ohne Eigenschaften,* Musil appears to treat irony thematically, while insisting upon all of the following features of irony: experimentality, its treatment of history and language in terms of its moral practice and ideology, social significance, and its psychological context:

Ironic novel of education Agathe-Ulrich?
Ironic portrayal of the most profound moral problems;
Irony is in this case gallows humor.
Irony: Agathe takes seriously what she is told: father, teacher and male
ideology, etc. . . .
Ironic: The man inclined to God is psychologically an individual who lacks
a sense of community. The pseudo-neurotic.
Ironic: The religious person as the evil one. The criminals—the women.
(DMoE, 1843)

That irony is treated less as content and more in terms of discursive
practice becomes more evident in the following qualification of it as a
search for a new narrative technique. This technique, in turn, is strictly
tied to the existential emphasizing of the direct tie between narrative and
life, where both are taken as discursive practice: "Satiric narrative technique can usually be reduced to the formula: play dumb. Assumed na-
iveté. This is also the essence of those who make compliments which
leave one in doubt as to what is meant" (Tgb., 584).

In the interview with Fontana, Musil says that he counterbalances a
tendency toward essayism with irony.[18] However, essayism, in Fontana's
sense of the word, is not the same as in Musil's description in Ulrich's life
and his own narration as essayism, as will be seen further on. Essayism is
rejected here in Fontana as a sort of classical reflective discourse, whereas
irony is featured as an active interaction and socially implicated practice.
Irony is that which counteracts a referential, reflective exposition:

> Interviewer: And are you not afraid that the structure of your novel might
> tend toward the essayistic?
> Musil: Indeed I am. And I have therefore employed two means of guarding
> against it. First, a basic ironic attitude, which, I hasten to add, does not
> mean for me a gesture of superiority, but rather a form of struggle. (G.W. II,
> 941)

Musil cites the following Schlegelian fragment whereby irony is seen as
the guiding principle of the novel as well as being inextricably tied to
Socratic dialogism. "Novels are the Socratic dialogue of our time. In the
face of school-wisdom, the wisdom of life has fled to this liberal form."[19]

In the *Tagebuecher*, Musil recognizes the close ties of modern irony to
Socratic irony and proposes irony as a compositional technique for a
forerunner of *Der Mann ohne Eigenschaften*, namely *Rapial:* "Note: Socratic and modern irony. See manuscript 'What is a Rapial' for the complete treatment" (Tgb., 964).

In another note Musil approaches very closely a Schlegelian notion of
irony as parabasic reflective distanciation and reserve in the face of that by
which one is impassioned—a form of renewed parabasis: "Satiric technique: Even what one loves must be thought through and mastered until it

appears satirical" (Tgb., 585, cf. Schlegel, *Kristische Fragment*, No. 37).
From his words about Pirandello and romantic irony it is evident that
Musil is thoroughly familiar with the narrative distanciation techniques of
parabasis in irony and with the close tie between romantic and modern
irony: "Set to rights: the romantic or even Pirandellian irony of it: the
character over the author" (DMoE, 1943).

The full epistemological consequences of ignorance are also associated
with modern irony by Musil who, while drawing upon the background of
Socratic maieutics, emphasizes that modern irony is not a feigned ignorance but a genuine, epistemological standpoint of uncertainty: "To be
Socratic is to feign ignorance. To be modern is to be ignorant" (G.W. II,
920).

That Musil considers irony to be manifest as discourse practice or as
discourse presentation, rather than in the content of the representations
themselves, is evidenced in this next remark, which also links discourse
practice with the pragmatic context of opposing self-presenting ideologies: "Irony is: to portray a cleric in such a way that it could also be a
Bolshevik. To portray a fool in such a way that the author feels: yes, in a
sense, I am like him too. This kind of irony—constructive irony—is relatively unknown in today's Germany" (DMoE, 1939). By his concluding
remark in this passage, Musil is affirming the limitations of his contemporaries' theories and practices of irony, a limitation which he says a modern, constructive, and ideologically conscientious practice and theory of
irony must overcome.

Irony is constructive in that it mixes various character types, various
ideological positions, presented in discourse. This interaction relativizes
and hence destroys the absoluteness and the ensuing power of each
discourse; hence it explains irony's contentiousness, its battle plan, as
well as its sociopolitical utopian role, i.e., to destroy ideology. Furthermore, the author himself cannot enjoy a privileged position of absolute
power over discourse or over his representations since he must admit his
discursive similarity to the presentations of the "fool." The authorial
enunciative position is "deabsolutized" by irony. Irony constitutes a utopian constructive vector pointed against and away from the totalitarianism
of self-sufficient, isolated, impermeable, ideological positions.

Hochstaetter perhaps best of all illustrates the epistemological and
ideological import of "constructive irony" in Musil. He describes it as that
which relativizes falsely grounded arrogance, places reality into doubt,
and situates the hero in a larger totality than that of the illusions of realism
of "Seinesgleichen":

> This kind of constructive irony corrects false pride by bringing the arrogant
> but uncertain spirit face to face with the phenomena of reality. It mediates
> the destructive aspect of the irony and the hero's constructive efforts in the
> superior knowledge that in the end both that which has been rejected out of

prejudice and that which has been provisionally affirmed somehow carry the mark of a lost or utopian common interest. This irony is constructive, because it secretly makes a concession to that which has apparently been condemned once and for all, because it corrects the prejudice of the narrator and his heroes and thus transcends the realm of the possible. In addition, it is constructive because it relegates to the realm of generality the apparently singular and eccentric endeavors of the hero.[20]

The relation of this "constructive irony" to the problem of values, taken as a problem of justification or legitimation of social practices, cannot be overemphasized. Irony is not merely a reversal of values but an essential uncertainty or "ambiguity" of value, where there is a "good-bad" ("Gut-Boeses") and a "bad-good" ("Boeses-Gutes"). Constructive is that which, ". . . by recognizing that there is something false and something true in everything, shows that everything is false, so that it will be kept in mind that everything is on the way to becoming true."[21]

Finally, irony is constructive in that it rejects the discursive procedures of the classical episteme. Musil rejects the principle of excluded middle in another definition which he gives to his novel, which is itself a constructive definition in that it aims at a *"performance"* of the replacement of traditional, classical metalanguage about his novel: "This book is not a satire but a positive construction. It is not a confession but a satire" (DMoE, 1939).

Irony is also to be seen as utopian and constructive in that, by relativizing closed ideological positions which are not utopian, irony "prepares the way" or leaves the way open for what would eventually be utopian. But this negative dialectic will be seen to be not the only way in which ironic discourse is utopian.

"Irony is not a gesture of superiority, but rather a form of struggle" (G.W. II, 941). Battle or conflict may be seen in terms of an antagonistic interrelation of various discursive positions. These positions are no longer able to exclude each other by claiming absolute truth and power for themselves. Musil's irony will be seen to be not a referential, metalinguistic reflection upon ideology, but a discursive, interactional conflict, a type of unreduced, radical dialogue. This relationality of irony is insisted upon once again as the relationality of things and not merely as mockery and funmaking: "It is out of the connection between things that irony nakedly appears. Irony is considered to be mockery and ridicule" (DMoE, 1939).

Given the above remarks, those who would hold on to a restricted definition of irony in Musil (such as Allemann gives when he says that irony in Musil is merely a self-parody of the author's own point of view[22]) must yield before the enormous, far-reaching, epistemological, and ontological complexity that Musil reads into this term. There is no dominant, parodying voice of irony in Musil's narrative; Musil himself describes his narrative in terms of the lack of a first principle or an epistemologically certain or non-contingent ground (DMoE, 133). Irony is the discursive position left once the transcendental guarantee of knowledge and power is lost.

Whereas Candace Lang in her recent work *Irony/Humor*[23] comes down in favor of the play on the signifier or trace and the postmodern dispersal of the subject at the expense of the self-reflectiveness of irony, we would tend to define irony as infinite semiosis where each new sign-relation radically de- and recontextualizes meanings. Nevertheless, meaning, however mobile, does exist as constituted pockets of linkage between a sign-vehicle, an object, and its effect upon a sign-user. Meaning is not "le manque" (Lacan). Also the subject is not eliminated, as postmoderns would contend. It is not "Qualities without the Man" but rather *The Man without Qualities*. In other words, man as himself a sign is a subject in constant process such that the meaning constellations he assumes constantly vary. This is not tantamount to de-ontologizing the subject! These partial, ever-surpassable fields of meaning and identity are partial meanings within possible contexts all potentially alterable within other contextual productions of signs by sign-users. Musil's practice of "essayism," we will wish to argue, was just such an attempt at partial meanings, in the realm of possibility: whence the potential of modern discourse. It is this aspect of modern discourse that we will insist upon as an alternative to the "deconstructionist" insistence on lack of meaning and dispersion of subjectivity.

0.8 "Modernity" and irony

This definition of irony as a potentially modern discourse taken as radically contextualized production of meaning throughout constantly substituting sign-fields also goes in a somewhat different direction from that of Linda Hutcheon's recent work on irony as a key theme in postmodernism, where she emphasizes the paradoxical relation of the parodic and ironic to the past. For Hutcheon postmodern fiction is historiographic metafiction that is self-reflective yet historically grounded. Postmodernism for her is paradoxical or doubly encoded. Language is arbitrary yet frontiered. Even Lyotard's declaration that we have lost faith in our master narratives becomes itself a master narrative.[24]

But we would disagree that the modern vs. postmodern debate between Habermas and Lyotard is merely an issue of Marxism vs. neo-Nietzscheism as Hutcheon contends when she argues that the former "inscribes a metanarrative with precise values and premises," whereas the latter "problematizes both the product and the process of inscription."[25] We will argue that modern discourse is not confident in the capacity of metanarrative to refer to object narrative, nor is the question of value precise and simply grounded. What is more, we will attempt to illustrate that not only Joyce but also Musil, one of the great modern narrators, though in a different vein, problematizes the product and the process of narrating/writing/inscription, but without neglecting the question of values and ground.

When Hutcheon argues that postmodernism cannot step outside that which it contests, that it is implicated in the values it chooses to challenge, we would propose that this is precisely the modern dilemma of a Musil, a Peirce, and the Copenhagen interpretation of the results of quantum mechanics experiments. What is more, we will argue that there is much potential in this very modern dilemma.

In short, much of what Hutcheon would call the ironic mode of postmodernism we will find to be quite modern. Since the turn of the century "moderns" have been preoccupied with the crisis of representation, the problematization of the status of reality, the distinction between fact and telling and between narrated and narration, the self-reflexive acknowledgment of the subject's complexity within the system under study, the inadequacies of totalizations, and the melting of disciplinary boundaries such as literature as distinct from science.

However, where we will define irony as the radical contextualization of meaning production whereupon one text is then repositioned within other sign-fields, this does not deviate substantially from Hutcheon's definition of parody as the ironic mode of intertextuality which enables critical, non-nostalgic visitations of the past. Peirce would refer to such intertextuality simply as inevitable semiosis. Again, however, we will attempt to show this to be a fundamentally modern development, one which can contend with the problems facing modern society, as opposed to a postmodern reduction of all to simulacrum (Baudrillard).

Musil constantly couples the words "irony" and "modern." Although we have circumscribed the word "modernity" chronologically it is not wise to do so restrictively or exclusively. "Modern" and "modernity" refer rather to a discursive episteme as characterized by specific postulates of discourse, just as "classical" refers to a set of other discursive postulates. Irony has disrupted the discursive postulates of the classical episteme, namely referentiality, analyticity, representation, true and false value systems, scientificity, absolute knowledge, taxonomy, and systematization, all represented in the discourses of Descartes, Newton, Locke, Chomsky, and the structuralists, among others. To a certain extent, the modern episteme is characterized by an exposition and interrogation of the classical postulates. Irony taken as a dislocation of codes, and as negative self-critical process in discourse, would reflect these aspects of anticlassical modernity. However, both irony and modernity are characterized by other than purely negative means. Modern discourse is more than a negative determination. This is where the difficulty of talking about discourse and modernity begins, i.e., at the place where modern discourse transcends itself as solely a negative transgression of classical discourse. To suggest but a few of the possible traits of (ironic) modern discourse which we will elaborate upon, we might mention:

- dialogism,
- continuous progression and productivity,
- constant interaction of various discourses and their situating fields,
- replacement of representation by re-presentation,
- emphasis upon the materiality of the discourse as opposed to its referent or signified,
- a "performative" quality replacing a metalinguistic/critical quality of one discourse's relation to another and to the whole epistemic field in which it is situated,
- relativity, indeterminacy of truth, or object of knowledge,
- mobility of the moments of observation and object of observation.

Such varied discourses as those of Cervantes, Kierkegaard, Joyce, Sollers, Musil, and Pirandello might fit into the "modern" episteme, all by virtue of their resistance to classical representation and the creation of new procedures. One other theorist to see the diachronically transcendent, epistemological modernity of irony and its consequent destruction of the classical representational episteme is Foucault, in the following remarks upon the irony in Cervantes (who, it must be remembered, was described as a complete epistemological "perspectivist" by Spitzer's somewhat Nietzschean criticism of *Don Quixote*):

> Don Quixote stands for the negative of the Renaissance world; writing has ceased to be the prose of the world, resemblances and signs have untied their old alliance; similitudes are deceiving, becoming illusion and delirium; things remain obstinately in their ironic identity: they are no longer anything but what they are; words wander off to adventure, without content, without resemblance to fill them; they no longer designate things; they lie dormant between the pages of books amid the dust . . . the signs of language have no more value than the flimsy fiction that they represent. Writing and things no longer resemble each other. Between them, Don Quixote wanders off to adventure.26 (our translation)

Where the modern and postmodern part ways, we will argue, is around the notion of the simulacrum (Baudrillard), the total Nietzschean negation of the real and the Derridean, Lacanian declaration of the sole existence of the trace in the absence of meaning and wholesale substitution of signifiers for each other. For with these declarations the modern historical project of linking ethics, politics, and discourse of knowledge must be relinquished.

These postmodern tenets would spell the end of Freud's very modern hermeneutic project and thus we can only disagree with Hutcheon's citation of Lyotard that postmodernism is psychoanalysis, the attempt to understand the present by examining the past, the orientation toward the presence of the past. This superpositioning of sign-fields throughout time would be the way toward accomplishing the impossible task of grasping what Peirce called the "ultimate interpretant."

Whereas antitotality is certainly not invented by postmodernism, since Schlegel and Adorno both directed it against Hegel, Habermas may be correct to state that such tendencies as the evacuation of the subject, meaning history, and value from discourse "do not emit any clear signals." Is, as Hutcheon argues, postmodernism's problematization sufficient? Habermas is well aware of the German philosophical significance of ironic "infinite negativity" when he asks, "but where are the works which might fill the negative slogan of 'postmodernism' with a positive content?"[27]

To this we will answer that they are less in a Nietzsche, a Lacan, a Derrida, or a Baudrillard and far more potentially in a Musil, a Peirce, or a Heisenberg.

0.9 "Apologia"

Finally, given all of this talk about a new discourse, some apologies are due before embarking fully upon an investigation of Musil and Peirce. What we undertake in Part One is little other than a rather straightforward thematic/semantic, perhaps almost hermeneutic interpretation of *Der Mann ohne Eigenschaften*, whereby we illustrate an interpretation of Musil, whom we regard as dealing with the same epistemological impasses and as making the same critique of classical, referential, scientific discourse as do Heisenberg and Peirce.

One consolation may be that our thematics does tie into pragmatics in that it recognizes its own interpretant determination, seeks to establish a consensus, and allows various discourses to interact. We hope to have avoided a Boothean or Hirschean-type hermeneutics, which has been practiced as a critique of Musil by F. G. Peters, *Robert Musil: Master of the Hovering Life*.[28] Their assumption is that interpretation can (is morally obliged to) grasp the initial unique authorial intention. This obviously is not our task here. The aim of this reading is to show that possible triadic, contextual positionings of *Der Mann ohne Eigenschaften* may occur among various other epistemologically oriented discursive practices. Still, one may consider this "hermeneutic" attempt to be a sort of interim stage, one which from within the hermeneutic, logical space of critical discourse tries to show the necessity of getting out of it and the possible directions to take in doing so. This quest is but a continuation of Janik and Toulmin's:

> Is there any method of doing for language-in-general what Hertz and Boltzman have already done for the language of theoretical physics? Is there (that is) some way to map the scope and the limits of the "sayable" exhaustively from within, so that in *both*, it can be seen how descriptive language in general used to give a *bildliche Darstellung* in the Hertzian sense of a representation in the form of a mathematical model of all matters of fact, and *also* the "transcendent" character of all ethical issues—which make them amenable only to "*indirect communication*"—at the same time *shows itself* as the byproduct of the analysis.[29]

Musil asked that he be read twice, once in his entirety and once in part (DMoE, 1941). First we must do a rather inadequate hermeneutic reading of the whole in order to seek directions on how we should read Musil a second time, in part, "*in potentia*," in "Teilloesung." Parts One and Two of this study might be read as just that: two readings of Musil and Peirce.

PART I

THE POTENTIAL HABIT OF MANY REALITIES
THE EPISTEMOLOGICAL PROBLEMATIC

1.0 "Seinesgleichen geschieht": The Crisis of Synthetic Knowledge

In *Der Mann ohne Eigenschaften* "Seinesgleichen geschieht" refers to the epistemological contention that the naked appearance of the world is the real: "das bloss aeusserlich Wirkliche" (DMoE, 1424). "Seinesgleichen geschieht" reigns as the theory of knowledge in Kakania, a theory which the hero of the novel, Ulrich, contests and in lieu of which he presents a theory of reality as "Moeglichkeit" (possibility). Ulrich is convinced that, instead of this systematization of reality as appearance, reality is that which possibility awakens: "die Wirklichkeit, welche die Moeglichkeit weckt . . ." (DMoE, 17).

1.1 Toerless: The rejection of synthetic knowledge

Young Toerless, the hero of an earlier novel by Musil, also questioned the priority of synthetic knowledge based on appearance in "normal" life, when in a boarding school's sordid event, the Basini experience, "reality was transformed." The transformation of and the mystery of knowledge of reality were also posed for Toerless by his inability to comprehend the significance of "imaginary numbers" in mathematics.

Seeking an answer, he visited his mathematics master. The master, somewhat uncomfortable with the subject matter, suggested as a solution Kantian synthetic knowledge, whereby, although we could not know the essence of reality, the thing-in-itself, knowledge could be based upon pure, synthetic, a priori features which are the "axioms of intuition," the "anticipations of experience," the "analogies of experience," and the "postulates of empirical thought in general."[1] Various aspects of knowledge such as Euclidean geometry, causality (in the sense of antecedent-consequent legality between successive phenomena), and the permanence of "substance," were universal and necessary aspects of scientific thought because, for Kant, they belonged to the intentionality structure of every

23

scientific question.[2] In other words, there was a synthesis between universals and particulars in the Kantian theory of knowledge.

Only one problem persisted, however, one which has discouraged more people in their quest of synthetic knowledge than the young Toerless. The basis for the intentionality structure of every scientific question was a *transcendental* one which could not be known but which must be supposed to exist if knowledge were to be possible at all—a sort of epistemological leap of faith. Premodern or classical knowledge depended on a transcendent. So the master explains to Toerless. So Toerless attempts but fails. And so Kant is rejected:

> "You know, I am quite prepared to admit that, for instance, these imaginary numbers, these quantities that have no real existence whatsoever, ha-ha, are no easy nut for a young student to crack. [. . .] "My dear young friend, you must simply take it on trust. Some day, when you know ten times as much mathematics as you do today, you will understand—but for the present: believe!" [. . .] On a little table lay a volume of Kant, the sort of volume that lies about for the sake of appearances. This the master took up and held up to Toerless. "You see this book. Here is philosophy. It treats of the grounds determining our actions. [. . ."] (Y.T., 111–12) When after perhaps half an hour he stopped, exhausted, he had reached only the second page, and there was sweat on his forehead. [. . .] But then he clenched his teeth and read on, and he got to the end of one more page before the break was over. [. . .] That evening, however, he could not bring himself even to touch the book again. (Y.T., 118)[3]

In Toerless, then, two modern problematics are introduced; (1) that of the impossibility of synthetic knowledge without a transcendent, and (2) that of the ability of the categories or structures of our language to represent the intentionality structure of our knowledge and of reality.

1.2 Exactness and soul

Ulrich later seeks to unite the exactness of the empirical, positivist sciences ("Genauigkeit") with the indeterminacy and the infinite vagueness of the soul ("Seele"): "We do not have too much understanding and too little soul, but rather too little understanding in questions of the soul" (G.W.II, 1092).

Early in *Der Mann ohne Eigenschaften*, Ulrich is portrayed as a typical empirical positivist ("Genauigkeit") which counters the verbal irresponsibilities of a Clarisse or of a Walter with a somewhat Wittgensteinian approach: "What we cannot speak about we must pass over in silence."[4] However, the limitations of such a position triggered Ulrich to end his career as a scientist and to begin an experimental year in quest of some access to the knowledge required by an intelligent person to live in both interior and exterior "reality" of the modern age. Ulrich states that at twenty-six he had the world in order but at thirty-two he suspected something ungenuine about it all.

This schism of universal and particular becomes most poignant as concerns the category of the subject. When Walter dubs Ulrich the "Man without Qualities" as "Eigenschaftslosigkeit," he deprives the subject of any constant essence, thus leaving only the various particular manifestations of the person. These particulars cannot be universalized, generalized, or abstracted from in order to reduce the character to the status of an essence, bestowed with qualities:

> "He is a man without qualities!. . ."
> "You can't guess at any profession from what he looks like, and yet he doesn't look like a man who has no profession, either. And now just run your mind over the sort of man he is. He always knows what to do. He can gaze into a woman's eyes. He can exercise his intelligence efficiently on any given problem at any given moment. He can box. He is talented, strong-willed, unprejudiced, he has courage and he has endurance, he can go at things with a dash and he can be cool and cautious—I have no intention of examining all this in detail, let him have all these qualities! For in the end he hasn't got them at all! They have made him what he is, they have set his course for him, and yet they don't belong to him." (M.w.Q. 1:70- 71; DMoE, 64–65)

Both Nuesser and Loebenstein situate the core of Musil's theory of knowledge/consciousness ("Erkenntnistheorie") and its relation to his "Dichtungstheorie" (theory of poetry) in the antithesis between "ratioidem" and "nicht-ratioidem Gegenstand und Gebiet" (G.W. II, 1025ff.).[5]

The impossibility of synthesis lies in the following: if a system of rationality has no ground outside of itself the classical one that Toerless had refused (i.e., belief in some transcendental unknowable synthetic structure), then, not only the mystical, the spiritual, the inexact, but also the findings of exact science are left absolutely ungrounded, relative, and dependent upon the subjectivity of the individual scientist. "The most basic fundamentals of mathematics are not logically guaranteed, the laws of physics are only approximately valid, and the stars move in a coordinate system that has no fixed place" (G.W. II, 1027).

The exactness of science, which is in doubt anyway, cannot, then, satisfactorily deal with problems of the soul or of the spirit, such as ethical problems. Musil mocks this attempt: "The ruling ethic of the day is like its method in that it is a statistical ethic which has stability as its basic concept" (G.W. II, 1027).

But Musil did not dispense with the problematic of synthetic knowledge light-heartedly. He thoroughly investigated the alternatives, first that of reducing all to the particular, as did Mach, and then that of abstracting from the particular to the "other state." It is this trajectory that shall be traced in what follows.

1.3 Mach: The positivist side of the coin

Perhaps the clearest statement of Musil's problematization of classical scientific knowledge is to be found in his initial interest in and ultimate refutation of the empirical positivism of Ernst Mach. Musil wrote his doctoral dissertation on this topic.

Mach resolved the dilemma of synthetic knowledge by dispensing with the universal term of the elements to be synthesized. For Mach, there is *no universal essence to be united with particulars.* All that Mach admits to exist are particular sensations, to which he gives the status of reality, with no postulate of an essence behind these sensations which is causing them: "The world consists only of our sensations, in which case we have knowledge only of sensations."[6]

By reducing essence to fact, which is in turn reduced to sensation, Mach does away with any need to synthesize essence and appearance, since they are one and the same to begin with. In one stroke, Mach does away with any conflict between knowing subject and known object:

> Ernst Mach's doctrine of elements is an excellent example of positivism's attempt to justify the object domain of the sciences as the exclusive sphere to which reality can be attributed. But the positivist concept of fact first attains ontological dignity by being burdened with the critical burden of proof against a shadowy world of metaphysical illusion. . . . According to Moritz Schlick, Mach's follower, there is only one reality, "and it is always essence." In the positivist concept of fact the existence of the immediately given is asserted as the essential. Mach's doctrine of elements is an attempt to explicate the world as the sum total of facts and, at the same time, the facts as the essence of reality.[7]

For Mach, knowledge is not based upon some absolute, transcendental category; rather it is based upon particular experience.

Eventually, in his thesis, although he did not embrace a Kantian theory of universals, Musil also refused Mach's reduction of all knowledge of the world to the status of sensation, due to the latter's lack of regard for the activity of the perceiving and cognitive consciousness. However, with Mach, the problem of synthetic knowledge had not disappeared for Musil. The problematic relation of experience to experiencing subject could not be so easily dispensed with. Musil states that the most pressing questions about society and praxis in life cannot be answered by reducing everything to atomistic, simple sense impressions. He criticizes Mach for a type of atomism ("Erlebnisatomik") which is out of the context of knowing consciousness, of discourse, and of action. "Erlebnisatomik" ignores the constant dialectic of exterior world and interior world, of object to be known and of knowing consciousness, of the sensation and the essence behind the sensation.

But also Musil insists "that behind appearances lie true events to be discovered."[8] Knowledge for Musil cannot be considered "unabhaengig von den subjektiven Bedingungen der Wahrnehmung."[9] We cannot simply abstract from the world nor from the knowing subject. Interestingly enough, Habermas, many years later, in his quest for a knowledge not divorced from human "interest" in the Kantian sense of the term, reiterates this very same critique of Mach on the grounds that the positivist did not consider the action of the knowing subject upon the reality of what it claimed to know.[10] Habermas clearly illustrates that Mach falls back into the classical discursive paradigm of referentiality by attempting to dispense with the role of the knowing subject in a definition of truth and reality. Mach divests color of its subjective quality in both cases. Both investigations proceed within a physicalist system of reference, regardless of whether we talk of bodies or sensations.[11]

But what, then, are these roles of the knowing subject and the knowing subject's representations? Whereas Mach saw no problem in this area (we could perceive sensations directly and objectively), Musil describes perception of reality as an active and varied procedure, far from being neutral and objective. For example, in Toerless, "seeing" is described in all of the following ways, which indicate the variety of very active and qualitatively modifying ways in which the subject perceives: "Seeing as observation," "seeing as fantasy," "seeing and consumption," "seeing, fire, enlargement," "seeing as unsuccessful transcendence."

Much later, in the "Nachlass" for the completion of *Der Mann ohne Eigenschaften,* Musil associates not only thought, but also *presentation* ("*Darstellung*") with the active production of one's time, with the 'constitution' of relations, and all of this in opposition to naked empiricism ("empirisches Denken"):

> A portrait of the times? Yes and no. A presentation of constitutive relationships. Not topical, but rather on a deeper level. Not skin, but joints. The problems do not have the form in which they appear? No. The problems appear unmodern. The problems of the present day are unmodern! . . . The basis is the spiritual constitution of an epoch. Here lies the contradiction between empirical thinking and emotional thinking. (DMoE, 1938)

1.4 Non-synthesis of "representation" and "object"

The second side of the coin of synthetic knowledge, it will be recalled, is that of adequate representation, a theme brought into the open by the above mention of the problem of "Darstellung," which is inextricably related to actively constitutive thought or knowledge. For example, the classical grammarians (Port-Royal) derived knowledge from the way in which language was patterned or structured. They claimed that it "represented" or was "analogous to" the intentional structure of knowledge. In this case, the representational capacity of knowledge did not come into question. And, as we have argued elsewhere, much contemporary theory of language, more specifically structuralism and semiotics, functions on the basis of a similar assumption.

Musil criticized Mach for not considering the subject of knowledge to be the relation of the cognitive subject to his environment. Subsequently Musil began to explore this problem himself in and through writing. Much later Habermas was to echo Musil's dissatisfaction with empiricism in his explicit critique of Mach by showing how he is stuck within a copy theory of reference and representation on the part of scientific discursive models, without considering the active role of the subject and the non-transparency of his discourse in so doing:

> In the framework of an ontology of the factual, knowledge can be defined only negatively: The *replication* of what is the case must not be obscured by admixtures of subjectivity. The cognitive act itself is designated with the trivial commonplaces of traditional realism and its copy theory of knowledge: "All science aims [. . .] at representing facts in thoughts."[12]

Mach's positivism amounts to a reductionist dismissal of the dialectic of representation, whereby science is founded upon the complete transparency of its symbols and models for reality: "Stipulating the object domain suffices as a criterion of the demarcation between science and metaphysics: all statements intending to describe facts and relations between facts are to be considered scientific. The positivist criterion of demarcation is copying reality."[13] Thus the crisis of synthetic knowledge translates into the discursive crisis of representation. Musil, also, according to Arntzen, was aware that a synthesis of soul and exactness should hypothetically require an adequate language, a sayable foundation: "The synthesis of exactness and soul [is] achieved from the beginning in the connection between the ape-like dance of words and the untold underground in which one is rooted."[14]

However, language should be the mediator of knowledge of the world and of men, as Mauthner was one of the first in "Wittgenstein's Vienna" to point out: "Just because language is a potential mediator it can simultaneously become a barrier to the desire to know."[15]

The theme of the closure off from knowledge and reference, due to language's non-transparency, is set by Toerless' recognition of the need for, yet impossibility of, expression of the "reality" of inner self in and through exteriorized language:

> . . . the words did not say it . . . it is something mute. (Y.T., 17; G.W. II, 18)

> . . . the words meant nothing, or rather, they meant something quite different, as if, while dealing with the same subject, they were taking it from

another side, one that was strange, unfamiliar and irrelevant. (Y.T., 88; G.W. II, 62–63)

As Musil moved away from pure science and philosophy into the literary realm, knowing, truth, and reality became problematized in terms of discursive representation, i.e., in terms of the impossibility of representation in and through the dynamics of discourse: "One must not believe that something must be said correctly in order that it be correctly understood; and therein lies the secret of the living language" (G.W. II, 694). However, the role that Musil attaches to the knowing subject does not make him an idealist in the Fichtean sense. "Reality" is material for the former and not merely a product of the transcendental ego. For Musil, "reality" is a creation of the relations between a constituting discourse, an object-reality, and a knowing subject. Discourse is a part of an active constitution of "reality." Writing "gives" or "constitutes" meaning or models and divisions of "reality"; it does not merely copy it:

> Writing offers symbols. It is interpretation. The interpretation of life. For its reality is material (however: it also offers models and makes partial suggestions). . . . Meaningful consideration is different from sober understanding. It is not only the ordering of understanding, but, more importantly, the ordering of feelings. Interpretation is in every case also the interpretation of life from within. (G.W. II, 970)

1.5 Mach and the beginnings of relativity

At one point, Max Planck,[16] making what he believed to be a most scathing rebuttal of Mach, suggested that if Mach's theory of sensations as reality is adhered to, then it would be conceivable that atoms are no more than the products of experimental sensation and really do not exist as bodies at all. (That, of course, is more or less the affirmation that did arise in postmodern physics.) This would tend to suggest that there are two readings of Mach, the empiricist positivist one just presented, and a far more "relativist" one.

A look should be taken at the controversial question of the extent of Mach's relativism. Where knowledge is based on sensations and experience as opposed to some absolute transcendental category, then there is no real truth in a genuine sense, but only a practical conservation furthering convention.[17] Such is Musil's not necessarily pejorative interpretation of a relativity position in Mach. Furthermore, Einstein's relativity theory is often seen to owe its origins to Mach because of such statements as this one: "Time and space and causality, the Kantian transcendental categories, are not absolute, rather . . . only secured through the meaning of relations in experience."[18] (Einstein himself often proudly declared Mach to be the inspiration for the relativity theory, whereas at the end of his life, in a posthumously published work, Mach openly rejected the relativity theory and any responsibility for it.[19]) The philosopher of science Milic

Capek, as well, attributes an attitude of indeterminacy and relativity to Mach: "Mach clearly seems to correlate the fact that something is going on in the universe with the mathematical indeterminacy of the universe."[20]

It was not on account of the ensuing relativity of reality that Musil criticized Mach in his dissertation. Rather, Musil found fault with Mach's failure to recognize a relativizing factor other than the succession of "Erfahrungen," namely that of the perceiver as subject of knowledge, which undermines the absoluteness of any transcendental categories of reality. In a remark concerning "human uncertainty," Musil does not seem about to escape from the relativity aspect of Mach's thought. He says that there is a small unelucidated remainder of indetermination which resides in every moral experience (DMoE, 813), and considers this to be the cause of human uncertainty.

Whether due to the influence of Mach's real or fictive propensities for relativity, there is no doubt that Musil foresaw the type of *uncertainties* that did arise in postmodern physics: "It is precisely when it is at its strongest that a feeling is most uncertain" (DMoE, 1228). And elsewhere, Musil draws the "Distinction between self-certainty and the uncertainty of feelings" (DMoE, 1227).

If the above seems to vacillate between indeterminacy in fiction and indeterminacy in physics, this is because Musil had begun to see an analogy between problems of representation in narrative and those confronting the pure sciences.

1.6 Perturbation and indeterminacy in quantum mechanics

In the 1920s Werner Heisenberg began to philosophize about the broader impact of quantum mechanics' reduction of the wave packet. The results were more than sufficient to place the classical assumption of objectivity of scientific observation of "reality," and of scientific models into doubt. Indirectly, at least, in the realm of the pure sciences, Musil's literary struggles with the problematics of knowing and of representing "reality" found some consensus.

In the reduction of the wave packet certain inconsistencies arose. The observable coordinates did not correspond algebraically with the corresponding momentum observable. Their probability distributions—but not their ranges of possible values—were coordinated.[21]

Because of these inconsistent results of wave packet reductions, confidence in the empirical was destroyed and along with it the classical confidence in referentiality. By virtue of the fact that the various symbols (i.e., the experimental results, such as the trail that an elementary particle produced in the reduction of a wave packet leaves in a cloud chamber), while supposedly referring to the same "reality," constantly differed from one another. Such a disparity placed into doubt the stability and accuracy of the signifier-signified or word-referent relation. Not only was the supposition that nature was simply "out there" placed into doubt, but also the idea of nature's accessibility to objective description, i.e., to representation.

All that the physicists could observe was the trace produced in one particular experiment, under one particular observer's methodology, eye, and apparatus. The disparity of the symbols throughout a number of experiments proved to be the flaw in the "representationality" of scientific models and instruments. As Hans Reichenbach writes in *The Rise of Scientific Philosophy*: "The *and* joining both wave and particle is not in the language of physics, but in a language which speaks about the language of physics . . . it does not refer to the physical object but to possible descriptions of the physical object and thus falls into the realm of the philosopher."[22]

Facts, reality, and objects are not just directly and transparently accessible to our consciousness and to our discourse. Rather what are perceived are already only symbols, or discursive models. What is more, the faults in these models are not merely due to the instruments or critical tools, but are also due to the interpretation of the results which these instruments yield. One might, thus, compare the instrument to various critical models or tools of discursive criticism.

The scientific observer's role and expectations might correspond to those of the individual critic trying to render a given discursive model operational for textual analysis. For example, the diversity of interpretations of Shakespeare might correspond to the plurality of experimental results. The distance from the "object" is at least two-tiered.[23] Not only is there a "deficit" in the perception of the "object" but there is also what is called an "enrichment" or, in a less positive, a "perturbation." In the reduction of the wave packet, what is being reduced are elementary particles. But, what is being used to reduce the wave packet are also elementary particles. Both are endowed with energy—indeed, both are energy which takes various forms as produced in and through experiment. Reduction of the wave packet suppresses certain physical correlations and in doing so changes the very physical aspect of the "reality" of the object being measured: ". . . since the measurement process is part of the activity whereby we contact and so observe physical reality, it has a disturbing effect on reality and tends to limit our access to the objective properties of atomic realities. . . ."[24]

The analogy between wave packet reduction and discursive critique still holds. We may define perturbation in relation not only to physics, but also to discursive criticism of discourse, as the inability to "separate the physiognomy of the strict object from the matrix of scientific methodology in which it makes its appearance," and the subsequent permutations which the object undergoes.[25]

The inevitable consequence of this perturbation is the impossibility of identifying our scientific models and categories of knowledge and representation with the "object" they seek to know and to represent.[26] Habermas would seem to have inherited this schism noted by Heisenberg when he suggests that the alternative to Mach's "Erfahrungsatomik" is precisely the recognition that science is the "result of *interaction* between the knowing subject and reality,"[27] whereby we may include the discourse and instruments of that knowing subject.

Nevertheless, quantum mechanics is far from having completely succeeded in removing the myth of the Enlightenment or of classical discourse from contemporary practices of discourse of pure science and of the social and human sciences. These myths still flourish today.

Elsewhere, in my work on new communications technology, *Powermatics: A Discursive Critique of New Communications Technology,* I have shown how these classical, instrumentalist procedures of a discourse of knowledge are still fully functioning in all of their hegemonic glory in the "information age." As late as the 1970s the cybernetician-anthropologist-psychologist Gregory Bateson found it necessary to level yet another blow at the arrogance of classical science at work in anthropology. Bateson places both transcendental and empirical theories of knowledge into question, while simultaneously pointing out the perturbations of the anthropological object of study by the subject. This time not only individual, observational factors come into play, but also ethno- and culturocentric factors:

> From this it follows that our categories "religious," "economic," etc. are not *real* subdivisions which are present in the cultures which we study, but are merely *abstractions* which we make for our own convenience when we set out to describe cultures in words. They are not phenomena present in culture, but are labels for various points of view which we adopt in our studies.[28]

What is more, Bateson explicitly outlines the implications of perturbation in terms of a disturbance of our confidence in referentiality. He dissolves the myth of the identification of icon with the object that it represents, the identification of the map with the territory. "Representation," "science," "referentiality," are all submitted to this epistemological critique:

> We say the map is different from the territory. . . . What was on the map is a representation of what was in retinal representation of the man who made the map; and as you push the question back, what you find is an infinite regress, an infinite series of maps. The territory never gets in at all—the territory is Ding an Sich and you can't do anything with it. Always the process of representation will filter it out so that the mental world is only maps of maps of maps, ad infinitum.[29]

1.7 The crisis of representation as epistemological crisis

In the preceding discussion, the access of science to naked external "reality" has been placed radically into question. What is more, inextricably linked with the placing into doubt of synthetic knowledge is the non-identity of sign and referent, i.e., the non-equivalence of scientific or interpretative discourse to that about which it speaks and which it claims to know. The epistemological significance of these developments is vast. Where the empiricist readings of an Ernst Mach do not manage to compensate for the inability to espouse Kantian transcendentalism, where science can neither have transparent access to its object nor faith in any universal or necessary principles, then "knowledge" and "representation" are no more than pieces of groundless fantasy. Unless, of course, some alternative status for the discourse of knowledge can be elaborated.

However, this crisis of classical representation and knowledge was not to go unanswered by modern discourse. C. S. Peirce who, in an article fittingly titled "Questions Concerning Certain Faculties Claimed for Man," seems to begin to find a way out of having to choose either a naked empiricism or a Kantian transcendentalism, a way which will provide us with some guideline for how to use modern discourse to overcome the limitations of classical scientific discourse: "Thus, the sensation, so far as it represents something, is determined, according to a logical law, by previous cognitions, that is to say, these cognitions determine that there shall be a sensation" (5.291).[30]

Peirce is suggesting here that the cognitive framework of the knowing subject determines even what will be perceived. Whence the positivism of Mach's "Erfahrungsatomik"? It is giving way to a modern phenomenology, whereby reality is coconstituted with frameworks of perception and cognition, which is where Musil will be seen to take us with his notion of "many realities."

2.0 Toward the Alternative Discourse of Knowledge

2.1 "Viele Wirklichkeiten": Many realities

In *Der Mann ohne Eigenschaften*, Ulrich's main objection to the Diotimas and the Arnheims who inhabit the land of Kakania is precisely that, for them, there is no other "reality" than "Seinesgleichen" (appearances). Says Ulrich to Diotima: ". . . you have spoken of wanting to fly away together with Arnheim into some sort of sanctity. So you imagine that as a kind of second reality. But what I have been saying means that we must regain possession of unreality. There is no more sense in reality now!" (M.w.Q. 2:338; DMoE, 575).

In opposition to what was shown to be the epistemologically untenable position of affirming a singular, absolute "reality," Ulrich counters with the argument that *there are many "realities"* and that, subsequently, "reality" in the classical sense of the term no longer has any meaning, either as empirical or as transcendental "reality." One may as well suggest a host of other "realities," including a "super reality":

> I do not believe that I see the truth, but what I experience is surely not
> subjective either; it reaches out for truth with a thousand arms. . . . So what
> is left? It is neither imagination nor reality; and if it is not suggestion, then I
> would almost have to conclude that it is the beginning of a super reality.
> (DMoE, 1429)

Despite the plurality of "realities" including "Wirklichkeit als Ver-
wirklichte," "Wirklichkeit als Gueltige," etc., each member of the "Collateral Campaign" will be seen to hold firmly to his or her notion and
discourse of "reality." Just as in the case of the disparity of experimentally
produced symbols in a quantum mechanics experiment, these "realities"—results—do not correspond to one another. Yet they all simultaneously claim to possess the absolute representation of "reality."

A refusal to conceive of more than one reality, of a reality other than the
doxological reality of "zweimaalzweiistvier," is flagrantly mocked by
Musil in the Tagebuecher, yet without relinquishing the need for certainty:
"Do you know what a street looks like? Yes? Who is it that tells you that a
street is simply that which you consider it to be? You cannot imagine that
it could be something else? That comes from the logic of 'two times two is
four.' Yes, but two times two is four!" (Tgb., 8).

2.2 Perspectivism

To positivist empiricism or to transcendentalism, Musil at first seems to
counterpropose an almost Nietzschean perspectivist theory of consciousness and a corresponding theory of "reality." Depending on the
perspective, reality may belong to the "normaler Zustand" or to the "anderer Zustand." Depending on the perspective, good may be bad or vice
versa, a phenomenon referred to by Nietzsche as "transmutation of
values."[31]

> . . . passionate experiences after a while become comical in a changed
> perspective, as though one were seeing them at the far end of a series of
> ninety-nine opened doors. (M.w.Q. 3:115; DMoE, 764)
>
>   . . . certain infinite perspectives that today still lie on the threshold of the
> unconscious . . . become clear and understandable. (Tgb., 53)

"Wirklichkeit" becomes, from a perspectivist point of view, a representation ("Bild") of the world from a certain viewing angle, for example:
"through a narrow, mud-caked window" (DMoE, 459), or through a
"blurred, multiplying lens" (DMoE, 1768).[32]

This perspectivist rendering of "reality" is closely linked to Musil's
theory of irony which is described as "variable functions" where the
meaning of a statement depends upon "Funktionswerte": "The meaning is
determined by the constellation" (DMoE, 37). Such a theory of meaning
seems to correspond to a pragmatic theory of meaning, such as that of a

Peirce or a Wittgenstein (*Investigations*), where the sense or value of a sign depends upon its functional relationship to the other signs and sign users which position it. Such a theory of meaning is truly relational. Furthermore, this relationality has implications for a theory of language. For Musil, the sense of a word is not only functionally relative but also multiple and changing, which implies a principle of relativity of meaning, dependent upon the discursive context in which it is employed: "But words have so many double and auxiliary meanings, so many double and auxiliary connotations, that one would do well to keep at a distance from them" (DMoE, Tgb., 2).

Perspectivism projected onto the field of discourse amounts to a plurivalence of meaning, whereby it would be impossible to fix a reference or a denotation since all meanings are equally valid and equally "real," from within that context or that perspective.

> God is far from meaning the world literally. The world is an image, an analogy, a figure of speech, that He must make use of for some reason or other, and it is of course always inadequate. We must not take Him at His word; we ourselves must work out the sum that He sets us. (M.w.Q. 2:65; DMoE, 357–58)

2.3 Discursive contextualization as "reality"

One must, however, be careful not to oversimplify the connection between "Erkenntnistheorie"-perspectivism and discursive perspectivism. The former does not cause the latter, nor does the latter *represent* the former. They are inextricably tied up with one another. For Musil, it is this very irreducible, contextual perspectivism of *discursive meaning* that is responsible for the pluralities of knowledge. A radically contextualized discourse implies a radically contextualized epistemology, and vice versa.

> In both cases [past and present] it was inexactitude and the ignoring of the decisive differences that played the greatest part. A part of what was great was taken for the whole, a remote analogy for the fulfilment of the truth; and the emptied-out skin of a great word was stuffed according to the fashion of the day. (M.w.Q. 2:190; DMoE, 458)

Quantum mechanics placed the onus for the plurality of reality, or at least for its unknowability, upon the instruments of experimental observation, analogous to the contextualization of discourse and of the discursive tools used to talk about reality: "The difference between observation, language and explanatory language, then, is *not that they deal with different sets of referents* but that they consider the same set within different contexts."[33]

This contextualization amounts to a redefinition of terms in relation to other discursive terms, whereby, under various contextual conditions, varying relations of likeness or identification are established. Musil thus describes "high humanity" (treated here as synonomous with "Enlightenment") as the belief that these likenesses are "identical to reality": "Without doubt what is called the higher humanism is nothing but an attempt to fuse together those two great halves of life, metaphor and truth, after the preliminary of carefully separating them" (M.w.Q. 2:362; DMoE, 593).

Traditional Musil scholarship widely recognizes this disturbance of a singular, absolute view of reality or meaning by the various contextualizations of discourse, whereby various relationships occur differentially. This perturbance is referred to by Karthaus as the "metaphorische Mutation" in Musil's writing.[34]

Maurice Blanchot, one of the most, if not the most, perceptive critics of Musil, associates this contextualization of truth and meaning in and through discourse directly with Musil's irony: "the spirit of the work—a spirit under the guise of irony. Musil's irony is a cold light which invisibly changes from one moment to the next the lighting of the book, and even though often indistinct, it does not allow us to arrive at a definite, pre-established meaning."[35]

We might also recall here that Cleanth Brooks defined irony as a radical contextualization of meaning. However, what Blanchot does not develop in his brilliant essay on Musil is a way of describing precisely how the contextual perspectivization of meaning and reality in *Der Mann ohne Eigenschaften* functions. Musil himself suggests that this effect is due to *the interaction of various words with each other.* He speaks of the ". . . irrational effect of words simultaneously irradiating each other" (G.W. II, 1147). It is this radically contextualizing relationality of modern discourse that we seek to find in Musil and Peirce as the beginning of a new way to speak.

2.4 Relational constitution of "reality" and "meaning"

Reality is relationally constituted but all of the elements in the relation contribute to its determination. One must not assume that perspectivism and contextual uncertainty of meaning are due to any subjective, capricious priority of a transcendental ego over the world. We are not thrown back to idealism. Rather, they are due to the relations which occur at every instant between man, his language, and the world.

> The way I'd put it . . . is that it's like looking out across a wide glimmering sheet of water: the eye seems almost to be seeing darkness, everything's so bright, and on the far bank things don't seem to be fixed on solid ground but floating in the air, in a delicate over-distinctness that's almost painful . . . bewildering. . . . One is linked with everything. . . . (M.w.Q. 3:99; DMoE, 751)

To return to quantum mechanics for a moment, we find a very similar explanation of the instability of reality based on *relationality*: ". . . the basic observables of physics are essentially constituted as relations between things and things, based upon so many different ways in which things act mutually and reciprocally upon one another."[36]

Arntzen describes the effect of this discursive interrelationality in Musil:

> . . . the single passage attains its actual effect only in context, i.e., as a structural moment. The satirical commentary, especially, can be fatally misunderstood if this is not taken into account, since this commentary not only appears in a wide variety of forms, but also in a variety of contexts and on different levels. (Arntzen)[37]

This postulate of interrelationality answers a definite "no" to the question whether there is a privileged reality among the plurality of realities, i.e., one more real than the others: "The goals, the voices, the reality, the seduction of it all, luring and leading one on, all that one follows and plunges into—is it the real reality. . . ?" (M.w.Q 1:149; DMoE, 129).

And Musil writes in his thesis on Mach that reality must ever be changing since it is only ". . . secured through the meaning of relations in experience."[38]

So far relationality has included two terms, the perceptual apparatus of the knowing subject and the discourse or sign-vehicle deployed to portray the world. The third term, the natural object, is still missing, but without it one would fall back into idealism.

2.5 Triadicity: Three-way relationality

At one point in the *Nachlass*, Musil delimits his epistemology as an interrelation of three aspects.[39] Although it would be dangerous to find a one-to-one correspondence, Musil's reference might be seen to justify an attempt to find a way of speaking about the relativity of reality and meaning in discourse by way of Peirce's notion of semiotic triadicity.

Although Peirce's work has given rise to many radically divergent interpretations, there is one aspect which is generally accepted. Peirce's philosophy of language and theory of knowledge, which he unites under the concept of "semiotics," is triadic, that is to say, it is based upon the interaction of three "categories" or "functions." Reality, truth, and meaning are also the changing products of triadic relations, as opposed to deriving from any absolute value: "The 'realistic view of reality' is the reality as the normal product of mental action, and not as the incognizable cause of it" (5.257).

Reality, then, must be redefined and reconsidered in nonabsolutist, nonclassical terms. But rather, for Peirce, reality and meaning are understood in none other than triadically relational terms. "Not only is every fact really a relation, but your thought *implicitly* represents it as such" (3.417). In a letter to Lady Welby, Peirce defined his philosophy as one that was convinced of the "triadic organization of all things," and then proceeded to delimit what he meant by his triadic categories: "Firstness," "Secondness," and "Thirdness."[40]

However, it should also be recalled that, for Peirce, knowledge of reality was knowledge of signs. *All knowledge was semiotics*, and as such dealt with signs, with sign-systems, and with the production of signs.

> It has never been in my power to study anything—mathematics, metaphysics, gravitation, thermodynamics, optics, chemistry, comparative anatomy, psychology, phonetics, economics, the history of science, whist, men and women, meteorology—except as a study of semiotics.[41]

As will be elaborated upon in the next section, everything, for Peirce, could appear and be known purely as a sign. We refer to the manner in which the plurality and shifting of reality and truth is due to the plurality of contextual meanings in various sign-relations.[42]

Peirce's triadic semiotics may provide the best opportunity for elucidating a new concept of discourse, one which could eventually be made operational. Signs as the constituting aspect of semiotics are also themselves relationally triadic. Each sign is composed of three elements, *an Object, a Representamen,* and *an Interpretant* (from now on we will refer to the sign which relates these three aspects as a "sign-function," although sometimes the Representamen alone is simply called "sign"):

> My definition of a representamen is as follows: A Representamen is the subject of a triadic relation to a second, called its Object, for a third, called its Interpretant, and this triadic relation is such that the Representamen determines its Interpretant to be situated in a similar triadic relation to the same Object for just any Interpretant. (1.514)

> A sign, called the *representamen,* in every case is used to "stand for" an object independent of itself. (2.303)

> [A sign is] anything which determines something else (its *interpretant*) to refer to an object to which itself refers (its *object*). (2.3030)

> The plurality of truths or references is a result of this triadicity:

> Now a sign has, as such, three references: first, it is a sign *to* some thought which *interprets it;* second it is a sign *for* some *object* to which in that thought it is equivalent; third, it is a sign, *in* some respect or quality, which brings it into connection *with its object.* (5.283)

Briefly, it is possible to draw some parallels between this semiotic triadicity and the elements involved in the quantum mechanics experiment. The Object would be the wave packet which is supposedly out there in brute Nature, there to be reduced or measured. This Object must not be confused with the "real." Secondly, the symbol which the sign leaves as a vapor trail, a particle, or whatever, already produced in and through experiment, and without which we would not suspect any Object to exist at all, is the equivalent of the Representamen. So too would be the image in the lens of a microscope or a telescope. The scientist's interpretation of the results of the experiment, or his observation (in the simplest sense of the image on the retina) are examples of more or less complex Interpretants, whereby Interpretant may be seen to derive from the words "interpret" or "translator." That which is translated? One sign-function substitutes for another, by virtue of the effect that the sign-function has on the use of the sign.[43]

Triadicity, as well as defining meaning and truth relationally, also refuses to give any preferential status to any one particular sign-function as more truthful or more referential than another. Peirce's sign-theory leaves no room for a biplanar semiotic assumption that referentiality-denotation represents a literal or objective reality, whereas connotation represents a contextually relative idea. The distinction between denotation and connotation is eliminated. All signs depend upon triadic constitution, as opposed to biplanar, bilateral correspondence: ". . . the dyadic relations of logical *breadth* and *depth,* often called denotation and connotation, have played a great part in logical discussions, but these take their origin in the triadic relation between a sign (representamen), and its interpretant sign." (1.538)

2.6 The Interpretant as Phenomenological Dimension

The importance attached by Musil to the necessity of a theory of the knowing subject/consciousness, and of Heelan's description of quantum mechanics as having pointed out that there is a "World-for-us"[44] and not just a "world-for-it," is also reflected in the relatively strong insistence placed by Peirce upon that aspect of the sign known as "Interpretant."

Here it should be stressed that, for Peirce, the Interpretant is *not a person*, rather it is *the effect* that a sign-function has upon an interpreter or user of a sign, be it human or other:

> . . . anything which is so determined by something else, called its object and so determines an effect upon a person, which effect I call its interpretant, that the latter is thereby mediately determined by the former.[45]
>
> (A sign) has an object and an interpretant, the latter being that which the sign produces in the quasi-mind that is the interpreter by determining the latter to a feeling, to an exertion, or to a sign, which determination is the interpretant. (4.536)

The Interpretant seems to be at the heart of Peirce's theory of meaning, where "by the *meaning* of a term, proposition or argument, we understand the entire general intended interpretant" (5.175). "The interpretant as it is revealed is the right understanding of the sign itself" (5.175).[46]

Where meaning is described by Peirce as the "proper significate outcome of a sign," the ties of meaning to Interpretant effect become even clearer:

> For the proper significate outcome of a sign, I propose the name, the interpretant of the sign. . . . Whether the interpretant be necessarily a triadic result is a question of words, that is, of how we limit the extension of the term "sign"; but it seems to me convenient to make the triadic proposition of the interpretant essential to a "sign." (5.474)

One should not overlook the question posed here by Peirce as concerns the triadicity of the Interpretant itself. It is essential. Whereas other theorists of consciousness posit a knowing structure, e.g., the Hegelian dialectic, which itself does not change, Peirce posits his mediating term as itself determined by previous and future sign-relations. "It is not necessary that the interpretant should actually exist. A being in future suffices" (2.92). Hence, meaning and truth, defined even in terms of its Interpretant effect or significate outcome, is irremediably triadic and relational. How can an Interpretant be triadically determined? It is so because throughout the production of sign-functions along a diachronic axis, various aspects of the sign change functions within different relational triads. Hence, what was a Representamen in one sign-relation may become an Object for another sign-function or again an Interpretant, and so on, ad infinitum. We may now understand why Peirce defines meaning as "the translation of a sign into another (sign) or system of signs" (4.127).

Given the triadic relationality of signs and their situation in various moving sign-relations, meaning and reality must be understood as a radical Contextuality. As Foucault was to argue much later, signifying discourse may no longer be considered as a fixed, abstract, absolute system, nor as an isolated discrete unit.[47] The sign or the discourse production must have its meaning and truth situated not as an extra-discursive referent but within the process of discourse taken as sign-triadicity which constantly evolves triadically as well. Context may be understood as the triadic relations of sign-functions of various degrees of extension ranging from the simple Object-Representamen-Interpretant relation to the whole diachronic context of human and non-human semiotic production, where the sign-functions continuously relate to and substitute for each other.

This past, present, or future concrete relationality of elements taken as the context which defines and positions all sign-production was subsequently to be seated at the heart of Foucault's definition of discourse, although the triadicity per se is not mentioned:

> Utterance is not a structure, in other words a set of relations between varying elements allowing for a possible infinite number of concrete models: it is a function of existence belonging exclusively to signs about which we can decide by analysis or intuition if they have meaning or not, according to what principle they are connected or juxtaposed, what they represent and what kind of act is effected by their expression (oral and written). (author's translation)[48]

Foucault, in the pragmatic tradition of Peirce, is insisting on the actual use or act of language situated in a relational context as the only object of

study possible for discourse analysis. He is excluding the biplanar semiotician's insistence on some absolute, abstract, generative system—
"langue." "Langue" is as absolute as the would-be absolute picture of
reality in classical science. The on-going practice, relationality, and contextuality render the "truth" of "langue" non-pertinent just as the disparity of quantum mechanics results rendered absolute physical
coordinates relative. It is for this reason that I would disagree with those
who label Foucault a structuralist.

Bateson also develops this pragmatic potential, insisting upon the actual, contextualized practice of discourse as opposed to the premise that
contexts are always conceptually isolatable—since the universe is a complex system of interrelated contexts. He speaks of:

> [a] weaving of contexts and of messages which propose context but
> which, like all messages, whatsoever, have 'meaning' only by virtue of
> context . . .[49]

> It is important to see the particular utterance or action as *part* of the
> ecological subsystem called context and not as the product or effect of what
> remains of the context after the piece which we want to explain has been cut
> out from it.[50]

Habermas, as well, carries forward this pragmatic solution. With direct
reference to Wittgenstein, he suggests the pertinence of a theory of language which would replace generative grammars of abstract syntax or
semantics with a greater consideration for the actual or possible use-
contexts (employment relations) of language: "The use theory of meaning
developed from the work of Wittgenstein has shown, however, that the
meaning of linguistic expressions can be identified only with reference to
situations of possible employment."[51]

Peirce's triadic description of semiotics seems to have given us a starting
point from which to talk about the interrelationality of "reality," "meaning," "truth." Indeed, it insists upon this contextualized relationality in
each and every practice of discourse. However, lest one succumb to the
hubris of many Peircean disciples and rejoice in a typology of signs, be it
triadic or not, several other aspects of the Peircean semiotic will be seen to
pose some problems to analysis. We refer here more specifically to the
reduction of everything to the status of the sign and the infinity of sign-
production and triadic substitution. Does saying that everything is a sign-
relation including man, as does Peirce, entail the postmodern murder of
the subject? Is the Man without Qualities the evacuation of the category of
the person?

3.0 *Der Mann ohne Eigenschaften:* Man as the Particular Manifestations of Signs

At this stage of our argument we would like to suggest that Musil, as
well as Peirce, couples a theory of man and of consciousness with a theory

of discourse. Musil attributes the status of sign and sign-production to man.

3.1 Man is an inference of signs

Musil criticized Mach for reducing bodies to the status of "thought symbols for complexes of elements." This reduction did not, however, entail a reduction of the basic "Erfahrungsatom" to the status of a sign. Indeed, for Mach, the body as a sign *refers to a non-sign*, i.e., to the reality of sensations: "Sensations are not signs of things; but, on the contrary, a thing is a thought symbol for a compound-sensation of relative fixedness."[52] Musil did not contest so much Mach's emphasis on the thought-symbol as his emphasis on the sensation as the sole reality, leaving out any conception of constituting mind.[53]

It is to C. S. Peirce that we may look to provide a way of conceiving of the "left-out" subject in relation to its manifestation as sign, without reducing it to a collection of sensations. His solution, briefly, is that sign processes are themselves cognitive systems and processes, i.e., references and not merely atomistic, dispersed elements. In other words, the cognitive subject/mind are inferences of signs. The cognitive process is discursive at every stage:

> Now thought is of the nature of a sign. In that case, then, if we can find out the right method of thinking and can follow it out—the right method of transforming signs—then truth can be nothing more nor less than the last results to which the following out of this method would ultimately carry us. In that case, that to which the representation should conform is itself something in the nature of a representation, or sign—something noumenal, intelligible, conceivable, and utterly unlike a thing-in-itself. (5.553)

Peirce reinforces the argument that the crisis of knowledge, of being, and of reality was a crisis of discourse's capacity to represent or to refer transparently, by saying that there is nothing new in considering "being" as a function of language. Aristotle (whose categories are parts of speech) considered it so, as did Kant (whose categories are the characters of different kinds of propositions) (5.294). From this standpoint Peirce goes on to say that "all thought occurs in signs" (5.253) and that "Man himself as a being of habit, as a mediator between denotation and law, is 'himself a sign'" (6.344). The argument that man is a sign follows the following lines (5.250-282). By refusing the possibility of original intuition, Peirce claims that the self is a learned entity, an inference, and not an intuited entity. And, since everything that is learned is a thought, the self is also a thought. But, since every thought is a sign, therefore man himself is a sign.[54]

3.2 The materiality of the sign

At this stage some warning should be made against considering Peirce to be a nominalist. "What is reality coincides with what we can truly state about it," says Peirce. However, this view is quite a materialist position in that the sign relations constituting our statements are material, are sociohistorically situated occurrences which relate extant Objects, Interpretants and Representamen. Later it will become more evident how Peirce justifies this assumption that man is a sign and that reality coincides with what we can say about it, without becoming a Kantian or a Lockean.

Foucault and Bakhtin, for the present, two other discourse theorists for whom everything is a material production and relation of signs, have developed and clarified this position that discourse is at the heart of material existence without evacuating that materiality.

For Foucault, discourse consists in: "practices that systematically form the objects of which they speak."[55] The relations of discourse are the relations of all types of social institutions and practices: "These relations are established between institutions, economic and social processes, behavioral patterns, systems of norms, techniques, types of classification, modes of characterization"[56] (author's translation). However these relations "are discourse itself as a practice."[57] What is more, "it is always on the level of materiality that it [discourse] takes effect, that it is effect."[58] If it is recalled that "effect" taken as Interpretant is the meaning, the significant outcome of a sign, for Peirce, then it becomes obvious that sign production and its meanings are real in a way far different from the referential manner. They are real as practice, as event, as relation, all of which manifest the materiality of discourse: "[discourse] has its place and it consists in the relation, the coexistence, the dispersion, the intersection, the accumulation and the selection of material elements; it is neither the action, nor the property of a body; it is produced as an effect of and by a material dispersion."[59]

It is Bakhtin who most clearly distinguishes between, on the one hand, referentiality or representation as a classical discursive procedure which yielded only a reflection, a simulacrum of reality, and, on the other hand, an interactive, interrelational discourse—*pragmatic* practice. This latter enjoys not only the status of material reality but also the *conditio sine qua non* of the realization of the consciousness. The following quotation from Bakhtin is a very clear refutation of the accusation that pragmatics is pandiscursivist idealism or nominalism:

> Every ideological sign is not only a reflection, a shadow of reality, but is also itself a material segment of that very reality . . . of sound, physical mass, color, movements of the body, or the like. A sign is a phenomenon of the external world. Both the sign itself and all the effects it produces . . . occur in outer experience.
> . . . consciousness itself can arise and become a viable fact only in the material embodiment of signs.[60]

Considering man to be a sign is the only way to ground the mediation or relationality spoken about in the preceding section, without positing a Kantian transcendental unity of consciousness. Only via the process of inference mediated by signs is understanding constituted:

> Man makes the word, and the word means nothing which the man has not made it mean, and that only to some man. But since man can think only by means of words or other external symbols, these might turn round and say: "You mean nothing which we have not taught you, and then only so far as you address some words as the interpretant of your thought." (5.313)

Considering everything to be a sign has vast consequences for the practice of discursive interpretation. First, it eliminates both the necessity and pertinence of intentionality-oriented hermeneutic criticism, whereby the critic 'guesses' some pre-discursively intended meaning unsupported by any discursive manifestations at all, e.g., the 'little black box' of the intentions of the sign sender. Character, authorial intention, receiver effect, sociohistorical background, all must be studied as sign relations. Secondly, the "reality" of the interpretation will not be situated in abstract categories of signs but in the signs and sign-relations themselves, those of a textual, paratextual and extratextual nature, including the sign relations, taken as Interpretant-effects of ourselves as sign perceivers/critics.

The alternative to recognizing the impact of Peircean semiotics would be to go on talking about essences, and structures of language divorced from the actual, materialized practices and interrelations of signs.

3.3 Is the man without qualities a sign?

Traditionally, James Joyce's work is thought to be far more radically modern or even postmodern than Musil's, precisely because of his treatment of the subject in narrative and in narration. The evolution from *Portrait of An Artist* through *Ulysses* to *Finnegans Wake* is seen to be the move toward the postmodern evacuation of the subject from the source of discourse. Instead, the subject flows out of discourse, is spoken by the host of discourses that subsume it. A closer comparison of these two authors, however, reveals that both were struggling for a postclassical conception of the subject in discourse, and that Musil's attempt is as innovative as Joyce's, though differently so.

From Musil's remarks concerning Joyce it would initially appear that Musil gives thought processes in consciousness some distinction from, and priority over, speech processes. These latter are the *sole* consideration of James Joyce, for which Musil chides him:

> Joyce. A profile: spiritualized naturalism—A step that was already due in 1900. His punctuation is naturalistic. So is the "obscenity." Appeal: How does the average person live? In comparison I practise a heroic conception of art. Question: How does one think? His abbreviations are short forms of linguistically orthodox forms. They copy language processes that take years. Not the process of thinking. (G.W. II, 858)

Although Musil, perhaps not without "sour grapes" (he disagreed with those who found Joyce more innovative than himself), begrudges Joyce for only imitating banal speech processes, it would be a mistake to see Musil as totally separating speech and thought processes. Musil is exploring thought processes but he is doing so, indeed there is no other way to do so, through a study and practice of *discourse processes*. For example, Musil proposes that discourse be considered to be a social product, i.e., a product of interaction, and he goes on to state that the logic of thought follows that of language:

> Collectivism. Language [is a] social product. Overcoming of the primeval beast of prey through the horde. Thinking [is a] result of language. Individual achievements are negligible compared to the knowledge and skills possessed and transmitted by society. The individual today is quite hopeless without society. (Tgb., 593)

In another passage, Musil illustrates that it is impossible to narrate life directly without mediation. All that can be narrated, if even that, is the "Widerschein"—reflection, or representation of life. This reflection occurs in the "mind" of literature and men. But as a reflection, it is indeed a sign of life, and hence an aspect of sign-relations and sign-productions. The opposite would be the naked presence of life itself, which Musil does not even try to represent. Everything else is semiotic: "Readers are in the habit of demanding to be told about life and not about the reflection of life in literature and in the heads of people. But this is justified only when this reflection is an impoverished and conventional copy of life. I am attempting to offer them the original" (DMoE, 1937).

In *Der Mann ohne Eigenschaften*, narrative does not occur in the sense that Pelć defines it, i.e., as saying "how things are."[61] Narrative occurs rather as saying *"how things are mediated"* in man's consciousness, as present in his discursive procedures. For Peirce, semiotics is triadic mediation and mediation is itself semiotic. Musil also explicitly states that man is only a "Gestalt"—a configuration in a book, a possibility, a contextualized semiotic appearance:

> . . . that history should be invented and that one should live the history of ideas instead of the history of the world, that one should clutch hard at everything that could never be quite realised in practice, so that one might ultimately reach a stage of living as if one were not a human being at all, but merely a figure in a book, a figure with all the inessential elements left out, the essential residue of it undergoing a magical integration. . . . (M.w.Q. 2:360; DMoE, 592)

If one were tempted to argue that Musil holds onto an anthropocentric view of consciousness,[62] one which would postulate man at the heart of all life and the source of discourse and thought, Musil's own distinction between a "man without qualities" and a "world of qualities without a man" indirectly dispels such an interpretation. Ulrich, the "man without qualities," is a man composed of his actual discourses, acts, and assumed roles, with no transcendental essence of consciousness apart from these material, interactional actualizations. On the other hand, in the land of Kakania, i.e., classical Vienna school thought, there existed a current belief in essences of character, in qualities, regardless of their being actualized or mediated in and through experience and material performance. Such a belief would hold that there are a priori facts and thoughts independent of their manifestation in and through discourse and actualized interaction. The narrator in *Der Mann ohne Eigenschaften* makes much fun of such a world of qualities or essences, without a man, a world without actualization and mediation in existence:

> There has arisen a world of qualities without a man to them, of experiences without anyone to experience them, and it almost looks as though under ideal conditions man would no longer experience anything at all privately and the comforting weight of personal responsibility would dissolve into a system of formulae for potential meanings. It is probable that the dissolution of the anthropocentric attitude (an attitude that, after so long seeing man as the centre of the universe, has been dissolving for some centuries now) has finally begun to affect the personality itself; for the belief that the most important thing about experience is the experiencing of it, and about deeds the doing of them, is beginning to strike most people as naive. (M.w.Q. 1:175; DMoE, 150)

In short, for Musil, consciousness, man, and thought processes are *not* essences which need not be mediated, manifested, or materially present. Perhaps less explicit metalinguistically, but nevertheless very obvious in Musil's narration, and as we shall show, in his own discursive practice, is the position that man and thought processes are mediated in and through discourse processes. Whereas Joyce's work has been described as writing the *work in progress*, whereby the subject has become the sum of its surface practices and the medium of infused discourses, Musil's work is the *subject in process*, whereby the relational production of discourses constitutes the subject and its thought in ever-changing or processual ways. Two very different concepts of the subject in discourse—both very different from that of the classical episteme.

But this does not mean that Musil's novel is not also a work in progress. Indeed, he never finished it! As we shall discuss next, however, this progressiveness and incompleteness of the narration was itself an epistemological solution or alternative to classical discourse, rather than the defeat of modernism.

4.0 "Essayism": Infinite Continuum of Sign Interaction, and Infinite Series of Contexts

In *Der Mann ohne Eigenschaften*, an impersonal, distanced narrator writes of Ulrich's chosen form of expression, "Essayismus," which corresponds to his attempt at "hypothetical living," an attempt to unite exact and inexact ways of knowing:

> In this manner an endless system of relationships arose in which there was no longer any such thing as independent meaning, such as in ordinary life, at a crude first approach, are ascribed to actions and qualities. (M.w.Q. 1:298; DMoE, 251)

> It was approximately in the way that an essay, in the sequence of its paragraphs, takes a thing from many sides without comprehending it wholly—for a thing wholly comprehended instantly loses its bulk and melts down into a concept—that he believed he could best survey and handle the world and his own life. (M.w.Q. 1:297; DMoE, 250)

4.1 Infinite process

In the *Tagebuecher*, speaking once again of the problem of exact and human knowledge, Musil proposes that the solution lies only in *infinite process*: "The answer to such questions lies at the end of an endless process" (G.W. II, 810). "Essayism" is the culmination of the attempt to unite exact and human knowledge in a new form of composition which emphasizes infinite process, perspectivism, relationality, and interaction. What is more, this discursive procedure corresponds existentially to "hypothetical living" and attempts not only to provide an outlook on, but also to legitimate certain social practices over others.

Elsewhere, Musil accentuates the continuous becoming of man's person and development as well as the becoming of his poetry. [Poetry] ". . . contains the not-yet-at-the-end of man, the fascination of man's development in consumption" (G.W. II, 1255). In this regard, at least, Musil approaches the Joycean concept of "work in progress."

The continuous production of various interrelations of words is reaffirmed as a principle of art by Musil: "The principle of art is infinite variation" (G.W. II., 868).

This principle is designed to destroy the systematic, overused, "conventional," repetition (could we say rigid "habit"?) of art works. It is as though there were a *compulsion toward this infinite production of discursive variations*, a sort of "Delight in speaking: one must talk in order not to lose the faculty of speech" (DMoE, 1671). And, again, this discursive movement entails a similar existential movement in the same practice of relationality:

> The task is: to discover ever new solutions, connections, constellations and variables, to produce prototypes of occurrences, enticing models of human existence, to discover the inner man. (G.W. II, 1029)

4.2 Uncertainty versus closed system

The discursive process known as "essayism" arose from Ulrich's discontent, not with the vague subjectivism of the escapees from science who proclaimed absolute "uncertainty" and the right to say "n'importe quoi," but rather from a dissatisfaction with "exactness," with the systems of science which had been his "metier" at the age of twenty-six but which at thirty-two seemed somewhat "ungenuine": ". . . a paradoxical combination of precision and indefiniteness. He possesses that incorruptible, deliberate cold-bloodedness, the temperament that goes with exactitude; but apart from and beyond this quality all is indefinite" (M.w.Q. 1:292–93; DMoE, 246–47).

In the totalized philosophical system, Ulrich saw a sort of tyranny, describing philosophers as aggressive people who, ". . . having no army at their disposal, bring the world into subjection to themselves by means of locking it up in a system" (M.w.Q. 1:300; DMoE, 253).

The absence of a structure or of a system, as well as the infinite continuous progression of discourse is an avowed compositional procedure used not only by Ulrich, but also by Musil:

> Were I to let my thoughts go beyond the bounds of that which I could possibly justify, I would call that an essay, an attempt. And since everything good has rules but evil does not yet possess a system and is treated as an exception and thus always remains personal, I, who am neither scholar nor character, but in this case still want to be a writer, can only give my thoughts a personal connection. (Tgb., 643–44)

4.3 Incompleteness

Indeed, "process" was so important to Musil, it was so essential not to give the impression of a finished structure, that he once told a friend how he would finish his novel, which of course is not only unfinished but *unfinishable:* "At the end of a page in the middle of a sentence with a comma." Incompleteness and process infiltrate the style and punctuation of *Der Mann ohne Eigenschaften:*

> One could put it all more briefly. The new cure for syphilis was making . . . Research into plant-metabolism was becoming . . . The conquest of the South Pole seemed . . . Professor Steinach's experiments were arousing . . . In this way quite half the definiteness of things could be left out, and it did not make much difference. (M.w.Q. 2:68; DMoE, 359)

What marks Ulrich off from the rest of the characters in the novel is the "fertige Weltanschauung" as closure of discourse possibilities of the latter as compared to Ulrich's "essayistic" plurality of perspectives and discourses. The disturbances and constant hovering, or "Schweben," of essayism are what destroys the fixed systems and ideologies of closed discursive perspectives.

("Schweben" is a term from Schlegel's romantic irony that was very dear to Musil—"hovering." It is also how Aristophanes portrayed Socrates.)

> There was something in Ulrich's nature that worked in a haphazard, para-
> lysing, disarming manner against logical systematisation, against the one-
> track will, against the definitely directed urges of ambition; and it was also
> connected with his chosen expression, "Essayism," even although this
> something in him contained precisely those elements that he had, in the
> course of time and with unconscious care, eliminated from that concept.
> (M.w.Q. 1:300; DMoE, 253)

In short, essayism tends toward a new type of discourse of knowledge
while simultaneously dismantling both exact systematic and capriciously
subjective kinds of knowledge.

4.4 Experiment

The German translation of "essay" is "versuch," which can mean "*attempt*" but which can also mean "experiment," for example, an
experiment with the discourse of knowing (DMoE, 253). Essayism no
longer fits into traditional categories of knowledge, namely true and false,
or smart or stupid (DMoE, 253). Essayism makes random elements interact
which have not yet come into contact (DMoE, 252). Essayism is a way to
learn the interplay of internal and external aspects of things (DMoE, 252).
Essayism is an experiment with the impersonal ("unpersoenlich") knowledge of "das Persoenliche."

The various discursive procedures that could be seen to constitute this
experimental discursive practice are disturbance, discontinuity, infinite
process, infinite interaction, impersonality, asystematicity, incompleteness, and perspectivism. These are the traits of a new type of
discourse of knowledge—"essayism"—which both Musil and his hero
Ulrich metalinguistically thematize and discursively practice.

4.5 Essayism and irony

Essayism in *Der Mann ohne Eigenschaften* is comparable to romantic
ironic infinite parabasis in the way that a perspectivist reflection relativizes all previous narrative positions, thereby destroying the illusion of
any absolute discursive position.[63] Herman Pongs suggests that constructive irony in *Der Mann ohne Eigenschaften* is less the connectedness
of things—"Zusammenhang der Dinge," as Musil said, and more a lack of
system, a lack of structure, a readiness for new relations and new experiences, an infinite continuum of experiment and relationality of dispersed
elements. Or again, as Pongs would say, irony, like essayism, is dispersion
or disconnectedness—"*Zusammenhangslosigkeit*": "Der Roman dagegen
spiegelt die 'Zusammenhangslosigkeit.'"[64]

But how do we talk about such a discursive process without once again
freezing it into the very categories of knowledge and discourse which it
had tendentiously contested and surpassed? Again we may look to C. S.
Peirce for such a reformulation of semiotics.

4.6 Infinite sign-production

Although it is impossible and perhaps nonessential to determine which comes first, or if they are separable at all (i.e., Peirce's triadic theory of sign-production or his cosmology), the latter may serve as a basis of explanation of the fundamental principle of interrelational dynamics of signs, thought-signs, and man-signs. In Peirce's cosmology, "Synechism" refers to the *constant extension, interaction,* and *continuous production* of the elements of the world, which are *guided by convention and chance—"Tychism."*

Tychism is the principle of evolution by absolute chance in the world which generates new habits, laws and associations. These new habits transcend fixed laws or mechanistic models.[65]

Synechism is:

> That tendency of philosophical thought that insists upon the idea of continuity as of prime importance in philosophy and, in particular, upon the necessity of hypotheses involving true continuity. (6.169)

> . . . there is only one mental law, namely that ideas have a tendency to continually extend themselves and to affect certain others which are situated in relation to them in a particular relation of affectibility. By this extensive action they lose their intensity, and in particular their power to affect others, but they gain in generality and are tied to other ideas. (6.04)

Synechism gives continuity and continuous interrelations to sign-production, whereas the element of chance involved in Tychism explains how it is that *new* ideas or hypotheses are formed.

This cosmology of continuity applies to things, feelings, ideas, thoughts, in brief, to the whole of semiotics. It makes for a new concept of time and space as an infinite continuum, without any fixed starting or ending points. Current, previous and successive stages of the continuum constantly interact:

> [In] what [does] the flow of time consist?. . . Between any two states [. . .] lies an innumerable series of states affecting one another. . . . Every state of feeling is affectible by an earlier stage. . . . In time, there must be a continuity of changeable qualities. . . . When any particular kind of feeling is present, an infinitesimal continuum of all feelings differing infinitesimally from that is present. (6.128–132)

> Since space is continuous, it follows that there must be an immediate community of feeling between parts of mind infinitesimally near together. Without this, I believe it would have been impossible for minds external to one another ever to become coordinated, and equally impossible for any coordination to be established in the action of the nerve matter of one brain. (6.134)

Therefore, signs are not only triadically organized and interrelated, but this interrelation is continuously expanding throughout time and space, without any clear demarcations or frontiers. Triadicity occurs as infinite progress and infinite regress, forming an open area or space of all sign-productions which, hypothetically, would have to be known in its totality were the "whole" of "truth" or "meaning" of any one sign-relation to be adequately, contextually understood:

> [. . .]each former thought suggests something to be thought that follows it, i.e., is the sign of something to this latter.
>
> Our train of thought may, it is true, be interrupted. But we must remember that, in addition to the principal element of thought at any moment, there are a hundred things in our mind to which but a small fraction of attention or consciousness is conceded. It does not, therefore, follow, because a new constituent of thought gets the uppermost, that the train of thought that it displaces is broken off altogether.
>
> [. . .]there is no intuition or cognition not determined by previous cognitions, it follows that the striking in of a new experience is never an instantaneous affair, but is an event occupying time and coming to pass by a continuous process. (5.284)

The infinite process, the continuous interaction, the infinite number of possible experiences; all were described by Musil, though somewhat more vaguely, with regard to essayism. However, Musil also overtly describes this continuity in terms of an unarrestable continuum of time and space: "Through history we create a similar feeling of the locality of the point at which we find ourselves, just as we continually orient ourselves in time and space" (Tgb., 637).

Just as essayism could come up with no fixed truth or falsehood to a thing, just as it must hold only a perspectivist semantic value system, so too does continuous sign production and interaction in Peircean semiotics imply an uncertainty of reference and a radical temporariness of meaning and "truth" ever to be surpassed throughout a diachrony:

> For what does the thought-sign stand—what does it name—what is its suppositum? The outward thing, undoubtedly, when a real outward thing is thought of. But still, as the thought is determined by a previous thought of the same object, it only refers to the thing through denoting this previous thought. . . . the subsequent thought denotes what was thought in the previous thought. (5.285)

4.7 Peirce's discursive "performance" of continuous sign-production

One cannot overemphasize the "ad infinitum" added at the end of Peirce's most cited definition of sign: "anything which determines something else (its interpretant) to refer to an object to which itself refers (its object) in the same way, the interpretant becoming in turn a sign, and so on ad infinitum" (2.300).

It has been convincingly argued by Timothy Reiss that Peirce not only defined the sign as continuous interrelation, interdetermination, and contextualization of meaning/truth, but also that Peirce semiotically *performs this definition* in his own writing. Peirce, argues Reiss, spent his life naming and renaming types of signs, a typology which continually changed throughout the diachrony of Peirce's work. Reiss gives an example of one performative definition of signs by Peirce which is itself a relational, relative, expansion of the field of definition of sign:

> By a *sign* I mean anything which conveys any definite notion of an object in any way, as such conveyers of thought are familiarly known to us. Now I start with this familiar idea and make the best analysis I can of what is essential to a sign, and I define a *representamen* as being whatever that analysis applies to. If therefore I have committed an error in my analysis, part of what I say about signs will be false. For in that case a sign may not be a representamen. (1.540)[66]

Nor does Peirce regret this lack of certainty or precision, but rather he sees it as a liberation from one's own self-delusions in the recognition and acceptance of the relativity of the results of one's investigations. Peirce considered that it was praise and not blame when: "It was a critic who said of me that I did not seem to be absolutely sure of my own conclusions. [. . .] To negate our inherent prejudices in pretending to liberate ourselves from universal doubt is nothing more than a form of repression" (1.10).

4.8 Interaction

Uncertainty, lack of structure, and the continuous transformation of sign-relations throughout a diachrony of sign-production, all of these traits were spoken about by contemporaries and successors to Musil—they form a consensus, so to speak. Mauthner, one of the fathers of pragmatics and a contemporary known to Musil, described language as always in "*statu nascendi*," which made it impossible to fix a conceptual content.[67] Much later, Bateson develops the continuous relational production of signs and the consequent relationality of meaning independent from any structure as due to an infinite series of contexts: "we are left regarding each step in a communicational sequence as a transformation of the previous step."[68] "Message material, or information, comes out of a context into a context, and in other parts of the book the focus has been on the context out of which information came."[69] The very absence of structure is the *conditio sine qua non* for the message, described cybernetically as a state of "readiness": "But structure alone is not enough. . . . But every meridian must be *ready* for the activating message, its 'readiness' being given direction but otherwise restricted by structure. Readiness, in fact, is precisely not-structure."[70]

Indeed, it is precisely this continuity of interaction which, for Bateson, defines language as "communicational," that is, as opposed to some absolute logical, transcendent, frozen form, or category of language.[71] We refer to Bateson's communicational theory here because we believe it most cogently points out how the development of the pragmatic potential of modern discourse could lead to a genuinely communicational view of language, rather than revert to a Saussurean semiotics reification of it as "langue"—structure.

Bateson also suggests the political implications of an interactional approach to discourse (be it pedagogical, therapeutic, or political discourse) over its *monological* counterpart; this latter he associates with "*theories of control*" and with "*theories of power.*"[72] In a similar vein, Patrick Heelan writes that Heisenberg described not only the scientific world of discourse, but all worlds, in a manner which accentuates the interactional aspect as a necessity of communication, and of reality taken as "public objectivity,"[73] i.e., consolidated by interactional consensus within the "public sphere." These "democratic" facets of such a communicational view of language will be seen later to become the crux of Habermas' communicational theory of society.

Foucault seems to be elaborating a similar theory of continuity of sign-production and interactivity when he suggests that discourse is not a fixed referential language, but rather something operating according to the principles of "*additivity,*" and "*interdiscursivity,*" taken as discursive procedures which merge together, annul one another, exclude one another, complement one another, and form groups that are in varying degrees indissoluble and endowed with unique properties. "It is to leave oneself free to describe the interplay of relations within it and outside it."[74] Often Foucault is read as positing no emancipatory ideal, and yet, as the above shows, such ideal is added in his pragmatics of discursive relations.

Finally, it is Bakhtin who provides the most operational notion to account for the continuous interaction of sign-relations when he speaks of "*dialogism,*" about which we will speak at greater length further on. Briefly, dialogism is the discursive procedure of allowing many voices and perspectives to coexist and interact without reducing or subsuming one to the other.

4.9 The potential of interaction

The interactional view of discourse is a radical deviation from classical discourse. It is this "modern" view of discourse as continuous interaction, amounting to a perspectivist and continuous redefinition of meaning, truth, and reality, which not only makes sign-production or essayism impossible to describe in a classical way, but also suggests the possible solution to the problems of traditional classical discourses of science and of power. Later on, Habermas and Bakhtin will be seen to suggest several social advantages of a dialogical practice of communication, truth, and knowledge, over a monological, absolutist theory such as that proposed by Kant:

> . . . the context is no longer that of Kant's monologic knowledge, but that of communicative or dialogic understanding. . .
> (a) the model of an ideal speech situation which operates counterfactually and makes it possible to diagnose the splitting of symbols in distorted communication. . . [75]

However, the notion of discourse as a temporally and spatially continuous process and as transformational interaction poses problems to would-be analysts of discourse. If "meaning," "truth," and "reality" are constantly evolving, changing, and growing as more and more discourse is produced or "pulled into the context," how then do we decide upon and speak of "truth" and "meaning"? An element of uncertainty and indeterminacy arises just as it did in the continuously evolving experimental relations of quantum mechanics. The earlier-cited performative definition of a sign (infra note 66), illustrated that Peirce fully accepts this uncertainty, as he does the probability of our error. Peirce describes and practices a semiotics in which, due precisely to the continuous production and interrelation of meaning, all knowledge and meaning is accepted as but a relative moment in an ever-changing diachrony: "all the cognitive faculties we know of are relative and consequently their products are relations" (5.262).

Musil's concept of "Essayism" also acknowledges the impossibility of fixing truth and falsehood, good and evil, once discourse is recognized as relation, interaction, transformation, and expansion of fields of reference. This recognition incites Musil to form a method of discourse which he calls the "method of unknowing"—"Methodologie des Nichtwissens."[76] Musil accepts uncertainty as the nature of existence: "Man's uncertainty about his value or perhaps also about his true nature and that of the person closest to him" (G.W. II, 956). Nor should the relationship which he establishes between modernity, Socratic irony, and epistemological uncertitude be overlooked: "To be Socratic is to feign ignorance. To be modern is to be ignorant" (G.W. II, 920). He renounces what Nietzsche calls the "will to truth." The solution to the uncertainty of the continuous production and interrelation of signs accepts uncertainty and attempts not to deform it by trying to fit it back into traditional, frozen categories of discursive absolutes from the classical, scientist episteme. No experiment can give absolute results and as such it must be unsuccessful in absolutist terms. But this failure of experiment to produce absolutely true results, or of language to produce absolutely fixed meaning or reference, is what Musil qualifies as "New Irony." Could modern discourse, then, under the auspices of "new irony," be the solution to the uncertainties of discourse production by virtue of its respect for those very uncertainties?

"New Irony." Social forms, morality, etc., are totalities in which the particulars appear to be determined. In terms of world history, however, they
are "Gestalts" formed by attempts at living, just like the dinosaurs, which
were also formed in this way and which superseded one another like
unsuccessful experiments. Seeing life in this way leads to a complete lack
of (religious) respect. (Tgb., 631)

However, a vague, fluctuating doctrine of uncertainty does not solve the
problem of *how to talk about* the continuous production and interaction of
discourses which produce meaning, truth, and reality (if only in an un-
decidable way). Where not only language, but the whole of culture as well,
is continually in a state of transformation, where "Nothing stands still," as
Toerless would say, how is it possible to isolate even partial meaning and
truth without contradicting the very continuity and relativity that have
been substituted for classical categories of discourse in the discursive
theories and practices of Peirce and Musil?

Although some critics of Peirce hold that this process will one day stop,
as ultimate Interpretant,[77] this is doubtful. It may stop in *death for the
individual* but not for the history of a community although, on second
thought of course, the possibility of death of the terrestrial community is
now very real. Barring nuclear annihilation, then, what we require is a
partial solution for experimental or analytical purposes to establish the
pertinence and epistemological justifiability of rendering Peircean semiotics operative for discursive criticism. We propose tentatively to freeze
pockets of discourse temporarily in order to obtain such results. However,
these results, "meaning," "truth," and "reality," have a rather distinct
epistemological status, that is as "partial solution" ("Partialloesung"),
"Possibility" ("Moeglichkeit"—Musil), "Potentia" (Heisenberg), or "Fields
of Habit" (Peirce).

5.0 Potentia—Partialloesung—Habit

In coping with the problematic question of the epistemological and
ontological status of reality, truth, and meaning posed by discourse taken
as a continuous, relational, triadic process, or as an infinite series of
experiments providing infinitely variable results, one might look to how
Heisenberg chose to speak of "reality" in relation to the contradictory
results of quantum mechanical experiments. Heisenberg finds both an
epistemological and a practical "sortie" from the contradictions of uncertainty and perturbations. The solution lies in the concept of "potentia" or
"dunamis," a notion which gives a new way of interpreting experimental
results as well as of defining "reality."

Musil's notions of "Partialloesung" and of "Moeglichkeitssinn" will be
seen to correspond very closely to the epistemological status attributed to

"potentia" by Heisenberg. And a semiotic correlate to these terms may be suggested by Peirce's notions of "immediate Interpretant" and "habit."

5.1 "Potentia"

In classical physics the results of the observation of physical objects—laws—are conceived of as idealized normative abstract objects (rather like the unknowable but reaffirmed existence of the *noumena*) or as real causes. Then the disparities in the results of quantum mechanics experiments required a new interpretation of the "reality" that these results reflected or discursively represented.[78] What is more, there had to be some way of temporarily stopping the on-going movement of the elementary particles if they were to be measured. Still, one must continue to take into account the movement and energy of the wave packet. The same requirement applies in discourse analysis to the need to stop the continuous expansion of sign-production and to isolate certain triadic relations without ignoring the fact that these relations are contextually situated in relation to a diachronically infinite field of other relations.

Heisenberg would say: "You can temporarily halt the flux of movement and isolate the quantity of energy but it must be recognized that these results (for example, observations of time space and causality) do not refer to anything other than *points of observation*." Experimental observation *produces* a moment of stability. This stability is not pure, naked "reality," but rather a stability produced by the momentary interaction of (1) the subject, (2) the subject's apparatus doing the measuring or the trace as "signifier" and (3) the Object being measured. This Object is unknowable except *in, through* and *as* an experimentally measured or interpreted entity.

Potentia, otherwise referred to by Heisenberg as "objective tendency" or as "objective possibility," is neither a pure idea nor an actual event, neither a transcendental category nor a particular substance, neither an object nor an interpretation. Rather, potentia refers to the possibility of producing laws or models of objects in and through experiment and interpretation. What the model represents is just the dialectical interaction of knowing subject, object to be known, and the traces left by both.[79] We have no direct knowledge of the object as brute reality or of the universal organization of our knowing categories. *Apart from the symbols or traces produced by their encounter*, within the particular conditions of experiment, i.e., within a particular context, we know nothing.[80]

The epistemological status that Heisenberg attributed to experimental results and labelled "potentia," according to Heelan, derives from a sort of synthesis of Kant, the categories of knowing, and Aristotle, the experience of known. The "reality" of the quantum mechanical results is a "dunamis" or "potentia," as opposed to an "in-itself," "physics" or "noumenal" reality, which exists only in relation to the act of observation. For example, energy is a condition of possibility characteristic of a particular physical milieu, whereas "potentia" would be the statement of the possible ("Moeglich") types of systems and processes permitted by that milieu taken as the context of experimentation and interpretation. Therefore the Kantian universal laws of nature are transformed into *laws of the possible relationships* holding between subject and object. Similarly, Heelan says, "reality" is described by Aristotle as the composition of two hylomorphic principles, not simply as external world, but as the mutual presence of *knowing subject* and *object to be known.*[81]

That the elementary particle would not have any existence (for us) were it not produced by the experimental reduction of the wave packet is an hypothesis proposed by Heisenberg to account for the fact that sometimes light is observed, i.e., is produced in experiment, as particle and sometimes as wave. The measurement of elementary particles is but a possibility. It may possibly be produced with certain other possible coordinates in and through the active, subject-performed experimental event of the reduction of the wave packet. The elementary particle is not a fact or object, such as that described earlier by Foucault as "de l'expérience originaire." The tendency of light to behave as a particle with certain other properties when acted upon in experiment is "potentia," a correlate of a possible union of subject and object in the act of observation or interpretation under certain conditions. Once again, at this stage it should be noted that we are no longer speaking of a *representation* of "reality" but of an interactive *production/presentation* of it. What is changing here are the limits and definition of the type of "reality" that we can know. One can know possible results only of the observational event and only as interaction of (1) the empirical behavior of the world, (2) our forms of thought or our instruments, and (3) our discourse for speaking about them. Heisenberg first poses the problem of the status of "reality" and then answers that it is one of potential results of interaction:

> . . . the search for the natural laws of the [ultimate structure of matter], entails the use of general principles of which it is not clear whether they apply to the empirical behaviour of the world, or to the a priori forms of our thought, or to the way in which we speak.[82]

> The atomic physicist has had to resign himself to the fact that his science is but a link in the infinite chain of man's argument with nature and that it cannot simply speak of nature "in itself".[83]

> . . . the true object of quantum mechanics was not nature but man's relationships with nature.[84]

Here, Heisenberg is really presenting an alternative ontology for the results of experiment. Hence, if science comes up with certain experimental results or with certain formulae, these "represent" not a noumenal "reality" of pure nature nor an empirical object in-itself. Rather they "present" potential configurations that *may be* actualized or that *probably will be* actualized in the event of experiment, in the encounter at a given moment of experimenter, experimenter's instruments and discourse, and object. Truth exists as potential.

The result of experiment has no absolute "truth," only *validity*. Validity is the result of a frozen moment which accepts its own partiality in relation to a diachrony of other experimental interactions. A potential formula would express "laws of atomic physics [which] are irreducibly probabilistic,"[85] laws which are not universal at all. These laws are simply more or less applicable to certain well defined domains of experience, i.e., their validity is contextually delimited. Though physical laws may seem to be Kantian universals they are only applicable as:

> possible or hypothetical ground for the construction of the scientific object; a process of empirical testing has to be employed to ascertain whether or not possible and hypothetical ground is *an explanation* in fact in this domain and where the boundaries of its domain of applicability are to be found.[86]

5.2 "Partialloesung" as "Moeglichkeitsepistemologie" ("partial solution" as the "epistemology of possibility")

This notion of ever possible new interactions is transposed to the realm of the language of ethics and the ethics of language; Musil plays on the word "actualities" to show that the validity of a solution is always only the potential, ever surpassable by another essay.

> But something else was contained in the claim: namely, the irrationality of morality (as of the essay). This is in any case the "morality of the work of fiction." It must not be the creation of a system but rather the unfolding of continuous "actualities." New moral experiences are always arising. Partial solutions are related to this. . . . [Such a morality] cannot form a system if it is not strictly conceptual. It is creation, not theory. At the moment it is very unclear, but there are many starting points in the book! The utopia of the essay simply branches off from the utopia of exactitude. (DMoE, 1880)

Robert Musil describes what could well be a quantum mechanical experiment in the following way:

> . . . [one can nowhere discover any sufficient reason] for everything's having come about as it has. It might just as well have turned out differently. The events of people's lives have, after all, only to the least degree originated in them, having generally depended on all sorts of circumstances . . . and have, as it were, only at the given point of time come hurrying toward them. (M.w.Q. 1:151; DMoE, 131)

The results of the experiment/experience are potential in that they could just as easily have been otherwise. They are circumscribed by particular temporal points and dependent upon the experience of the subject, "von ihnen selbst ausgegangen."

The experiments that Musil is describing are those of living and writing (perhaps for both Ulrich and himself). Nevertheless, the pertinence of indeterminacy in the realm of physical science to the uncertainty of the realm of the ethical and the compositional does not escape Musil: "Then all moral events took place in a field of energy the constellation of which charged them with meaning, and they contained good and evil just as an atom contains the potentialities of chemical combination" (M.w.Q. 1:297; DMoE, 250).

The continuous processes, the interrelationships, the uncertainties that earlier were seen to characterize Musil's theory of knowledge and of discourse, are often described in terms of the ever-pending "realm of possibility" ("Rand des Moeglichen") for different results in the experimentality of the world laboratory ("Weltlaboratorium"). Musil and Heisenberg have perhaps found the solution to the problem of the infinite variability of the various experimental results in life as well as the solution to the impossibility of believing in Kantian transcendentals or in Aristotelian naked experiences. The alternative: "Potentia" ("Teilloesung") and "Possibility" ("Moeglichkeit").[87]

In view of the flux of existence and the impossibility of exactness ("everything is fleeting and fluid," DMoE, 1651), yet with the desire to avoid completely relativistic subjectivity, the solution proposed by Musil was that of partial solution ("Partialloesung"). As was the case of "potentia," "Partialloesung" admitted of its limitation to the status of possibility ("Moeglichkeit"). "Moeglichkeit" is a *possible configuration* of "reality" under given, partial conditions of observation. Potentia and Moeglichkeit are not deontological, rather they bestow a new ontological status upon the results of experiment—being as possibility, circumscribed by actual contexts of experimentation.

5.3 Partialloesung as narrative procedure

For Musil, this partial solution of possibility applies both to the perception of, and action in, the world *and to the practice of narrative discourse:* "Speed up a hundred-fold the course of human history and describe what comes out" (Tgb., 684). "Today only the mathematician has the possibility to experience such a fantastic feeling" (G.W. II, 1006).

Albrecht Schoene deals with the possibility of various contextually situated results in terms of the use of the *subjunctive conditional verbal mode* in Musil. Schoene illustrates the direct connection between uncertainty and possibility in modern science and Musil's own narrative technique. Both present events as if they only *possibly* could occur or could have occurred. Neither presents events as *actually* having occurred or necessarily occurring according to some universal law: "Out of the experimental attitude of the scientist and the constructive fantasy of the logician and mathematician arises the novelist's passion for the subjunctive conditional. 'What would happen if . . .'" (Schöner).[88]

Musil himself stresses that his technique of narrative, derived from his inability to describe duration ("das Dauernde"), was based on narrating things, not as they had occurred but as they *may have occurred*. Furthermore, Musil's narrative techniques attack the problem of representing "reality" as a problem to be solved by *partial solution*, according to the process of "der kleinste Schritt," the smallest step: rather than as one of an absolute, totalizing representation: "My conception of fiction or the task I set myself: a partial solution, a contribution to a solution, investigation, etc. I feel released from [the necessity of providing] definitive answers" (DMoE, 1837).

"Roman" is a "Gestalt" in which he relates—the partial realities ("Teil-wahrheiten") of the partial solutions ("Partialloesungen") (Tgb., 448). By doubting the status of reality not only in science but also in the realm of narrative, Musil practices narrative sign-production not as representation, but as an experimental "Roman" within which there are pockets of discourse that one might classify as partial solutions to problems not only of representation but of knowledge, of the ethics of choice and of action (Tgb., 1243–44). Musil renders this technique operational in part via the use of the subjunctive, but also via the incessant changes in pragmatic use-contexts of discourse and of discursive pockets, which we shall identify later in Part Two as "potential habits." This technique is a form of irony which destroys the totality of each habit before it can lay claim to classical truth, to referential knowledge, or to the power that accompanies these concepts. Such irony, as a constant proposition of partial discursive solutions and as the relegation of all reality to the status of a contextualized "ought," will be seen to provide a narrative practice of the epistemology of "potentia."

"Reality" is not narrated as a referential "reality"; rather, "reality" is the interaction of narration—the subject's discourse and the event to be recounted, an event which cannot take place outside of its realization in and through narrative discourse. However, the "reality" of the narrated event "could" be otherwise if "told" otherwise, such as it is in the various perspectives of Ulrich's essayism as well as in the alternative endings to Ulrich's life. From the beginning, *the narrative poses a narrated meaning as a "partial" or "possible" "reality"* only subsequently to negate any tendency to take it as a naked, bare reality outside of the subject's narration which mediates and produces it:

> Let us assume that their names were Arnheim and Ermelinde Tuzzi. . . . So we are confronted with the enigma of who they were. (M.w.Q 1:4; DMoE, 10)

> . . . even God probably preferred to speak of His world in the subjunctive of potentiality . . . for God makes the world and while doing so thinks that it could just as easily be some other way. (M.w.Q. 1:15; DMoE, 19)

5.4 The possible implications of potentia for discursive criticism

Credit must be given to T. J. Reiss for having demonstrated the usefulness of Heisenberg's notion of "potentia" as a possible way of talking about meaning in an episteme based on infinite sign production, relativity, and triadicity. Reiss starts from the assumption that, as "potentia," the only object of science is the measurement produced by the interactional act of observation/intervention—affecting the activity in the process of being measured.[89] The only experimental truth is the isolated measurement and the knowledge of a stability of transformation. Reiss then suggests that in critical, interpretative discourse, "*meaning*" occurs as a relational production and not as something "out there," independent of interpretation: "The production of critical discourse is its meaning, a meaning which depends on the production of the discourse criticized."[90]

Meaning, says Reiss, results from an activity in a space (the contextual interpretation/measurement/experiment), whose boundaries are delimited by an epistemology of the observing/interpreting language, on the one hand, and by an analysis of objects/events producible according to a particular experimental order/context, on the other hand. In discursive theory, potentia is the possible stability of results which could arise due to possible triadic encounters of (1) text-object, (2) observing-subject, and (3) the subject's discursive models. Therefore, "meaning" and other discursive categories such as "types" or "genres" are none other than potentia or possibilities circumscribed within a particular limited context of interpretation and production. Accordingly it would only be fair to say that this, our present listing and elaborating of discursive procedures of the "modern" episteme, are also no more than potentia—an interrelational critical production. There are (contrary to the affirmations of traditional criticism) no absolute, transcendental meanings or classes of discourse. Critical results all correspond to the meeting of critic and text, as well as to historically determined contexts which situate these results.

However, the fact that the onus is placed upon both the text-object (which is only realized in interpretation), and the subjective categories of the observer, indicates that the results of experiment/interpretation are not purely subjective or open-ended in the sense that such critics as Eco give to this term, i.e., as dependent uniquely upon the receiver's categories.[91]

Potentia is the result of the dialectical interaction of both subject and object. It does not stem from a one-sided idealism, an abandon to capricious subjectivity, anymore than it arises out of naked empiricism.

5.5 How to render operative?

Rendering the notion of potentia objective for discourse analysis proves more difficult than drawing thematic epistemological parallels between quantum mechanics and textual theory. It may be suggested that potentia be considered as the generalization of a series of synchronic cross-sections (but complemented by their immediate contexts) or experimental snapshots taken throughout the diachrony of sign-production. Each synchronic cross-section would be isolated, as a temporary result of the interaction of (1) text-Object, (2) subject-critic, and (3) the subject's discourse. Any laws or regularities of these synchronic cross-sections throughout diachrony would not have the status of absolute laws of structures. These laws do not apply exclusively to either text-Object or context. Rather they would be "probable"—"possible" regularities within a historical and cultural discursive context.

Each individual result, each synchronic cross-section, must in turn be reinserted within the diachrony of possible relations, making any particular critical result valid or objective only within the context of the interpretation. Results of discursive interpretation are not universally valid, nor are they justified in calling themselves *the true interpretation* of such and such enunciated. Rather they are: (1) temporally frozen, (2) epistemologically and contextually relative, and (3) possibly probabilizable in a series. Such would be the qualification of the results of criticism if understood and practiced as potentia.[92]

C. S. Peirce viewed *experiment* in a way not unfamiliar to the type of critical procedure suggested above. He situates the results of experiment and their validity in relation to the isolated observational act or experiencing act, and in relation to its idiosyncrasy. What is more, the results vary because they are superseded by more experiments and experiences, for other individual Interpretants, and by new relations with other Objects and Representamen. The individual experimental event is a fact in its individuality, which must subsequently be placed in relation to other experimental observations in the relational continuity of the representations of objects for other Interpretants: "How can an experiment, in itself, reveal anything more than that something once happened to an individual object and subsequently some other individual event occurred?" (5.424).

However, Peirce partially solves the problem of the idiosyncrasy of each individual experimental triad by saying that the synchronic series of experiments can constitute, in their diachronic sum, an experimental result: "every connected series of experiments" (5.424). This is tantamount to saying that the collection of results of a *potentia*, or generalization of a series of synchronic cross-sectioned results, placed in connection within a diachrony, amounts to an experiment and a result in itself *which is more "valid" than the isolated individual result.*

In that potentia implies a recognition of the interrelational constitution and does not make the same claims to absoluteness or idealness or universality that the results of generative grammar or structuralist semiotics do, we believe it to be justifiable to relate the notion of potentia with Peirce's concept of a *series of possible experimental results.*

The notion of "instantaneously stopping" and of temporarily isolating a sign-relation from the infinitely expanding context is comparable to what Peirce calls the *"immediate Interpretant"* (4.539). This procedure of temporarily freezing and isolating experimental results allows one to consider a sign-relation despite the impossibility of ever analyzing the whole infinite continuum of sign relations. History would have to stop for this to be possible. At the same time one acknowledges that each result is only a part of this continuum. Elsewhere Peirce describes the immediate or explicit

Interpretant in terms which indicate this temporary stopping of sign-production and limitation of contextualization: "all that is explicit in the sign itself apart from its context and circumstances of utterance" (5.473).

In analysis, the partial halting of the process, the isolation of a particular sign-relation, seems to be the only operative way to proceed while *simultaneously* acknowledging the partiality of results and the need for a view of the *series* of synchronic results. The "immediate Interpretant" must always eventually be submitted to the "dynamic, living, self-analysing habit" of what Peirce calls the "ultimate Interpretant":

> The habit conjoined with the motive and the conditions has the action for its energetic interpretant; but action cannot be a logical interpretant because it lacks generality. The concept which is a logical interpretant is only imperfectly so. It somewhat partakes of the nature of a verbal definition, and is as inferior to the habit, and much in the same way, as a verbal definition is inferior to the real definition. The deliberately formed, self-analyzing habit—self-analyzing because formed by the aid of analysis of the exercises that nourished it—is the living definition, the veritable and final logical interpretant. (5.491)

5.6 The potential of the modern: Continuity of sign-production vs. the dead end of the postmodern—"absence" and "différance"

. . . *Irony* has become a, if not *the*, privileged term for supplementarity or symbolic deferral/mediation in critical texts of the past decade or so. It has in fact become virtually synonymous with the now-(in)famous *écriture*, or writing, in the Derridean sense. In the mouths of signified-oriented critics, it has a variety of negative connotations (frivolity, bad faith, onanism, etc., i.e., deviation or perversity), while on the tongues of those with post-structuralist sympathies it often takes on the positive overtones of liberation (with play, self-referentiality, etc., considered as healthy manifestations of a naive good faith).

The conception of discursive meaning production as an ongoing process has been compared to contemporary French discursive theories, e.g., the Lacanian notion that all we do is string together chains of signifiers to overcome the everlasting absence of the signified, and the Derridean notion of the difference residing between signifiers and between signifier and signified. However, it seems that Peirce does not create a philosophy or a semiotics of *"absence,"* rather one of true continuity. *"Meaning"* (the word "signified" is not really pertinent here since, for Peirce, meaning is not fixable to any one sign unit nor to any one signifier on a biplanar level) is not absent, but rather it is relative to and co-constructed within the various sign-fields which situate it. Meaning is not absent but rather it is uncertain, since it depends upon the possible configurations of habit in all possible future and past and coexistent triadic relationships. Meanings constantly substitute for each other within the process of the triadic discursive practices.

Peirce does not distinguish between signifier and signified, between sign and object as is manifest in the semiotics of a Lacan or of a Derrida (différence-différance). Nor is *absence,* of signified or of meaning, a category in Peirce's semiotics. Rather, in Peirce, the notion of infinite semiosis, of continuity of triadic relations, between all three elements—Object, Representamen, Interpretant—replaces that of difference, or of total absence of signified.

For Peirce meaning is not absent; it is an infinitely ongoing *triadic* circuit of various interacting and mutually substituting conceptual/semiotic/discursive fields. For example, when Benveniste despairs of a Peircean semiotics, that it has no "point fixe,"[93] no "premiére relation de signe," he is pointing out only the possible infinite regression and progression of sign fields in Peircean semiotics.

Musil is *an author of infinite semiosis.* At first glance the interpreter may find no obstacle to interpretation. At each instant a possible triadic relationship may be isolated and a potential meaning derived—a "presence" as opposed to an "absence."

However, the meaning can never be finalized, universalized, or fixed in Musil. The meaning is in constant "mouvance." This is because Musil's production of discourse best performs the Peircean notion of infinite semiosis. If we take, for example, the Representamen 'Moosbrugger,' in *Der Mann ohne Eigenschaften,* we may see that it becomes the Object and the Interpretant for many interpreters, which at each instant are different and which interact with the preceding and following Interpretants, all situated in different but partially overlapping discursive fields.

Such is the indeterminacy of Musil's work. Such is its continuity, which is not reduced to pure absence but rather is constantly extended to include an infinity of sign-relations within discursive fields of both production and reception.

Meaning is not absent. Discourse is not pure difference or superficial traces. The potential of modern discourse is its preservation of the possibility of "meaningfulness" without resorting to a classical transcendental authoritarian absolute.

6.0 Habit

But, one may object, if modern discourse has practiced and theorized the infinite production of variable sign-relations, how does meaningfulness become possible? The loss of the transcendental guarantee of correct representation and of ordered systems does not imply necessarily the absence of patterns, regularities, procedures, or reliable relationships of the terms of the sign relationship. We do have pockets of stable semiotic relationships which, however, are not meaningful due to any absolute correspondence but merely due to conventional habit.

At one point in his text, Peirce classifies existence according to three categories—chance, law, and habit: "Three elements are active in the world: first chance, second law, and third, habit-taking" (1.409). "Chance is first, law is second, the tendency to take habits is third" (6.32). In other words, habit is a triadic configuration that contains chance and law. Even though the continuous interaction and expansion of sign-relations seem to add a chaotic element of chance and indeterminancy to sign-theory, one which makes speaking of regularities and order very difficult for discursive criticism, the tendency of all things to take habits corresponds to the possibility of finding generalizable probabilistic experimental regularities as potentia. The element of chance does not contradict regularities, which, it must be remembered, are triadic and therefore based on interaction of subject-object. On the contrary, habits are built up from chance occurrences by "a logical process which we may suppose takes place in things, in which the generalizing tendency builds up new habits from chance occurrences" (6.206).[94]

6.1 Bridging the gap—"différence"—with habit

Peirce proposes habit as the solution to the gap between human and exact, or between the continuous, dynamic, chance-generated, uncertain field of sign-relations on the one hand and the need to fix them and to find regularity in them, on the other: "It is clear that nothing but a principle of habit, itself due to the growth by habit of an infinitesimal chance tendency toward habit-taking, is the only bridge that can span the chasm between the chance medley of chaos and the cosmos of order and law" (6.262).

In Peirce, habit is sometimes referred to as Interpretant-habit, a label which points out habit's close relationship to the effect or significate outcome of a sign on sign-users. The effect (or meaning) is determined by the habits of past sign-relationships in connection with the interpreter. "Therefore there remains only habit, as the essence of the logical interpretant" (5.486).

6.2 The communicational aspect of habit

Habit may be closely related to semiotic notions of code; however, one must be careful to understand code not in the semiotico-linguistic terms that Jakobson read into it and that Barthes renders operative in S/Z, i.e., as a dyadic semantic transfer mechanism. Rather, habit as code must be understood in cybernetic terms which lend to it the "three-dimensional" pragmatic understanding of habit as a triadic, interrelational, *communicational* relationship. The habit does not directly and absolutely correlate a biplanar unit or sign-meaning. The habit is a regularity of transformations between objects, persons, and material symbols, or between Interpretant, Object, and Representamen.

Bateson's communication theory of code acknowledges the pragmatic dimension of code as habit. He insists on the three-dimensional, com-

municational aspect of code as opposed to the direct, semantic correla-
tional aspect, which merely unites the sign and a pre-established sense:

> The code, a transfer whereby *perceived* objects or persons (or supernaturals)
> are transformed into wood or paint, is a source of information about the
> artist and his culture.
>
> The essence and raison d'être of communication is the creation of redun-
> dancy, meaning, pattern predictability, information, and/or the reduction by
> "restraint".[95]

Habit, then, is a temporary limitation of possibilities or of relations
largely predetermined by the previous perceiver's sociocultural Interpretant-habits, which enable possible meaning configurations that are the
interaction of sign-functional habits, to be temporarily and potentially
isolated. To summarize, *triadicity, relativity, relationality, con-
ventionality, and communicationality,* are the properties which draw the
cybernetic notion of code and the Peircean notion of habit together and
make them applicable to the practice of communication and to the interaction involved in knowing objects discursively.

It cannot be overemphasized how much discursive habit-formation both
predetermines and governs our perception/interpretation and hence our
cognition in Peirce's semiotic theory of knowledge.[96] A habit is a regularity of discursive procedures. The perception of Object and Representamen, as an Interpretant-effect, depends upon previous Interpretant-
habits of attention or cognition which are stored in what Peirce calls
"memory" and "associations in memory."[97] But for Peirce this memory is
more social than individualistically anthropomorphic. Habit, then, is a
configuration of sign-relations which may be temporarily isolated but
which must be resituated in the historical mnemonic-continuum of other
habits in order to be more completely if not exhaustively interpreted.[98]

6.3 Habit constitutes belief

As if by way of an irony of the schoolmaster who told Toerless to take
the possibility of synthetic knowledge on faith, Peirce stands Kant on his
head to suggest that belief in an absolute transcendent—summum
bonum—is merely a pragmatic custom.

Very strongly formed habits are referred to by Peirce as "beliefs," which
illustrates the conventional and temporary side, not only of religious
convictions but also of what is normally called firmly grounded, permanent, scientific knowledge:

> For belief, while it lasts, is a strong habit, and as such forces the man to
> believe until some surprise breaks up the habit. The breaking of a belief can
> only be due to some novel experience, whether external or internal. (5.524)

> It now begins to look strongly as if perhaps all belief might involve *expectation* as its essence. (5.542)

Such also is the status of potentia: a probabilistic expectation which must nevertheless be "proven" with each new concretization of experimental interaction. Much later Bateson also argued that firmly embedded habits are removed from critical inspection, treated as undoubted beliefs, and ultimately survive as knowledge.[99]

6.4 The stochastics of habit

But habits are neither fixed laws nor parts of mechanical models, neither absolutes nor exempt from variation by evolution, by chance. In short, habit bears all of the epistemological flux, interrelativity, and possibility of "potentia" as was described earlier.

In his essay "The Doctrine of Necessity Re-examined," Peirce professes a theory of chance and hazard much in keeping with that of the "clinamen" developed by Lucretius, thus foreshadowing some of the "postmodern" stochastic, antistructuralist principles of Michel Serres' philosophy of communication[100] as well as Foucault's insistence on the role of chance as opposed to that of the volitional subject in changing history.

The acquisition of Interpretant-habits (and their interpretation for that matter) is always subject to growth, alteration, and relativity. This is so because these habits are interactionally-triadically constituted and are formed in the first place by chance occurrences. These chance occurrences include chance interactions between all of the following: the interpreter, his previous habits, the Object that he is observing, and the habits of his whole socioepistemological, discursive context (episteme).

6.5 Habit breaking

When Peirce speaks of the formation of new habits and of the endurance of old habits, he seems to be placing habit at the heart of a semiotics of innovation, a semiotics which will serve to circumscribe irony as a deviation from the norm without positing fixed, absolute, deep structures, or "langue," and which recognizes it own relativity and dependence upon the relation between interpreter and text at each instant.

First of all, Peirce speaks of the boredom of long-held habits and of the surprise and pleasure in the pragmatics of reception that the disruption of old habits, as well as the creation of new habits, causes:

> Everybody knows that the long continuance of a routine of habit makes us lethargic, while a succession of surprises wonderfully brightens ideas. . . . New mental commissures are habits. Where they abound, originality is not needed and is not found; but where they are in defect spontaneity is set free. (6.301)

Also, Peirce allows for a deliberate control over habits and actions based on habit. The individual "not merely has habits but also can exert a measure of self-control over his future actions" (6.301). Peirce speaks of the necessity of breaking up old habits as: "The operation of the environment, which goes to break up habits destined to be broken up and so to render the mind lively . . ." (6.301). However, certain habits are described as being stronger than others and as such are more resistant to change:

> Habits have grades of strength varying from complete dissociation to insep-
> arable association. These grades are mixtures of promptitude of action, say
> excitability . . . Habits also differ in their endurance . . . it may be said that
> the effect of habit-change lasts until time or some more definite cause
> produces new habit changes. (5.477)

Bateson's cybernetic definition of code, Paolo Altos' derivation from pragmatics, also insists on the necessity of changing redundancy. Such change is necessary for information to be conveyed at all, in that total redundancy, total codification and habit, would be tantamount to non-sense. Cybernetics defines meaning as either a difference on a background of redundancy or as a redundancy on a background of difference: "The technical term 'information' may be succinctly defined as any difference which makes a difference in some later event."[101] Furthermore, the need to change habits is referred to not only as the absence of absolute structure but as *potentiality* for change: "Flexibility may be defined as uncommitted potentiality for change."[102] Even in his theory of learning, Bateson suggests that the flexibility of ideas is derived from the stochastic, i.e. chance process in the evolution of learning.[103]

Habit, or the cybernetic theory of codes, allows for constant change as well as for the indeterminacy of all postulated habits due to the evolution or change of habit by chance. This notion is, of course, directly parallel to the concept of the random in quantum mechanics.[104]

In Musil, we run across a similar principle of knowledge taken as dependent upon discontinuity and chance—"Willkuer."

> There are truths but no [single] truth. I can quite well claim two di-
> ametrically opposed things and be right in both cases. One must not weigh
> one idea against another—each has a life of its own. Consider Nietzsche. As
> soon as one tries to find in him a system other than the spiritual ar-
> bitrariness of the wise man, what a fiasco. (Tgb., 12)

In providing a discursive theory for a semiotics of innovation, Peirce suggests that there are certain types of sign-activity or discourse-practices which cause more changes (or rupturing of habits) than others: "It natu-rally follows that the repetition of the actions that produce the changes increases the changes" (5.477). This might be read to mean that certain discursive activities are more transgressional and explosive of habits than others.[105] The transgression of the receivers' habits or beliefs is valorized by Musil as one of the capacities of the significant word: ". . . every meaningful word has the potential to overturn everything that was formerly believed."[106]

Furthermore, Musil sets up certain genres of habits which he then sets out to disrupt through irony, for example the "Apprenticeship novel" ("Bildungsroman" or "Ironischer Erziehungsroman") (DMoE, 1843) "Takes place in a museum so that both sides of culture (ironic Bildungsroman) are equal" (DMoE, 1927).

In a performative, ironic statement of what his novel is, it is very interesting to note that Musil defines it in terms of negative theology, i.e., in terms of the various narrative habits and expectations that the novel does not practice. Musil performatively describes his work as an innovative, habit-breaking function:

> In the case of a book with . . . pages, . . chapter, . . . characters, and 33 times as many lines, none of which is intentionally empty, the task of writing a self-advertisement presents so many obstacles that I prefer to say what this book is not.
> It is not the great Austrian novel for which people have been waiting since time immemorial, although . . .
> It is not a portrayal of an era in which Mr. . . . learns how to live and love. Neither is it a portrayal of society.
> It does not contain *the problems* that cause us suffering, rather . . .
> It is not so much the work of an author who has a task (to repeat what . . .), as it is a constructive variation.
> One could add: Since the author exists in the spirit of the whole, this book is idealistic, analytical, possibly synthetic.
> . . .
> It is not the book of a psychologist.
> It is not the book of a thinker (since it brings the mental elements together in an order which . . .)
> It is not the book of a bard who . . .
> . . .
> It is not the book of an author which *is successful* . . .
> It is not an easy book and it is not a difficult one, for that depends on the reader. (DMoE, 1939)

It is possible, based even on the limited information given above, to isolate some habits which Musil's discourse professes to violate or simply to ignore. And these habits might be seen to form a consensus of habits in relation to the participants, senders, and critics which constitute the positioning horizon of expectation for Musil's work. Musil rejects the following narrative habits: the nationalistic novel, the "roman à clef," the social-transgressive novel, the novel of the unhappy consciousness, the novel of philosophy of ideas, the satirical novel, the psychological novel, the novel as "travail sur la lettre," the novel of plot, the hermeneutic novel, the novel with either a difficult or an obvious meaning. The only positive descriptions of the book do not deal with habits but rather with the principle of constant variation and of the creation of new habits, i.e., the novel as constructive variation.

6.6 Phaneron: Fielding habits

The potential of modern discourse resides in replacing a correspondence theory of truth and meaning with the notion of contextual validity within a certain field of relations.

If triadic sign-relations are organized and perceived as past habits stored in memory and as future habits formed by chance, it remains to be seen how they are organized. How may one speak of the various possible configurations which habits may take? Peirce proposes the notion of *sign-field* or *"phaneron"* to explain the configurations which sign-habits take on: "Signs are irreducibly triadic—they function in relation to other elements of the triad in that they are situated in a field—ground—phaneron" (2.228). "Field is synonymous for relation of signs" (1.286). The sign-field describes all of the sign-habits present to the interpreter at the time of the reception of a particular sign-relation, a presence which necessarily governs the reception of or the contextualization of the particular sign-relation. The sign field, "phaneron," is the organization of sign-relations in a particular time and space which governs the functions of any new perception of sign-relations. The phaneron is the "collective totality of all that is present to the mind no matter what manner or sense, and *without worrying at all whether it corresponds or not to any real thing"* (1.285, emphasis added).

Phaneron, taken as a merely possible and temporarily relative configuration, approximates the types of laws formed as "potentia" in quantum mechanics. The sign-field provides a way of speaking of certain configurations of sign-relations, including other signs, Objects, Representamen, and Interpretants, which may possibly be related and provide the contextual background for positioning new sign-relations. A single triadic sign-relation looks like this (figure 1).

The phaneron should be pictured as an ever-expanding yet potentially delimitable relation of such triads throughout a three-dimensional temporo-spatial plane (figure 2).

Field also became an important concept in the development of cybernetic communications theory, whereby, Bateson suggests, various sign-relations or messages are situated within certain possible "frames" or "Gestalten"[107] (synonomous to contexts or to fields) which determine their perception and cognition: "This double framing is, we believe, not merely a matter of 'frames' within 'frames' but an indication that mental processes resemble logic in needing an outer frame to delimit the ground against which the figures are to be perceived."[108]

Other names for frames or situated information which remain stable for a moment, in Bateson, are "phenotype" and "genotype," whereby each stable configuration is nonetheless always potentially alterable and necessarily situated within much larger frames in a process called the *infinite series of contexts within the total "eco-system."*[109] The total "eco-system," in Bateson's theory, which necessarily positions all information and all partial fields, is the equivalent of the ultimate Interpretant or total field of sign-relations in Peirce's semiotics, which of course has not yet and probably never will be totally known.

The notion of field as a temporary and possible configuration of fluctuating, expanding, and interrelated elements does not elude Musil's theory of discourse. Essayism is described as a field of forces or as a constellation of events laden with significance: ". . . alle moralischen Ereignisse [fanden] in einem Kraftfeld statt, dessen Konstellation sie mit Sinn belud. . . ."

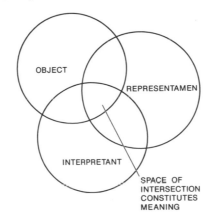

Fig. 1

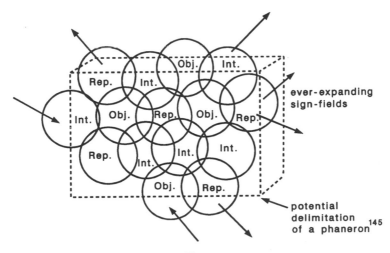

Fig. 2

(DMoE, 250). Elsewhere, Musil speaks of the novel as a "Feldbildung (of) Geschehnis," as "a temporary stationary state of events" (Tgb., 821).

Field ("phaneron") taken as a potential semiotic organization of sign-relations (since the constitution of a field is an interrelation between the existing sign-relations and the interpreter of these relations, who seeks some order in them), is a very promising concept for both the theory and practice of discourse analysis. Phaneron justifies positing certain delimitations and "types" or "disciplines" of discourse while avoiding a supposition that these categories exist absolutely or independently of a contextualized interpretation of them.

Indeed, Foucault was much later to question classical taxonomy and referred to such divisions of discourse sometimes as fields, "champs," sometimes as disciplines, and sometimes as "pratiques." If extended throughout a larger spatial and temporal context, these fields were called "episteme." No longer were the divisions absolute. All of these concepts are merely possible delimitations of sign-relations which nevertheless determine what is considered to be "knowledge," "truth," and "meaning" in any given historical context:

> A discipline is a group of objects, of methods, their corpus of propositions considered to be true, the interplay of rules and definitions, of techniques and tools.[110]

> The field of discursive events, on the other hand, is a grouping that is always finite and limited at any moment to the linguistic sequences that have been formulated.[111]

Whence the potential of modern discourse for what is often called postmodern inter- or transdisciplinarity.

6.7 Habit and community

These fields of habits or the spaces of habits which change throughout history and circumscribe what is considered to be knowledge in each epoch depend not only upon the interrelations of Interpretants, but also upon a whole community of interpreters. (Furthermore, in the case of the social sciences, the interpreters are not only fields of Interpretants but also the objects to be interpreted, as in the case of Alice's hedgehog croquet balls.) Says Peirce: "thought, belief, and its fixation are established in the community and vice-versa" (5.378).

Despite the relativization of classical categories of absolute truth and meaning due to the interaction and evolution of all things (as in both quantum mechanics and Peircean semiotics), one should nevertheless not believe that truth is to be abandoned to the capricious winds of relativity and subjectivity. Truth, meaning, reality, objectivity, all depend upon the criterion of the consensus of the community, a far cry from classical absolutes, but not total chaos either.

As soon as the postulates of a transcendental knowing subject, such as "la méthode" of Descartes, are placed into doubt, something must replace them as a justification of knowledge. Cohen, in the vein of Kuhn, and Feyerabend, suggests that, as early as Mach, conventional agreement among scientists became the basis for constituting knowledge: "By sharing knowledge in the human community, and through other communities, the individual transcends the limits of egoism, for Mach envisioned the world as a whole and man's place as the passing but yet integrated."[112]

Heelan, too, warns us against considering quantum mechanics to postulate a subjectivist theory of knowledge, insisting that Heisenberg replaces absolute truth as empirical or formal objectivity with "*public objectivity.*" For Heisenberg, "a wave function is 'objective' but not real; since 'real' implies an empirical content which is not at all 'objective'."[113] Public objectivity is defined as the consensus of the scientific community necessary for science to continue.

For Peirce, too, in the end truth and meaning depend not upon a singular habit, nor upon the habits of the idiosyncratic self, but rather upon the consensus of the community:

> The *real*, then, is that which, sooner or later, information and reasoning would finally result in, and which is therefore independent of the vagaries of me and you. Thus, the very origin of the conception of reality shows that this conception essentially involves the notion of a Community, without definite limits, and capable of a definite increase of knowledge. (5.311)[114]

Only in the public investigation, in the communal consolidation of beliefs and habits, do we move away from idiosyncratic error and toward the establishment of truth by the "community of investigators. The concept of truth [is] something which is public" (5.384).[115] [116]

In *Der Mann ohne Eigenschaften*, Ulrich makes a statement quite similar to Peirce's position that it is the *community* which must decide what is truth, and *not the isolated individual experimenter*: "The average, the sum of the experiments, then no longer comes about in the individual case, which becomes unbearably one-sided, but the totality is like an experimental community" (M.w.Q. 2:231; DMoE, 490).

Of course, the problem still remains as to whether either Peirce or Musil thought that an ultimate, final, complete field of truth could ever be reached in the form of a consensus within the vastest community conceivable.

The relations of habit and of fields of habits to the community is an extremely pertinent concept in that it replaces an idiosyncratic, individualist, elitist, classical notion of discourse and science with one that depends upon the discursive activities of a particular spatio-temporal context of sign-users. This notion approximates Heisenberg's concept of "*public objectivity,*" which replaces the category of absolute "truth." But also, the following definition by Peirce of the relation of habit to the community, for each "epoch", could just as easily have been made by the author of the quotation which follows it, Michel Foucault, in his definition of "episteme."

> Each epoch has certain beliefs, in placing one's own epoch in relation to other beliefs of other epochs one sees their relativity . . . The willful adherence to a belief, and the arbitrary forcing of it upon others, must, therefore, both be given up, and a new method of settling opinions must be adopted, which shall not only produce an impulse to believe, but shall also decide what proposition it is that is to be believed. (5.382)

> By *episteme*, we mean, in fact, the total set of relations that unite, at a given period, the discursive practices that give rise to epistemological figures, sciences, and possibly formalized systems; the way in which, in each of these discursive formations, the transitions to epistemologization, scientificity, and formalization are situated and operate; the distribution of these thresholds, which may coincide, be subordinated to one another, or be separated by shifts in time; the lateral relations that may exist between epistemological figures or sciences insofar as they belong to neighbouring, but distinct, discursive practices.[117]

In other words, what determines the various habits or discursive procedures that circumscribe knowledge at any given time and place is the community, and not some individualist absolutist standard; while, at the same time, these habits or practices also describe the Interpretant-habit of the community. Herein lies the major shift in epistemology between the classical and "interactional" episteme. Nor would it be too great an extrapolation to see here a shift away from a liberalist theory of knowledge grounded in the individual toward a more consensually based democratic one.

6.8 Habit and ideology

One great advantage of the concept of habit over the postmodern concepts of difference and absence is that it still allows us to take a critical stance toward social practices of discourse.

Earlier it was stated that firmly held habits were tantamount to beliefs, and that habit was comparable to the cybernetic understanding of code, in which case rigid habits would be tantamount to overcoding.

In his *Theory of Semiotics*, Umberto Eco, who is much influenced by Peircean semiotics, suggests that all coding is a type of overcoding, in the sense of an inference from a one-time occurrence to a generalized rule. All codes are, to a degree, a stratification and a fixing of discursive practices and rules of all types (not merely correlations of sign-meaning on a biplanar level). A code, to be formed in the first place, depends upon the fixing, if only temporarily and relatively, of certain conventions of sign-activity.

However, when these codes or habits become automatically accepted as transfers by a body of sign-users within a certain field (such as the associating of nuclear energy with danger, and the disassociation of coal power with danger) then, says Eco, the overcoding becomes extreme and is responsible for what is commonly called ideology:

> But, in general, any addressee will turn to his own cultural inheritance, his own partial world vision, in order to choose the subcodes that he wishes to apply to the message. To define this partial world vision, this prospective segmentation of reality entails a Marxist notion of ideology as "false conscience." Naturally from the Marxist point of view this false conscience is born as a theoretical disguise (with pretensions to scientific objectivity) for concrete social relationships and given material conditions of life.
>
> Ideology is therefore a message which starts with a factual description and then tries to justify it theoretically, gradually being accepted by society through a process of over-coding.[118]

Ideology, then, to begin with, is a justification of a partial world vision, or semiotic field, by taking it for the total world vision or field, i.e., by neglecting to insert it and relativize it within the larger context of semiotic fields. Ideology is the failure to recognize the relativity and partiality of one's own sign-field or episteme. Ideology could be described as a process of "over-habit-forming" or "overcoding," whereby the relations established as habits are not treated as relative and dependent upon a particular context, but as absolute relations not to be questioned.

In this case, such discursive "disciplines" as classical science, physics, or ethnocentric anthropology, not to mention jurisprudence and psychiatry, could be considered overcoded fields of habits, which have not been situated within larger fields of sign-production, but which have each been taken as a whole field in itself. This supposed whole field is unrelativized by any discourse exterior to the accepted paradigm that it represents or from which it originates.

Foucault, also, seems to associate ideology with an overstructuration or overlocalization of certain discursive practices, a phenomenon not uncommon to the "rigorousness and regularity of scientificity":

> . . . ideology, which is not identified with knowledge, but which does not efface or exclude it, is situated in it, structures some of its objects, systematizes some of its utterances, formalizes some of its concepts and strategies; this elaboration oversees knowledge, modifies and redistributes it on the one hand, and confirms and valorizes it on the other hand. It is to the degree that science finds its place in discursive regularity that it operates and refunctions in any field of discursive or non-discursive practices.[119] (our translation)

Ideology is the neurosis of society whereas schizophrenia is that of *the individual*. Both ideology and schizophrenia arise from an inability of the actors to examine their own habits and to control the contexts of their language and actions. Rather, ideologues and schizophrenics are merely positioned pawns within a pregiven context which they leave unquestioned and unthreatened. "Schizophrenics are rigidly committed to their patterns of inconsistency."[120] Of course, both of these cases of recalcitrant habits result in a diminishing of the arena of action, of free-will, or as Bateson puts it so well:

> [The forming of a genotype] is a process whereby the newer inventions of adaptive behavior are sunk deeper into the biological system of the organism. From planned and conscious actions they become habits, and the habits become less and less conscious, and less and less subject to voluntary control.[121]

> We have a habit of not re-examining our habits.[122]

Bateson's association of "over-habit-forming" or "overcoding" with madness, with the inability to change habits, reminds one of an explanation given by Ulrich justifying his constant switching of discursive habits. He states that the madman can never do anything else, cannot change his habits of thought or action, whereas the man of possibility, the sane man, can always do something else: A person who is responsible for his actions can always do the other thing, too, but a person who is not never can! (M.w.Q. 1:315; DMoE, 265).

The constant changing of habits, equivalent to a "decoding" or demystification of ideology, is described by Musil as an englobing of fields of discourse, and a refusal of any particular semiotic or discursive structure and semantic relation:

> Not only does the sentence get its meaning from the words, the words also get their meanings from the sentence . . . to a certain degree even in scientific language . . . the encompassing and the encompassed form their meanings mutually between themselves, and the structure of a page of good prose is, logically analysed, not something fixed, but rather the swinging of a bridge that changes the further one goes. (G.W. II, 1213)

Ulrich's position of possibility, and the freedom that it bestows, is not only an epistemological position which refutes absolute, classical knowledge; it is also a revolt against the ideological constraints of rigorously prescribed behavior in Wittgenstein and Freud's Vienna: "There are too many people in the world who say exactly what one should do and think for me not to be tempted by the opposite . . . strict freedom" (DMoE, 1941).

Thus the remedy to overcoding is none other than habit-breaking or "un-coding." "Un-coding" may be understood as a dismantling of the fixed discursive procedures, of the habits of sign-relations that, in ideology, are taken as total field and as absolute structures. "Un-coding" dismantles particular associations of sign-functions among each other, such as Representamen with Object or Representamen with Interpretant.

With the crisis of representation in classical discourse we no longer had the luxury of declaring things or texts ideological on the basis that they were false representations. A pragmatically oriented modern discourse makes it possible to declare ideological an overcoded text which excludes other potential relations. The hegemonic is the ideological. The potential of modern discourse, one which we wish to hang onto, is not to abandon the realm of ethics to the play on the surfaces of postmodern aesthetics.

6.8.1 Habit as a normative postulate of communication

Earlier, it was seen that a disturbance in the redundancy of habit, and vice versa, was a requirement of information. In other words, information may be portrayed as a breaking up of patterns and regularities in the signal, or as an introduction of patterns (habits) into noise.

Juergen Habermas will be seen to speak of the patterns or habits of communication in terms of "pragmatic postulates of communication," a notion not entirely unrelated to what Foucault called the procedures or practices of discourse, though more generalized and later to become normatively quasi-idealized.[123] Traditionally in the classical episteme, these include, among others, referentiality, exclusion, access to power via access to and desire for knowledge, as well as internal procedures of classification, ordering, and distribution.

Habermas distinguished from classical syntactico-semantic laws these postulates of communication which introduce pragmatic rules or habits of discourse and which are dependent upon the sign-use or upon the actual performance of speech:

> Like structuralist linguistics, it [syntactico-semantics] delimits its object domain by first abstracting from the pragmatic properties of language, subsequently introducing the pragmatic dimension in such a way that the constitutive connection between the generative accomplishments of speaking and acting subjects, on the one hand, and the general structures of speech, on the other, cannot come into view.[124]

The distinction being made by Habermas is one between competency or habits of communicational practice and fixed grammatical laws. There are habits or norms of communication which are defined by the pragmatics of communicating; they are what Habermas later refers to as "*validity claims*," which if followed, validate statements (where validity replaces truth):

> Whether or not they have an explicitly linguistic form, communicative actions are related to a context of action, norms, and values. . . . Without the normative background of routines, roles, forms of life, in short, conventions—the individual actions would remain indeterminate. All communicative actions satisfy or violate normative expectations or conventions.[125]

These habits of communication are what, in a given context, just as in a given experimental situation, justify the validity of a communication or of the results of an experiment: "validity claims are at least partially and implicitly related to discursive vindication."[126] Accordingly, they must be in "accordance with existing norms" and "must merge with value patterns."[127] "Universal pragmatics aims at a reconstitution of the rule systems over which adult speakers must have mastery in order to use sentences in utterances at all, regardless of the specific natural language to which the sentence belongs or the context in which it happens to be embedded."[128]

However, with the postulation of these "pragmatic universals" also arises the possibility of their negation or their fracturation, whereby their "being," for example, the validity claim of "truthfulness," turns out to be mere "appearance":

> As soon as these validity claims (truth, legitimacy, veracity, comprehensibility) can be hypothetically grasped and negated, then the individual domains are no longer taken for granted in their objectivity, normativity, subjectivity, or intersubjectivity, but become modal. [. . .] i.e., these regions are experienced or expressed with a view to the possibility of the negation of the form in which they present themselves. We impute "being" to objectified reality in view of the possibility that our experiences may turn out to be mere "appearance". . . .[129]

The status of quasi-universal pragmatics resembles that of habit or potentia. All these concepts are only possible claims to validity and must be, within each context, either reaffirmed or refuted by actual experiment or actual discursive practice.

Nevertheless, Habermas was to take one step further than Peirce's and Heisenberg's respective notions of habit and potentia. Habermas explicitly suggests that these validity claims may be disturbed or broken by distorted discursive practices such as irony and fiction. We can exploit modal errors intentionally. What is more, in intentionally practicing a rupturing of postulates of communicational validity, such discursive practices strip illusory phenomena (i.e., ideology, false conscience, etc.) of their subjective character and utilize them as media of communication and of knowledge. In other words, the ironic breaking of habits of validity for communication destroys the ideological illusion within meaning structures and breaks down the confusion between illusion and being and between literal and direct statements:

> In symbolic or allegorical representation, in the use of *ironic* or metaphorical language, we presuppose that a hypostatized appearance only seemingly represents a substantial content, i.e., is identified as an illusion. At the same time, we intentionally utilize the confusion between essence and existence, because it is precisely the irreality of appearance of the essence which provides us with the disclaiming clue that the literal meaning of ironic usage or of metaphor, i.e., that which is immediately perceived in an allegorical image, ought not to be taken literally or directly.[130]

For Habermas, alternative discursive practices such as irony are definitely strategic discursive distortions which disrupt or break with preset habits of discursive practice, i.e., they break with communicational validity claims or normative pragmatic postulates.

Alternative discourse taken as habit-breaking perhaps best explains the combativeness that Musil accentuated in his definition of irony, when he said that irony was a "Form des Kampfes," a type of battle. Irony is the battle against the overcoded habits which play the role of ideology (in the sense of false conscience) and which, if utopia is ever to be possible, must be exposed by some relativizing, de-legitimizing, and radically contextualizing discursive procedure.

This habit-breaking function is one which destroys false conceptions of reality by disrupting their validity claims, a process that can be likened to the habit-breaking or decoding which unseats mythologies (Adorno/Horkheimer and Barthes) and ideologies (Eco).

If we recall that habit-breaking was essential to communication in cybernetic theory (Bateson), we may also conclude that alternative discourses such as irony, as a disturbance of redundancy, are essential to communication. Otherwise we fall into redundant nonsense, of the ideology of what Musil called "das Immergleiche," the ever same.

But what occurs once the consensus of validity claims is broken? When the validity claims are no longer accepted, then, says Habermas, there are three choices. (Habermas himself strongly recommends the last choice, if communication is once again to become feasible). These choices are: (1) switching to strategic action (for example, taking up arms against the one who is no longer convinced of the validity of your claim); (2) breaking off communication altogether; or (3) recommencing action oriented toward reaching an understanding at a different discursive level, i.e., the level of *argumentative speech or discourse.*[131] Habermas uses "discourse" as opposed to "communication" to distinguish between talking and talking about the rules of talking.

This third choice involves doing away with the habits or validity claims which are contested. Then, at a level of discourse unconstrained by habit, one must interact to discuss "discourse" about the possibility of forming new habits or new constraints of discourse, which will avoid the pitfalls of those earlier rejected as invalid. This reevaluation of the rules of communicational competence calls for the recognition of the relativity and transformability of communicational habits. This evolution occurs via the ever-expanding practice of discourse: "Codes control the emission of messages. But new messages can restructure codes."[132]

In the above remark, Eco is suggesting something similar to Habermas' remedy to overcoding. Eco also distinguishes the formation of discursive habits from discourse-production which transcends and reconsiders these habits. Eco speaks of discourse as a "new set of cultural units thus introduced into the social competence (i.e., old set of codes) which modify the preestablished semiotic field."[133]

Earlier it was noted that modern discourse was characterized by the relativity and constant expansion of sign-relations, and that habit was not posited as the end product or final result, but as a possible, limited, and necessarily surpassable way of temporarily halting this process in order to talk about it or to operate within it. "Modern" discourse then, becomes the process of discourse taken as unconstrained by permanent habits. Such a discursive process nevertheless allows for the temporary formation of habits, a formation which is interrelationally dependent upon configurations of signs and upon sign-users within various contexts.

6.8.2 The epistemological advantages of "habit"

The advantage of speaking of habit lies in its epistemological justifiability as compared to the linguistico-semiotic use of the concept of code. This epistemological edge provides an alternative conceptual tool for discourse analysis.

The epistemological pertinence of habit, to speak of postclassical discourse exemplified by Musil as well as by the paradoxes of quantum mechanics and Peircean semiotics, seems to make habit suitable as an operational tool for the analysis of "postmodern" discourse as well.

(1) Given the fact that meaning, truth, and knowledge were seen to be triadically *produced*, as opposed to merely *correlated* on a bidimensional plane, Peirce's notion of habit fits the task of describing this triadicity. Habits produce meaning as patterns of triadic interactions of sign-relations.

(2) Apart from the relationship of habit to a theory of sign-production, it is accordingly inserted into a theory of interrelation, or of communication taken in the fully cybernetic sense of the terms. Cybernetics' use of the term "code" for redundancy and reduction of variation is very close to Peirce's definition of habit as a "limitation of possibilities" (6.132).

(3) Even though codes are posited in biplanar semiotics as conventional links between sign and meaning, signifier and signified, they are posed as absolute structures describing these conventional relations, such as, for example, the codes of classical narrative outlined in Barthes' S/Z. Habit, on the other hand, has the advantage of always including the subject who discerns the habit (i.e., the discourse critic), as the third term, Interpretant-effect. This inclusion serves contextually to relativize not only the type of sign-meaning transfers conventionally established, but also the type of transfers that the critics' own habits make in the critical process of isolating certain habits within other sign-fields. Habit is a conceptual tool which recognizes and accepts its own subject: the dialectical relativity of the sign-object relationship.

The Peircean postulate of infinite production of signs and infinite expansion of sign-fields acknowledges that there is no possibility of permanently fixing any habit, even in a partial context. Habit may only be postulated in a way that provides for its immediate surpassing throughout the spatial and temporal expansion of the sign-field. This means that any interpretation of signs must admit bias and acknowledge the eventuality of being surpassed or relativized by yet other interpretative moments from within different contextual fields of habits. This is something which Barthes does not do in S/Z.

One semiotician does come close to recognizing the relativity and surpassability of code-postulation due to the infinite production of discourse. Umberto Eco, drawing extensively upon Peircean semiotics, defines the limitations of codes in much the same way that Peirce defined the limitation of the categories of his semiotics:

> The creation of a complete semantic structure must thus remain a mere regulative hypothesis. Even if one ever managed to describe a system of this kind, it would already have changed and not merely because of the influence of various historical factors, but also because of the critical erosion to which it would have been submitted by analysis itself.[134]

> Meantime, if law is a result of evolution, which is a process lasting through all time, it follows that *no law is absolute*. That is, we must suppose that the phenomena themselves involve departures from law analogous to errors of observation. (6.101)

Habit may be thought of either as (a) temporarily stable within a community of sign-users or (b) temporarily isolated, with some stability, by a temporarily stable, critical habit which is shared by a body of interpreters. Whatever the case, habit always recognizes that it is interactionally determined, hence relative and subject to revision. This characteristic applies to the habits which seek to classify or delimit certain types or "genres" of discourse. These types or genres are composites of habits of relatively greater or lesser complexity and persistence; they are sign-relations which acknowledge their dependence upon the Interpretant-effect of their perception. In other words, the category "modern discourse" itself may be only a temporary sign-field of habits, or a temporary consensus of critical habits of metalanguage.

(4) Habit may be posited as a discursive category which operates according to categories other than those of truth and falsehood. Rather than being judged as either true or false, habits are considered in terms of their degree of contextual validity. This is an open deviation from the principle of excluded middle. A habit is valid to the degree that it applies to the other contextual fields of habit which position it; it may be invalid in other contexts, and hence can never possess a universal truth-value:

> . . . an inference is regarded as valid or not, without reference to truth or falsity of its conclusion specially, but according as the habit which determines it is such as to produce true conclusions in general or not. The particular habit of mind which governs this or that inference may be formulated in a proposition whose truth depends on the validity of the inferences which the habit determines; and such a formula is called a guiding principle of inference. (5.367)

(5) Finally, a conception of discourse based on habit disrupts referentiality. In the theory of habit, meaning is not attached to a sign by a habit. Meaning *is* the relation itself. Meaning *is* the habit, just as the result of a quantum mechanics experiment *is* the interactional relation of object, instrument and observer: ". . . the whole function of thought is to produce habits of action. . . . To develop its meaning, we have therefore, simply to determine what habits it produces, for what a thing means is simply what habits it involves" (5.400).

Habit refers to more than the relationship which holds between a one-to-one signifier-signified dyad. Habit leads the way toward a conception of discourse production as inter-actional, as a practice, and as a production of relations.

7.0 The Epistemological Status of Modern Discourse

In our introduction we summarily listed the traits of discourse which could be said to characterize the classical episteme. It is now possible to present the transformations of that episteme that constitute a modern discourse of knowledge.

Modern discourse grows out of the impossibility of synthetic knowledge and of synthetic representation. It is associated with the inability of modern physics and Peircean semiotics to continue to support either Kantian transcendental categories of absolute knowledge or the identity of reality and sense-perception at the basis of empiricism.

Perturbation and indeterminacy, in the discourse of modern physics, correspond to perspectivism, continuous sign-production, and interaction, all elements of semiosis. Meaning, truth, and "reality" are all the relative, related products of a triadic relation of Object-Representamen-Interpretant; they, in turn, relate to other triadic fields or contexts. Irony then is a kind of *extreme contextualization* of meaning, reality, and true-false values. Not only does this perturbation render the absolute value of natural objects indeterminate, but, furthermore, it shows that meta-language is unable to describe its object (i.e., discourse) either transparently or absolutely. Both the meaning and the metalinguistic categories of discourse are relational products of the text-Object, the discursive Representamen, and the Interpretant-effects. These triadic variables are all placed in mnemonic and future possible fields of triadic relations.

Triadicity, relativity, indeterminacy, and perturbation, in relation to meaning and metalinguistic results, are devastating factors for classical theories and practices of discourse. It becomes superfluous to ask which signified is referred to since all of these types of signs are relational and possible. Rather one asks: which relation in which context? There is an infinite number of possible contextualized meanings attached to every sign-relation.

Because modern discourse is associated with infinite sign-production and interrelation, its meaning and knowledge is an *inference*, i.e., determined by previous triads of sign-relations. Inference occurs as thought, and thought cannot occur outside of signs. Therefore, meaning and knowledge must be conceived of solely as a production and interrelation of signs. There is no way to study or to practice a discourse of knowledge other than as a relation of sign-production.

Although sign-relations are infinitely interrelated with other sign-fields, various configurations, called habits or fields of habits, may be temporarily isolated from the total context (which would be impossible to talk about in any case). These temporarily arrested and isolated sign-configurations have the same "possible" epistemological status as potentia enjoys in modern physics. They are possible, experimental, interpretative results produced by an interaction of subject and object.

(A) As a first corollary, any critical type or category of discourse may be considered to exist as a product of sign-interaction, temporarily frozen as an isolated pocket of habits. In this case, one may speak of pockets of discourse, as merely isolated, punctual examples.

(B) Secondly, critical metalanguage may also be considered valid within certain contexts, as opposed to postmodernly immediately deconstructible.

(C) Thirdly, where discourse is relational, both as practice (i.e., critical, interpretative practice) and as object to be known, and where meaning, truth, and knowledge are all contextually relative, then it must also be said of the existence or nonexistence of a critical discursive category that it is possible, a mere production dependent upon the Object-Interpretant-Representamen dialectic. Hence, the very existence of a discursive type such as irony is itself contextually relativized. Irony does not "exist" in an absolute ontological sense. It is constituted by contextually situated triadic interaction. In other words, it would be fair to consider any isolated sign-relation as a potential discursive procedure. The existence of a critical interpretation or finding is dependent upon the contextual Interpretant-relations and habits that ensue within each particular context, which itself is equally contextually positioned. For example, even such an evident category as irony in the phrase spoken during a rainstorm: "Nice weather we're having!" is potentially non-ironic if situated within the Interpretant-context of a Dutchman who likes rain, and, of course, vice versa (or if indeed we are sitting in the sunshine!).

(D) Finally, then, the only way to study discourse at all is to isolate certain contexts, while also taking into account our own critical-interpretative contexts. We may decide whether or not, within that particular context, it is valid to consider a discursive type habit, genre, or meaning to exist or not. However, we cannot pose laws of discourse as objects which are fixed and absolute.

What lends consolidation to any critical results would be only a certain consensus within a community of critics, within a particular context. (For example, we have tried to establish a certain consensus among Musil, Foucault, Peirce, Bateson, and Habermas regarding modern discourse.) As soon as the utterance is situated within a larger field of possible contexts, "it's an open croquet game" once again. In other words, not only is a type of communication, e.g. popular culture, contextually situated within a modern epistemic field as pragmatic contextuality, but it is also determined solely by contextual pragmatics.

In attempting to analyze modern discourse, one is obliged to isolate habits of sign-relation and to study their interrelations in a contextually restrained field while attempting, at a further moment, to resituate these isolated habits, these discursive types, as moments in a larger series of sign-production leading up to and surpassing present day discursive, social, political, cultural, and economic contexts.

7.1 Modern discourse: A definition

Modern discourse is habit-disturbance, e.g., the deviation from, interference with, opposition to, or destructuration of past habits of classical discourse. The initially posited habit, as well as the intention to break the habit, are both relative, interrelational considerations positioned within a sectioned-off context, this context being at least partially determined by the interpreter's context. Neither the postulation of habit nor of habit-breaking intention is an absolute.

7.2 The potential of modern discourse

Finally, once these contextually frozen habits lose their reconfirmation by means of the consensus of the community of sign-users, the temporarily arrested sign-production resumes as a continuous, unconstrained production of discourse. Once the communal acceptance of the validity of contextually relevant habits is destroyed, then, say Musil, Heisenberg and Peirce, later to be taken up by Habermas, Foucault, Bateson, and Eco, the process of discussion, of discourse, or of experiment unconstrained by habits or by strategic action should resume in order to arrive at new, communally accepted pockets of habits or validity claims. This stage of unarrested, fully interactive expansion of sign-fields has also been shown to be responsible for the dismantling of previous codes/habits throughout the evolution of discursive practice. As a process which resists overcoding and ideology (Eco), the emancipatory function of the discursive process is evident. *The potential of modern discourse is* this infinite, continuous, unconstrained production and practice of signs. The potential of modern discourse guarantees the nonabsolute, nonideological, nontyrannical overcoming of every partial sign-field, of every partial result, and of every partial truth.

7.3 Modern discourse: A second definition

Modern discourse, considered in the vastest epistemic sense, goes beyond any negative dialectical or apophatic function. In its fullest, most complete practice (which perhaps has never yet been fully realized) modern discourse is nothing more nor less than sign-production unarrested by constraining habits or fields of habits, although discourse eventually constitutes new habits. Modern discourse is infinite, free, unconstrained interaction. In this sense, modern discourse is fully communicational.

Modern discourse, in its broadest perspective, may be understood in terms of the continuity of triadic relationality, interaction, interference, and of the expansion of sign-relations—the infinity of possible sign-field productions, substitutions, interactions, and expansions. Consequently, modern discourse practices and reaffirms the relativity, the contextuality, the indeterminacy of truth, reality, and meaning.

In the Conclusion, we will draw out some of the social consequences that Habermas will come to associate with this conception of a potentially free unconstrained communication—the project for modernity which he refuses to abandon to the apositivities of postmodernism.

It now remains in Part Two, our second reading of Musil, to see if such a potential modern discourse can be put into practice simultaneously to "read" a literary text and to resolve certain inescapable practical ethical dilemmas in social, psychological and political realms of experience.

PART II

THE GHOSTLINESS OF NARRATIVE
DISCURSIVE PRAXIS OF THE
ALTERNATIVE EPISTEMOLOGY

> I am not interested in real explanations of
> real events. My memory is bad. Besides, the
> facts are always exchangeable. What inter-
> ests me is the spiritually typical, I might
> even say the ghostliness of the event.
> (Robert Musil, Interview with Oskar Maurus
> Fontana: "Was arbeiten Sie?" [1926])

> The story in this novel is that the story the
> novel is supposed to tell is not told. (DMoE,
> 1937)

The epistemic tenets of potentia and of a Peircean triadic semiotics apply
not only to Musil's discursive and epistemological theory but to his narrative or discursive performance as well. From the preceding it should be
evident that two notions are essential to any discursive criticism of Musil's
work and that both of them must be rendered operational in order for such
criticism to take place: (1) triadicity and (2) the contextualization of fields
of Interpretant-habits.

0.0 An Imbroglio of Phaenera

Among the infinitely expanding discursive fields which interact in *Der
Mann ohne Eigenschaften*, we have selected the following as essential for
an analysis of Musil:

(1) A field of *narrative* (i.e., *récit*), where narrative is understood as a
configuration of "representeds," i.e., the story of *Der Mann ohne
Eigenschaften*.

(2) A field of *narration* or of *enunciation* understood as the "apparent"
and "underlying" *sources* which produce or position the enunciateds. The
determination of the first field depends on this second one. However, it is

not in fact easier to *isolate* elements of this second field than it is to do so for those of the first field.

(3) A field of extraneous discourses—a sort of intertext including other so-called narrative texts, literature, journalism, societal doxa etc. This field emerges when one questions the assumption that the second field (narration) is a single fixed identifiable, human source. It is seen that, in fact, these other discourses work to position the discourse in *Der Mann ohne Eigenschaften*.

(4) A field of metadiscursive consensus—such practices would include not only Musil's metalinguistic commentary about his own discursive production, but also a certain representation of the "Musilkritik" including, for example, Blanchot's interpretation of Musil's narrative as one that heralds the reign of "impersonality."[1]

(5) An interdiscursive epistemic field. As has been illustrated, *Der Mann ohne Eigenschaften* is situated not only by literary or "narrative" discourse fields, but also by discourses from other discursive series (Tynianov), including the philosophy of language, modern science, and sociohistorical theory. As Janik and Toulmin's *Wittgenstein's Vienna* and Schorske's *Fin de siècle Vienna* both so well portrayed at the turn of the century all discourses were thoroughly interconnected; i.e., Wittgenstein's *Tractatus* could not be fully understood without relating it to other discourses or to other disciplines of past, present, and future fields (Kant, Mach, Musil, Freud, Kierkegaard, Heisenberg, Einstein, etc.).

(6) A field comprising, last but not least, our own critical interpretive discourse, which is responsible for choosing and relating the former five fields, must also be acknowledged as having certain epistemological biases and as being composed of certain limited fields. In this way the choices in relating these fields also become somewhat relativized. The configurations which are placed into relief are de-absolutized because they depend to a degree upon our own strategic choices and interpretive filters. Just as Musil claimed to be writing for no one in particular (namely for no one in the present generation), so too must the interpretations generated by our own discourse take into consideration other past, present and future interpretations: "Thomas Mann and people like him write for people who are here; I write for people who are not (yet) here" (Tgb., 880).

Our own critical discourse had indeed related many of the above-mentioned fields. Also, we readily would admit that much traditional discursive criticism, although sometimes unawares, relates many of these fields and seeks a consensus (if somewhat vicariously and selectively) of the various domains of discourse. In general, most critics of discourse would include among the possible domains of discourse the author's metalinguistic commentary, the comments of other critics, and the discourses from the surounding epistemic climate. However, most critics tend to refuse to see that their own critical discourse is equally as situated and contextually relative as are the discourses that they claim to say truths about. The best proof of this would be the pamphlet-type battles over "right" vs. "wrong" schools of criticism. Perhaps the drawback of such interactive criticism is an operational problem, that of simultaneously relating all of these various fields. Because triadic sign-field relations have been shown to be infinitely expanding and infinitely variably interrelated, a speaker would ideally have to talk about all of these fields simultaneously. At the same time he would have to relate his own interpretive fields to the host of others which belong to the community of investigators. No one critic of discourse has yet succeeded in transcending the classical discursive traits of exclusivity, possessiveness, and knowledge's "will to truth." No one has succeeded in an conscious attempt to remain fully open to the discourse-field of the community. The alternative to this scenario would be to undertake discursive criticism in conjunction with a *whole community of investigators* where many active Interpretant-fields are brought into play in search of a consensus, thereby avoiding confinement to one particular individual's limitations and prejudices. But even then, biases, in this case those of the epistemic *community*, would still remain.

Also, the continuum and flux of the various fields make it impossible to order or hierarchize definitively, or causally and linearly to link one field to another. For example, one cannot say that Musil's discourse was causally "influenced" by the fields of discourse of modern physics. One may only say that they interact more or less directly and that the temporary delimiting isolation of this interaction is a product of the Interpretant-discourses which postulate or produce the interpretive result, including this present one.

Within fields we find what Peirce would call habits of sign relations or what Foucault refers to as discursive procedures, i.e., regularities or constraints generalized from particular discursive practices. In the following analysis these levels will not always be extricable one from the other. Rather the level of the enunciated will be enmeshed with the enunciation, and so on.

1.0 A Partial Solution to the Irony in *Der Mann ohne Eigenschaften*

One could argue that, in Musil, irony sometimes functions as an isolated case of binary opposition of meanings/signifieds. For example, Musil himself refers to the double significance of Arnheim's and Diotima's communication when he calls their silence an 'ambivalent' one. At one point the narrator plays on the contradiction between the corporal, sensual and the "spiritual," lofty traits of Diotima's character. One could simply reduce irony to a pocket of oppositions of figural versus literal meanings as, for example, in the following: ". . . in the very moment, that is to say, when he wanted to fling himself down at Diotima's feet reckless of his beautifully creased trousers and, indeed, of his future . . ." (M.w.Q. 2:225; DMoE, 510).

Wladimir Krysinski, in an analysis of the first paragraph of *Der Mann ohne Eigenschaften*, locates Musil's irony in a narrative modalization which results in the following binary oppositions of "topoi": the "Tatsaechliche" vs. the "Gespenstische des Geschehens"; the factual vs. the ghostliness of experience; the scientific topoi of discourse vs. the human type of knowledge.[2] Of course, there is a wide consensus among critics that, in Musil, there exist both binary oppositions and a dependence upon changes in narrative perspective and voice. However, such "Partialloesungen" (pocket solutions) to irony in Musil, taken as binary opposition, not only remain within the classical, logical episteme of the "exact"—an episteme whose exclusivity was rejected by Musil—but also such an approach limits itself to one particular context, for example, the first paragraph.

Any study of Musil should contextualize any enunciated within a context which is far broader, dynamic, and complex than a series of binary, semantic oppositions. Indeed, we have seen the difficulty of isolating semantic categories, let alone structural configurations. The problem then is to find a new, or at least a more flexible, less classical way of talking about contextualization and modalization in *Der Mann ohne Eigenschaften*, a way that is consistent with the epistemological positions outlined in the preceding chapter.

1.1 Interference of discursive practices

It is possible, to a limited degree, to discern certain fields of enunciation which position an enunciated, often allowing for a partial, stable interpretation, a "Partialloesung" of irony as a binary opposition or as an interference of one field with another. For example, Clarisse's discourse addressed to Walter presents a case par excellence of *interference of one discursive habit or procedure with another*. Walter is carrying out a long diatribe when Clarisse interrupts him merely, or rather precisely, for the sake of disturbing him; she asks if he wants a beer when in fact there is no beer in the house:

> The lines floated in waves from his lips.
> Clarisse watched these lips in amiable astonishment, as though they had sent a pretty toy flying up into the air. Then, remembering her role of good little housewife, she interrupted:
> "Do you want some beer?"
> "Hm? Why not? I always have some, don't I?"
> "But I haven't any in the house!"
> "Pity you asked me," Walter said with a sigh. "I mightn't have thought of it."
> . . . But Walter had now lost his equilibrium and did not quite know how to go on. (M.w.Q. 1:69; DMoE, 63–64)

1.2 Multiplication of contexts: Frames of reference

On a level other than that of the "apparent" or represented senders and receivers in *Der Mann ohne Eigenschaften*, it is also evident that Musil was addressing his enunciation to a certain field of receivers who inhabited "Wittgenstein's Vienna." For example, it is well known that the character Arnheim is modelled after Walther Rathenau, the German author, industrialist, and statesman. Obviously, one context of reception would be the concrete sociohistorical one of those who would recognize this "personnage à clef." But is it really necessary to recognize this context of reception in order to appreciate the various discursive configurations around the character of Arnheim? Obviously not! "Arnheims" may be found in every context, culture, and time. The field of applicability of Arnheim not only extends further than the temporally and spatially limited cultural codes of "Musil's Vienna." What is more, the significance of this character grows and becomes potentially universal in relation to the development of Western history as it is progressively situated in more and more contextual fields. The fields of reception of the enunciated cannot be isolated or tied to the distinct, referential coordinates of any one particular field. Rather, these fields potentially spread out over infinitely expanding spatio-temporal contexts. A further example serves to illustrate how crucial it is to be able (or unable) to isolate and fix positioning contexts of discourse. If one takes the syntagm, "Collateral Campaign," and situates it purely in relation to immediately apparent enunciated contexts, one is constantly confronted with a great flux of all of the possible meanings that this term may cover.

In Book 2, Chapter 22 of *Der Mann ohne Eigenschaften*, the Collateral Campaign is described by the narrator (via Ulrich's focus) as incarnated by "an influential lady of ineffable intellectual charms, waiting in readiness to devour Ulrich." The Campaign, in the above context, is somewhat carnally reduced to the person (body) of Diotima and to a collection of elements or charms such as sensuality and ambition, which constitute this gracious lady.

In Part I, Book 2, Chapter 37 of *Der Mann ohne Eigenschaften*, the Campaign is described by the narrator, who adopts two foci, first that of Tuzzi and secondly that of the host of participants in the Campaign. Tuzzi's focus circumscribes the Campaign as what "beseiged Tuzzi's home." The rest of the participants see it as what "claims to find a chance to help truth come into its own at last." Ranging from Diotima's person through the status of a nuisance to the most universal of truths, the meaning of "Campaign" undergoes a radical metamorphosis depending upon the discursive context which situates it. The above are just two very limited, isolated examples of contextualization, from a great number which appear within the text itself.

Furthermore, if we position the meaning of the Campaign in relation to the time of writing of the novel, i.e., the extended period including the outbreaks of both World War I and World War II, its significance would change completely. The Campaign is understood as one of the paths leading to war. But what does it mean to understand the Campaign in relation not only to the two World Wars, but also to the "repetition" itself of such wars and such campaigns, both historically prior and subsequent to the death of Musil? In this case, one can see how the infinite expansion of situating contextual fields changes the significance of the syntagm "Collateral Campaign." This "repetition" adds a dimension of sinister ineluctability and cynicism to the roles of the discursive and political. It is far from original to suggest that discursive praxis constitutes "Campaigns" in society throughout history. The Campaign also finds a contextual home in the political and discursive practices at the time of this present reading of Musil.

At this stage of our reading of Musil we suggest that a host of currently popular critical tools and concepts have actually derived from the epistemology elaborated in Part One. Such concepts as dialogism, polyphony, and interdiscursivity all refer to the materiality of contextualized semiotic interaction as ongoing sign-production.

This explanation of contexts in relation to various fields of discourse is described by Bakhtin in a remark that gives us some direction as to how to begin to analyze this discursive phenomenon and its social and epistemological implications:

> . . . the discourse of our practical experience is full of words belonging to others; there are those we mix our voice with, forgetting to whom they belong, there are those we use to strengthen our own words, accepting them as an authority, finally there are those we people with our own expectations which are foreign or hostile to them.[3]

For Bakhtin, as well as for other pragmatists such as Austin and Habermas, what we study when we study discourse is no longer a syntactico-semantic structure, a "langue" or a grammar composed of atomistic elements. For Bakhtin, the basic unit to be studied in discourse analysis is the dialogue, i.e., interaction. For Austin, it is the speech act or utterance. And, for Foucault, it is the organization of the field of utterances, where they occur and circulate [and] the configurations of the enunciative field,[4] i.e., the relations between various discursive practices.

These theorists have begun to study how various enunciateds are positioned in relation to the events in which they are manifest in order to see how they are understood in relation to many fields of origin and shared meaning.

A word's meaning and truth can no longer be said to exist outside of its contexts of use. Indeed, the word's meaning and truth are *constituted* or produced by this use, just as the result of a scientific experiment is constituted in and through that experimental interaction.

Foucault describes how one may view discourse in relation to its social contextualized configurations, i.e., discursive interrelations: "I am supposing that in every society the production of discourse is at once controlled, selected, organised and redistributed according to a certain number of procedures, whose role is to avert its powers and its dangers, to cope with chance events, to evade its ponderous, awesome materiality."[5]

Perhaps the key to an alternative mode of discursive "analysis" of complicated communications such as *Der Mann ohne Eigenschaften* lies in a study of the materiality of these internal discursive procedures as interrelated events, as well as of the configurations that they form and the claims that they make on the social order in which they appear. Rather than undertaking yet another semantic analysis of content, one would analyze the habits of procedures of the discourse-event itself in relation to as many other discourse-events as possible.

2.0 Expanding Triadicity: One Enunciated, Many Contexts

One of the most striking examples of ironic contextualization in *Der Mann ohne Eigenschaften* is the *mis en relief* of certain singular triadic sign-functions and the constant positioning and repositioning of them within various other sign-field relations or discursive practices. First, an enunciated is isolated and defined in a more or less stable, "referential" way. Then this stable definition is destabilized and destructured. The utterance recurs, but in a qualitatively different way since it occurs in a different contextual field. We shall refer to this operation as a form of "deterritorialization" in the sense of Deleuze's definition of this term.[6]

As will be seen, the shifting from one contextual field to another is carried out in *Der Mann ohne Eigenschaften* by almost all of the characters as well as by the narrator. The receiver is also provoked by the text to reposition sign-functions. This deterritorializing shifting occurs most evidently around the following sign-functions: "Geist" (DMoE, 152–158), "Erloesung" (DMoE, 517ff.), "Genie" (DMoE, 33–35, 44–47, 1254–71), and "Liebe" (DMoE, 191, 144, 355, 496, 521ff., 744, 901). However, although many enunciative fields effect this deterritorialization, what is of interest is the particular way in which each does so. It will be seen that while both Ulrich and Diotima deterritorialize others' discourses, Diotima does so in a way that lends itself to the ridiculous, whereas Ulrich does so in a way that provokes epistemological and ethical doubt.

Each contextual use of the particular sign-function may be temporarily isolated as a sign-functional "potentia" having a partial and temporary meaning ("Partialloesung"), which is immediately surpassed with each new context of use. When the interpreter of the sign-function tries to find an ultimate or total Interpretant for all of the potential sign-functional relations, he finds that the various meanings add to, interfere with, translate for, substitute for, overuse, and misuse each other, making it impossible to fix any single, absolute meaning. Within a synchronic instant there may exist a meaning which is temporarily isolated, but it cannot withstand the flux of relationally constituted meanings for any longer period of time. This discursive procedure of continually repositioning a sign within new contexts, of seeing the sign from new perspectives, of never arresting its sense, is of course, the procedure earlier referred to in *Der Mann ohne Eigenschaften* by the narrator as "essayism" and "experiment."

2.1 The many interpretants of "Genie"

A much-used word in the circles of the Campaign is "Genie." One particular use in the sense of Wittgenstein's term, "language-use," of this sign-function catalytically incited Ulrich to reflect upon the various meanings produced within the many contexts that situated this term.

A journalist had written that a certain race horse was a "genius" (DMoE, 44). Ulrich began his search for a recuperation of this use of the term first of all in relation to the dictionary definition of the term, as though looking for a fixed referential or at least literal value to attach to "Genie":

> "It is most evident," said Ulrich to his sister, "when, as usually happens only by chance, one becomes aware of a little-noticed sign, namely, that we have the habit of pronouncing 'genius' and 'genial' differently, and not as if the second came from the first". [. . .]
> "At that time, after the conversation with Stumm, I took a look in Grimm's *Dictionary*," Ulrich excused himself. "The military word 'genius', that is, the 'soldier-genius', naturally has come to us, as many military expressions have, from the French." (DMoE, 1257)

Then Ulrich proceeded to expand the situating discursive field. He gave the various etymologies of the word "Genie" ranging from Goethe to Kant, as well as the various ways that the term was used (DMoE, 1258).

Somewhat later, after this abundance of discursive complexes, we switch over to Stumm's reflective positioning of the word:

> "What exactly is a 'genius'," he asked. No one has ever called a general a 'genius'!" [. . .] I think I can tell you what a 'genius' is: It is not just someone who is very successful, but rather someone who also, so to speak, goes about his business backwards!" And Stumm went on to argue his point using the great examples of psychoanalysis and the theory of relativity. (DMoE, 1259)

Add to the above several remarks made earlier concerning Clarisse's expectation that Walter would become a genius, the social world's pronouncement that Walter *was* a genius, the remark made early in *Der Mann ohne Eigenschaften* by the narrator concerning the genius and ruin of Kakania: "Yes, in spite of much that seems to point the other way, Kakania was perhaps a home for genius after all; and that, probably, was the ruin of it" (M.w.Q. 1:34–35; DMoE, 35). The sign "Genie" combines with various sign-relations in many discursive fields in an infinite number of possibilities. These infinitely expanding combinations make it impossible to attach any single signification to the Representamen "Genie," to see meaning as anything more than a contextualized discursive production shifting throughout a variety of fields.

We may schematize the shifting sign-fields of "Genie" as in figure 3, whereby the various contexts produce various meanings, all of which battle with each other for supremacy.

2.2 "Erloesung"

The constant enunciative positioning and repositioning of a sign-function within many various use-contexts, is also effected by Stumm in relation to the "Wortgruppe Erloesen." The various over- and misuses of this term point to the "inflation of language" evident to both Stumm and the reader. Stumm's consideration of all of the uses of this term illustrates its "corruption," its inflation.

Stumm himself calls it a "geschwollenes Wort" (DMoE, 518). Once again, the result of his accentuated repositioning of each sign-function is the impossibility of associating an object, a denotation, or a referential meaning to any word: "The world of those who write and those who have to write is full of big words and ideas that have lost the objects to which

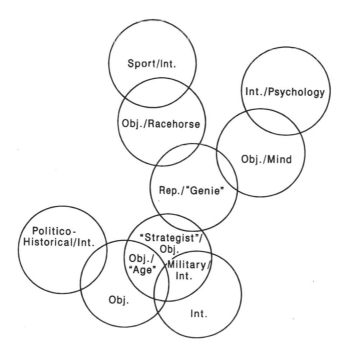

Fig. 3

they refer . . . and the surviving concepts must be used" (M.w.Q. 2:26; DMoE, 326).

We might then define the "inflation of language" as the overflowing of a word with multiple but unarrestable meanings given the complex fields of discursive circulation that assume the word.

2.3 "Geist"

Not only does the infinite contextualization of a sign-function disturb any referential meaning of the term, but also certain idealistic assumptions about certain terms are dismantled. This dismantling of ideology occurs as a sort of explosion of overcoding. For example, Ulrich initially attempts to hold onto the idealistic and ideological assumption that mind/ spirit/intellect ("Geist") is the highest human value: "Geist[gilt] als das Hoechste und ueber allem Herrschende" (DMoE, 152). Here "Geist" and "human value" are rendered synonymous by overcoding, or myth, as Barthes would say. Reflecting upon the various uses of this sign-function, Ulrich recalls many of the cliché, overcoded uses of the term, remarking that "Geist" is considered to be the highest manifestation of all things. "Geist" is even the superlative qualifier for aspects of life which are situated on the lowest link of the chain of being. Here Ulrich is faced with a conflict between a shifting contextualization which relativizes and a word-usage which absolutizes and mythologizes while simultaneously attempting to be applicable to even the most banal of concrete contexts:

> Mind and spirit [= Geist], when in combination with something else, are the most widespread thing there is. There is a masculine mind, a cultured mind, the greatest living mind, the spirit of loyalty, the spirit of love, 'keeping up the spirit' of this cause or that, 'acting in the spirit of our movement' and so forth. How solid and unimpeachable it sounds, right down to the lowest level! (M.w.Q. 1:177; DMoE, 152)

Musil, then, brilliantly *turns this contextualization into a decontextualization.* Many people had attributed an absolute value to the term "Geist," but when Ulrich tries to see what this value is, independently of the various contexts which have situated it, the word is emptied of sense, so to speak, once it is totally "decontextualized," "deterritorialized" or "demythologized," reduced to silence.

> But when the spirit stands alone, a naked noun, bare as a ghost to whom one would like to lend a sheet—what then? One can read the poets, study the philosophers, buy pictures and have discussions all night long. But is it spirit that one gains by doing so? . . . Perhaps, if one knew more about it, there would be an awkward silence round this noun 'spirit'. . . . (M.w.Q. 1:177; DMoE, 152)

In other words, the inability to fix any specific context if only for a moment leaves us with no meaning at all!

In another definition of "Geist," Ulrich sees this somewhat elusive term operating as an Interpretant-context which gives meaning to other sign-functions. "Geist" can cause the sign-function "beauty" to have fluctuating Interpretant-effects such as "good," "bad," "magical," etc.:

> The mind [Geist] has learned that beauty can make things good, bad, stupid or enchanting. The mind dissects and analyses a sheep and a penitent sinner and finds humility and patience in both. . . . It regards nothing as firmly established, neither any personality nor any order of things or ideas. Because our knowledge may change with every day, it believes in no ties, and everything possesses the value that it has only until the next act of creation, as a face to which one is speaking changes even while the words are being spoken. (M.w.Q. 1:178–79; DMoE, 153–54)

As this continuous, triadic situating and resituating of "Geist" unfolds, where first of all other words become Interpretants of the sign-function, "Geist," and then vice versa, "Geist" becomes all three functions; the Object is "Geist," the Representamen is "Geist," and the Interpretant is "Geist": "Geist" means nothing since it can only be reduced to itself in a tautologically sinister language game: "And all at once the whole thing presented itself to Ulrich comically, in the question whether in the end, since there was certainly plenty of mind and spirit knocking about, all that was wrong was that the spirit was mere spirit and the mind had no mind?" (M.w.Q. 1:180; DMoE, 155).

The destruction of any absolute meaning or even of any relatively stable meaning for such terms as "Geist," "Erloesung," "Liebe," and "Genie," illustrates the negative, aggressive, tendentious attitude of discursive practices traditionally associated with irony. The interaction of various contexts of discourse and the differential enunciative positioning leaves intact no myth, no ideology, and no value associated with any particular sign-function. An infinite discursive practice attacks and places into question the claims to exclusivity and power that Foucault associates with the specific, "undisturbed" discursive practices of knowledge.

While we have not devoted much space here to the discussion of the relationship between Nietzsche and Musil, this comparison having already made up a large body of traditional Musil critique, we might suggest that whereas discourse is the will to power in Nietzsche and in Foucault's renditions of him, for Musil, the discursive project is constantly to recontextualize, de-absolutize, de-exclusivize discourse and thereby mitigate its claims to power.

3.0 Discursive Habits Constitute the Subject: Infinite Sign-Practices Disperse the Subject

This radical contextualization of signs destroys the absoluteness not only of certain key-words, but of characters as well, since these are defined, indeed constituted, as sign-functions. As such, characters have no other status than that of the elements of the discourses which constitute them. To state it in yet another way, character is nothing more than a configuration or a habit of discursive elements which circulate within the field labelled by the proper name/"deictic"—for example, "Moosbrugger." This view and practice of characterization as discursive configurations of elements comes very close to Mach's reduction of the subject to nothing more than a series of elements: "[It is] not the ego that is primary, but rather the elements (sensations). . . . The elements form the ego."[7] Musil, too, expressed the decentralization and deessentialization of the notion of character: ". . . the personality will soon be no more than an imaginary meeting-point for all that is impersonal" (M.w.Q. 2:210; DMoE, 474), although he sees it as a condition of the age more than as a state of being to be advocated.

However, even where character is constituted by the discursive events that assume him/her, some characters are more rigidly constituted, so to speak, than others.

In the following quotation one finds the distinction between the ridiculous sense of contextualization and tragic discursive orientation. In Diotima's report to Ulrich of Arnheim's evaluation of his (Ulrich's) role in the Campaign, we may isolate three types of discursive procedures: (a) *Distortion* through rigid recontextualization: Arnheim's rigid, blind re-situating of humanist, aesthetic discourse into the realm of business, and vice versa; (b) *Acontextualization:* ignorance of the original context such as is the case with Diotima's unreflective imitation of Arnheim's discursive habits, and her application of them to the context of her adulterous and ambitious tendencies; and (c) *Super-positioning of contextualizations:* Ulrich's critical reflection on the habits of others and his inability to adopt one particular firm stand even in defense of this fluctuation of perspectives:

> "I [Arnheim] should be inclined to fear that his influence on Count Leinsdorf was not a fortunate one, were it not that this true nobleman is so securely enshrined in the great traditional feelings and ideas upon which real life is based that he can probably well afford to bestow this confidence."
>
> These were strong words, and Ulrich had deserved them. But Diotima did not take so much notice of them as she might have, because it was the other part of Arnheim's pronouncement that made an impression on her—his way of regarding estates not as something to be owned in an estate-owning spirit, but as a form of spiritual massage. She thought this magnificent, and let her thoughts wander after the idea, imagining herself as the lady of the manor in such a setting. "I sometimes admire," she said, "the broad-mindedness of your criticism where His Highness is concerned. All that is, after all, a vanishing period of history, isn't it?" "Yes, to be sure," Arnheim replied. "But the simple virtues, courage, chivalry, and self-discipline, which that caste developed in such an exemplary way, will always keep their value. In short, the noble lord and master! It is a type to which I have learnt to attach

more and more importance even in my business activities." (M.w.Q. 2:22–
23; DMoE, 323–24)

While Ulrich adopts a critical overview of all of these discursive idio-
syncrasies, Diotima is completely unreflective about the way that she uses
Arnheim's discourses "à la mode" to justify her infidelities and to glorify
her "arrivisme" (i.e., to displace the discursive sphere of aristocracy while
imitating it, situating it in the discursive sphere of bourgeoisie, since, as a
bourgeoise she can never belong to it, make her own discourse enter
wholly into the aristocratic sphere). Arnheim seems completely uncon-
scious of certain inconsistencies which arise between the fundamental
values of capitalism and those of honor, aesthetics, humanism, etc. Part of
Arnheim's success is due to his slipping contextual humanistic discourse
into the realm of economics, discourse based on exchange or the principle
of adequate mediation. The discourse of exchange lends power and cre-
dulity to all that he says, and humanism excuses or at least occults some of
the un-esthetic factors of Arnheim's profession (DMoE, 407ff.). But, one
must ask, does not what is described as the greed, power, and the exploita-
tion underlying the capitalism of the turn of the century somewhat betray
the precedents of these other "humanist" discourses? Or perhaps what is
made apparent here is that "humanist" discourses themselves are facades
of a common, underlying social and political power struggle in that they
too seek possession and power at the expense of the "Other's" discourses.
It is perhaps such contextual inconsistency between the humanist claims
and the capitalist procedures of Arnheim's discourses that causes Ulrich
and Tuzzi to reject them as a mixture of "soul and the price of coal":

> There was a confidence-trick involved in this union between the soul and
> the price of coal, a union that was at the same time a useful dividing-line
> between what Arnheim did with his eyes wide open and what he said and
> wrote when he was under the twilight spell of his intuitions. And there was
> something else, which caused an even greater sense of discomfort in Ulrich
> and which was new to him: things of the mind [Geist] in combination with
> wealth. (M.w.Q. 1:334; DMoE, 281)

> . . . but people believe Arnheim because they are at liberty to imagine him
> as a big, rich man who is sure to know all about what he is talking about, has
> been to the Himalayas himself, owns motor-cars and wears as many benzol
> rings as he likes! (M.w.Q. 1:253; DMoE, 214)

> This combination of mind [Geist], business, good-living and well-readness
> was something he [Ulrich] found in the highest degree intolerable. (M.w.Q.
> 1:207; DMoE, 176–77)

Diotima's and Arnheim's discourses are particularly overcoded because
of a hyperbolization of a certain lack of self-reflectiveness and because of a
certain rigidity with which they place one discourse into the context of
another discourse (i.e., soul into business) to which it does not apply

without great inconsistencies. What is more, both tend to *overhabitualize* or overcode the sign-functions within two or more seemingly incompatible contexts. This results in an inflation and "ideologization" of these sign-functions: in the following Diotima shifts from a "sacred or ritual" sphere to an everyday sphere: "She [Diotima] was capable of uttering the words 'the true, the good and the beautiful' as often and as naturally as someone else might say 'Thursday'" (M.w.Q. 1:43; DMoE, 42). [Elsewhere, the narrative commentary explicitly states that this lack of communicative competence, i.e., knowledge of contextually pertinent language use, in Diotima's discourse amounts to nothing more than "*cliche*" (DMoE, 277).]

Finally, in Ulrich's somewhat misogynous perception of Diotima's corporeal discourse, the inflexibility of her pseudointellectual, pseudospiritualist speech is exposed in all its distorted communicative incompetence: i.e., the voluptuous deictics of body language completely contradict—are split off from—the "pseudointellectual or reverential" enunciateds: "How pleasant she [Diotima] would be . . . if she were uneducated and easy-going and as good-natured as a big warm female body always is when it hasn't any particular idea in its head!" (M.w.Q. 1:328; DMoE, 276).

The bourgeoisie's constant displacement of the mediational trait of the discourse of exchange—capital—by those of intellectuality, of humanism, and of love, is exposed in all its confusion and inflexibility in the following narrative commentary which inserts a mixture of Diotima's language-use (i.e., "Seele") and Arnheim's discourse field (i.e., "Kapital") into the context of Diotima's struggle with carnal temptation and social ambition: "Probably what she called 'soul' was nothing but a small capital for love that she had possessed at the time of her marriage" (M.w.Q. 1:119; DMoE, 104).

One might add here that the *automatism* and *rigidity* of Diotima's transference of discursive contexts and the *unreflectiveness* with which she does so, are traits which Bergson, in *Le Rire*, attributes to the phenomenology of the ridiculous.[8] Diotima's discourse amounts to a kind of low comedy. She unreflectively and rigidly imposes the constraints of one context upon the enunciated from another without being aware of the curious shifts in meaning and "truth" that she operates by so doing. She rigidly recontextualizes. This makes her the perfect victim for Ulrich's destabilizing ironic recontextualizations.

4.0. Clearing the Way for Alternative Discourse: Disturbance of Communicational Postulates

The constitution of an alternative discourse must begin by breaking with the constraints of traditional discursive habits. Up to this stage of our analysis of *Der Mann ohne Eigenschaften*, what we have called discursive habits and configurations, as well as discursive fields and context, have been defined somewhat vaguely and elusively. It remains to be seen if there are any constants among these habits and if so, what their relations are, not only to character, but also to the structure of society.

According to Bakhtin, discerning various configurations of communicational habits and fields might also reveal the various social organizations of the epistemic climate in which a discourse was written, as well as something about the present context of textual reception or concretization: "Thought does not exist outside of its potential expression and thus not outside of the orientation and the thought itself."[9]

Relating irony to what Habermas terms a "mutation of certain communicational postulates" may indicate more clearly what the nature of the violated habits of discourse are. Later we will see that these communicational postulates may do more than *indicate* social relations; they may constitute them.

4.1 Opposition of "is" versus "ought": Irony as critical theory/praxis of communication

Habermas has stated that irony plays on the disparity between the modes "is" and "ought," whereby the communicational postulates that "are" are violated in order to propose what communicational postulates there *"ought"* to be:

> At the same time, we intentionally utilize the confusion between essence and existence, because it is precisely the irreality of the appearance of the essence which provides us with the disclaiming clue that the literal meaning of ironic usage or of a metaphor, i.e., that which is immediately perceived in an allegorical image, ought not to be taken literally or directly. . . . Because this intentional employment of illusory phenomena presupposes the mastery of the mechanism of illusion, we may, contrariwise, regard the understanding of derivative modalities of play, of idealized constructions, of symbolic imagery, of irony, of formalism, etc. as a test of stability of ego delimitations. The joke lends itself particularly well as a test case, because the comic effect of a joke springs from relief that one has not allowed oneself to be led into modal confusion.[10]

Habermas is referring here to Critical Theory's distinction between *facticity* and their duty to criticize it in relation to *utopian possibility*. Habermas' theory of irony corresponds overtly only to our first partial definition of alternative discourse as *irony, as "habit-breaking."* In our second definition of alternative discourse as infinite interaction, "modern" discourse will be seen not only to break habits, but to approach the Habermasian, utopian quasi-ideal of emancipated interaction.

From the above quotation it is apparent that discursive perturbance, in disturbing nonideal communicational postulates and in feigning these nonideal postulates, also presupposes the possibility of ideal postulates.

Habermas differentiates between the communicational postulates of everyday communication and those of "symbolic or allegorical constructions."
This suggests that the text of *Der Mann ohne Eigenschaften* must be related
to both utopian ideals and actual practices of communication if one is to
understand the "is" and the "ought" of Musil's communicational theory
and praxis.[11]

4.2 Disruption of validity claims taken as pragmatic rules of interaction

Habermas outlines three basic validity postulates of communication
which, if adhered to, would produce a "perfect" communication act.
These validity claims have the aim of "coming to an understanding" with
the other person, i.e., of tending toward a perfect communication. The
three criteria that must be adhered to are as follows:

(1) Propositional content: One must give the hearer something to understand. The proposition must be a true proposition, fulfilling the requirement called "Wahr" by Habermas. This condition does not deviate very
much from the classical criterion of referentiality, whereby Habermas is
trying to retain the last remnants of a semantico-referential paradigm: "To
choose the propositional sentence in such a way that either the truth
conditions of the proposition stated or the existential propositions of the
propositional content mentioned are supposedly fulfilled."[12]

(2) Second, Habermas postulates a claim of *sincerity, veracity or right-
ness ("Wahrhaftigkeit")* so that the hearer can have confidence in the
sincerity of the sender, i.e., in his intention to say the truth: "The speaker
must want to express his intentions truthfully (wahrhaftig) so that the
hearer can believe the utterance of the speaker."[13]

(3) The speaker must conform to recognized norms of communication
so that his utterance is likely to be "understandable" ("verstaendlich") by
the hearer. The speaker must choose a comprehensible (verstandlich)
expression so that the speaker and hearer can understand one another: "To
perform the speech act in such a way that it conforms to recognized norms
or to accepted self-images (so that hearer can be in accord with speaker in
shared value orientation)".[14] One may restate these postulates quite simply: (1) To represent something in the world; (2) To express the speaker's
intentions truthfully; (3) To establish legitimate interpersonal values.[15]

Within the third category there are three subcategories as exemplified by
the discursive behavior of Agathe in relation to her husband Hagauer.
Agathe leaves Hagauer without giving any reason except that she did not
want to return. This is a violation of the norm of "*Begruen-
dungsverpflichtung" (the obligation to provide grounds)*. Secondly,
Agathe, in suggesting that she would be perfectly capable of stealing a
gold cigarette case despite the fact that she has neither a need nor a motive
for doing so, demonstrates a case of *failure to provide justification
("Rechtfertigungsverpflichtung")*. Thirdly, Agathe's aim to disinherit
Hagauer, regardless of the law, to falsify the will, is an example of a

flagrant rejection of *the obligation to prove trustworthy* (*"Be-wahrungsverpflichtung"*).[16] Both Ulrich and Agathe, in delegitimizing these validity claims of social communication, carry out an ironic discourse and are dubbed the criminals/outlaws ("die Verbrecher") by some unidentifiable voice which provides the chapter headings: "And now here was Agathe on the point of leaving the confines of the moral territory, about to venture out upon those limitless deeps where there is no other criterion than whether a thing will lift one up or let one down" (M.w.Q. 3:155; DMoE, 797).

And, to this degree, Musil's heros, in their experimental year, radically violate the modern democratic project for an ideal society based on an ideal speech situation as proposed by Habermas.

4.3 New Discourse: Alternative pragmatic postulates

However, at the same time that this ironic revolt against such conventions of discourse is carried out by Agathe and Ulrich, both are simultaneously seeking to create their own ideal, mutual communication system where the postulates would constitute a *new discourse*. Their new discourse would be one where *the postulate of referentiality* does not hold, one which does not share the conventional constraints of comprehensibility in society; rather, it would be one which fashions its own ways of communication, unconstrained by society, i.e., the discourse of the other state ("anderer Zustand"). These postulates, however, have certain drawbacks for our argument here in that they are still very general and fail to illuminate the innovativeness and the complexities of the communicative practices in Musil's narration.

It might be more fruitful to postulate several other habits of communication from which Ulrich's and Agathe's discourses deviate. These habits will be seen to overlap with some of Habermas' *postulates of communicational validity*, as well as with several of what Foucault calls the *"internal procedures of the materiality of discourse."* Furthermore, some of these communicational habits approximate several of the categories posited by a semiotics of narrative (such as the code of character or that of mimesis). As with the communicational habits of referentiality and identifiability of participants, very often the Interpretant-intuitions may be quite similar to those found by traditional semiotic analysis of narrative. The main difference lies in the epistemological and ontological truth claims of the latter as opposed to the relativity of the validity of the former.

For example, in the first paragraphs of *Der Mann ohne Eigenschaften* and in some of the chapter headings, one finds *a violation of the romanesque communicational postulates of the identifiability of the participants of discourse.* The use of the impersonal: . . . "even though it is somewhat old-fashioned: it was a fine August day in the year 1913" (M.w.Q. 1:3; DMoE, 9) leaves the identity of the narrating subject—the subject of enunciation—in doubt. Also, in the opening chapter the identity of the dialoguing characters is first hinted at and subsequently repealed, leaving their identity an enigma which was never intended to be solved: The hermeneutic code is introduced only to be revoked. "Let us assume that their names were Arnheim and Ermelinde Tuzzi—but no, that would be a mistake, for Frau Tuzzi was spending this August in Bad Aussee, accompanied by her husband, and Herr Dr. Arnheim was still in Constantinople. Se we are confronted with the enigma of who they were" (M.w.Q. 1:4; DMoE, 10).

Or again, in the chapter title, "Wem gibst du Recht?" (DMoE, 119) ("Whose side are you on?"), there is a fundamental plurality and unidentifiability of the sender and the receiver. Obviously, from the specific context of the chapter, the question is posed to Bonadea by Ulrich. Still we would not have read the context before we read the title. However, this could also be a question posed by Ulrich to himself (an interpretation corroborated by the larger context of the whole novel), by the narrator to Ulrich, by the author to the narrator, by the author to the reader, by the reader to himself, and so on, depending upon the romanesque and extra-romanesque contexts of enunciation and reception which reposition this heading.

In the first chapter, one finds yet another postulate of communication disturbed, the *postulate of identifiability of levels and types of discourse*. To begin with, the headings of the opening of the book switch levels and types of discourse with no identification of the voices that "speak" in each case. The book begins with the heading, "Erster Teil" followed by the remark "Eine Art Einleitung" ("A kind of Introduction") followed by the title of Chapter 1, "Woraus bemerkenswerter Weise nichts hervorgeht" ("Which surprisingly enough does not get us anywhere"). Here there are at least two levels of discourse: a) that of the "author" of the book, the supposedly neutral and impersonal organizer who follows the standard divisions of the "novelsque" genre, and b) that of metalinguistic commentary, which, in both cases, mocks the standard divisions and the roles of the introduction and development of a communicational structure, in this case the "novel," in general.

In the first paragraph, there is a constant switching between at least three types or "fields" of discourse with no linguistic markers of subject of enunciation. In the impersonal voice and perspective of positivist "scientific" or "factual" discourse the geo-meteorological facts are "neutrally described": "There was a depression over the Atlantic. It was travelling eastwards, towards an area of high pressure over Russia, and still showed no tendency to move northwards around it. The isotherms and isotheres were fulfilling their functions" (M.w.Q. 1:3; DMoE, 9).

Then, once again with no formal mark of identification of the speaking voice, a metalinguistic voice takes over, interrupting the former discursive level or type in order to state: "In short, to use an expression that describes the facts pretty satisfactorily, even though it is somewhat old-fashioned"

(M.w.Q. 1:3; DMoE, 9). And finally, the type of discourse known as "common usage" enters into play, opposing scientificist discourse, to restate what the scientific discourse has already said: "It was a fine August day in the year 1913" (M.w.Q. 1:3; DMoE, 9).

Not only could the speaker of the last remark be millions of people and no one specific, but the repetition of the content of the weather report, where only the types and levels of discourse change, violates another postulate, that of *informativity,* i.e., adding to the reservoir of propositional content that the receiver is already supposed to possess. In terms of referentiality, no new information is added by restating the weather report. It is precisely this violation of the postulate of informativity that highlights the radical relativization of the various levels and fields of discourse. It is not the informational content, but the *triadically constituted message* which changes according to the discursive Interpretant-contexts that situate the Object—weather. It is this change, despite the fact that the Object remains fixed (i.e., the weather on an August day in 1913), that discursively practices triadic indeterminacy and dynamics.

The private holiday language ("Urlaubsprache") of Agathe and Ulrich, enclosed within its own diadic monad and cut off from society, is an example of a defiance of the *postulate of social comprehensibility.* The solipsistic relation of Ulrich to the other members of the Campaign is also a violation of this postulate. Defying the postulate of comprehensibility amounts to an anti- and asocial discourse, unconcerned with following the norms and values of society which are necessary for one's utterance to be understood.

The most accentuated case of the defiance of the principle of communicability is the discourse of Clarisse. Clarisse's discourse is an intertextual "take-off" on Nietzsche, whereby the progression begins with a disruption of normal laws of syntax and moves toward a complete neglect of any semantic coherence, in favor of pure phonetic play on the signifier:"My dar*ling*—my lord*ling*—my *ling!* Do you know what a *ling* is? I can't work it out. I think perhaps Walter's a weak*ling.*" (All the '-lings' were heavily underlined) (M.w.Q. 3:52-53; DMoE, 711).

The result of ignoring the principle of comprehensibility, in both Nietzsche's and Clarisse's cases, was total solipsism, where, on the island, even Ulrich could no longer communicate with Clarisse's new language, a stochastic conglomerate of hieroglyphs: "— — — —" (DMoE, 1753). Clarisse's practice of discourse gravitates rather toward the Derridian theory of language as "differance" and absence ("lack") of meaning than toward any dynamic and shifting triadic constitution of meaning.

The difference between a discourse which recognizes the postulate of comprehensibility and one which does not is what lies between a Kierkegaardian, solipsistic theory of language and the interactional practice of discourse as shifting fields of meaning. For Kierkegaard, both "indirect expression" and "infinite inwardness/subjectivity" were associated with ironic discourse. Communication, for Kierkegaard, was not comprehensibility; it was an indirect provocation of the receiver to inwardness: "[Indirect communication] is communication by means of reflection reflecting a subjective truth and a notion of an objective uncertainty held fast in an appropriate process of the most passionate inwardness."[17]

Some of the more severe critics of Lacan's concept of "le manque" ("l'absence") and of Derrida's insistence on "la différance" would insist that they go no further than a solipsistic performance of vocables—"du Bulgare" according to some. Furthermore, these same critics would insist that a theory of discourse based on the lack of meaning can only lead to a psychotic slippage along the surface of the signifier in the absence of any meaning to integrate the self. The psychotic play on the signifier ends up in the obsessive paralysis of a Kierkegaard, or the madness of a Nietzsche or a Clarisse.

But the constant narration of Musil's novel does not leave intact Ulrich's and Agathe's social discourse nor the Nietzschean play on the "supplement" of the signifier. As the novel unfolds, the demands of the social force these delimited sign-fields to open up.

An alternative practice and theory of the subject and discourse would have to surpass the confinement to the empty signifier were it to avoid paralysis or psychotic disintegration, the primary task to which this work addresses itself.

5.0 Interdiscursive Interference—Habit-breaking—Dislocation of Fields of Discourse

Certain habits of communication, articulated in certain fields or configurations, form either types of characters or types of discourses. Foucault speaks of these various configurations of discursive production as constituting societies of discourse, taken as institutions or disciplines, which are based on a certain hegemony of procedures of discourse and knowledge: ". . . the 'fellowships of discourse', whose function is to preserve or to reproduce discourse, but in order that it should circulate within a closed community, according to strict regulations, without those in possession being dispossessed by this very distribution."[18]

These disciplines or "societies" of discourse refer to certain institutionalizations of discourse, certain fields of practice and power. In Der Mann ohne Eigenschaften, much of the effect of irony is a result of the interaction of these various fields or disciplines which relativize and destroy each other's closure, absoluteness, and claim to validity and power. Each of these disciplines is constituted by a field of habits of discourse which, we shall argue, by virtue of their overcodification and unrecognized partiality, also constitute ideologies.

5.1 The fields or types of discourse in *Der Mann ohne Eigenschaften*

In *Der Mann ohne Eigenschaften*, one could present a typology of the various discourses that circulate throughout the field of the novel. Any such typology must, of course, acknowledge its own relativity and Interpretant-dependence. Nevertheless, it would serve as a heuristic way to describe which habit-configurations make up the discursive fields of *Der Mann ohne Eigenschaften* and of "Musil's Vienna," as well as describing how irony, as habit-breaking and discursive interaction, dislocates these fields. Where, as we argued in Part One, a fixed absolutized partial field is considered to be ideological (Eco) then a disruption of that field would amount to a demystification of ideology, a disturbance of its hegemony. Although it would be too tedious to present a justification of each and every type of discourse in *Der Mann ohne Eigenschaften*, it is possible to describe how certain types of discourse are practiced loosely and continuously throughout the novel. They interact with, come into conflict with, "prick leaks in," or try to exclude and even explode each other. There are many of these discourse-types. Each claims to be absolute and to enjoy power exclusively at the expense of other discourses. The sheer multiplicity of these discourses, each of which claims to be absolute, tends to self-destruct their exclusive truth claims. Knowledge, in the classical episteme, is based on a political economy of the scarcity of a discourse's ability to be "right." "Everyone can't be king!" But there are many types of discourse found in *Der Mann ohne Eigenschaften* which make classical discursive validity claims for themselves, which are in turn destroyed or relativized by the simultaneous presence of many other absolutist discourses, making the same exclusive claims.

As we have constantly suggested throughout, the potential of modern discourse is not dissociated from providing legitimated readings of texts nor from addressing ethical, psychological and political dilemmas confronting subjects of the postclassical episteme.

The canon of Michel Foucault has always been praiseworthy for applying his approach to discursive criticism to such social ethical issues as the penal system, medical practices, the treatment of the mentally ill, and the ordering of sexuality. To this degree his work is more "applied" than that of Habermas. In any case, neither of these thinkers would espouse a formalist divorce of aesthetics and ethics, nor be content to play on the signifier. Despite Foucault's critique of Utopianism, he follows in the modern project of seeking a more socially just, less authoritarian, less hegemonic order of discursive and social practices.

The work of Musil is very modern in this regard as well; it constantly raises within the narration a host of social, psychological and political practical dilemmas: How does an intelligent being live in modernity? As with Foucault a key dilemma is the relationship between reason, madness, and criminality.

	Economic	-----------------	Arnheim
	Political	-----------------	Leinsdorf
EXACT	Jurisprudential	-----------------	Schwumm and Ulrich's father
	Jurisprudential	-----------------	The courts of law
	Forensic	----------------	Police reports and Pfeiffer
	Psychiatric	----------------	Doctors in the asylum
	Journalistic	----------------	Newspaper accounts
HUMAN	Societal	----------------	Bonadea and Diotima etc.
	Philosophical	----------------	Nietzsche/Clarisse/Ulrich
	Idiosyncratic	------------------	Clarisse:
	?	----------------	Moosbrugger

Figure 4

5.2 Moosbrugger: Criminal or saviour? madness or reason?

One example of the proliferation and relativization or contextualization of discourses in order to address the issue of reason, madness, and criminality is that of the *Moosbrugger sign-function*. Around the sign-function "Moosbrugger" circulate many types of sign-productions which both triadically situate and are situated by this sign-function. Each of these discourses claims exclusively to say the truth ("Will to truth") about the object "Moosbrugger" and, what is more, claims to be in the field of truth (Foucault) in order that it may say and legitimize this truth. Among these discourses one may isolate the following fields or types in a sort of hierarchical order of the power that each exercises over the other in society (figure 4).

It should become obvious as the discussion of these types progresses that each of these discourses operates according to the classical episteme while claiming exclusive and absolute knowledge and power for itself. Their mutual exclusion make hierarchization necessary, i.e., for a system of power to make one subordinate to the other. All the while, the dynamics and elusiveness of the sign-function "Moosbrugger" place into doubt and provide an Interpretant-context for each of these other disciplines. At the same time, Ulrich's insistence on viewing the Moosbrugger case simultaneously from the perspectives of all of these various disciplines will be seen to expose the *occulted partiality* of each discursive field which takes itself for the totality.

Questions of context are questions of value. Who is Moosbrugger? Is Moosbrugger an Object to be studied by society? Is Moosbrugger a Representamen, a symbol of something about/for society? Or is Moosbrugger an Interpretant-effect, interpreting society for us through a certain very specific filter? Hinging upon the reply to these questions is the reply to the axiomatic question: "Is Moosbrugger a criminal or a crucified saviour?" Does society, including any of its discourses, have the right, the power or the validity to pronounce upon Moosbrugger and can it stabilize the contextual uncertainty of the very grave ethical value which the Moosbrugger case exemplifies? Inextricably linked to the semiotic questions of the Moosbrugger case are questions of ethic *value*, which is seminal to any discursive analysis that inscribes itself within the project of modernity.

The Moosbrugger case opens with the discursive proceedings of the police interrogation and investigation and their "interpretation" by the media (DMoE, 68, 119). These proceedings include a description of the forensic detachment of the police (Book I, Chapter 18), as well as a reproduction of a part of the juridical discourses that try to circumscribe Moosbrugger.

In the same chapter, the narrator reproduces some of the remarks likely to made by the doxological discourses of society: "Says the accountant to his wife as he slips into bed one night: 'What would you do now if I were Moosbrugger?'" (DMoE, 69).

In Chapter 30 of Book I, Ulrich "hears voices," and continues to reflect upon the complexity of the ethical decision in a labyrinthine way. Clarisse's discourses about Moosbrugger in Chapters 38 and 53 lend a Nietzschean perspective to the problem of morals. Ulrich's father, in Chapter 111, also discusses the juridical quarrel regarding the hypothesis of diminished responsibility. In Chapters 87 and 110, the reader is presented with Moosbrugger's own voice and perspective on the social discourses which attempt to interpret and manipulate him. In Book II, Chapters 32 and 33, preparations are made to visit Moosbrugger, on which occasion the psychiatric-medical discourses come into interaction with both the philosophical and the juridicial discourses. And earlier, Leinsdorf benevolently stayed the hand of the executioner, in a gesture of disinterested but omnipotent intervention, above and beyond the powers of all the previously mentioned discourses. Even Bonadea, Rachel, Diotioma, and Arnheim are periodically seen to concern themselves with Moosbrugger, and, what is more, directly or indirectly, Moosbrugger with them.

By positioning Moosbrugger in relation to some of the various discourses mentioned above, it will be shown that Moosbrugger is simultaneously Object of the others' discourses, Interpretant of their discursive functioning, and Representamen or symbol—a keyword to which one may attach many meanings. For example, Moosbrugger becomes a Representamen, a password for Bonadea, which has the Interpretant-effect of allowing her to infiltrate Diotime's circle. For Clarisse, as well, Moosbrugger is a Representamen. "Moosbrugger" is the Representamen which substitutes for both "God" and "Anti-Christ."

5.2.1 *Journalistic discourse* may be characterized by the following sub-habits of communication: (1) communicational claims of referentiality and factuality (i.e., presenting a true propositional content about something out in the world); (2) non-necessity of identifying the participants of the communicational act, whereby the (3) "impersonal," "objective" source of the journalistic "enunciated" is divorced from the status quo yet able to represent what the "public" ("everyman") needs or wants to know. (Journalism, under the guise of "objective reporting," traditionally acknowledges no bias of its own; any bias it might acknowledge is that of the discourses it reports, not that of the fields from which it itself originates.) The following report illustrates the so-called referential, objective factuality and shows how this discourse functions according to the principle of excluded middle. There is a victim and a henchman, a good guy and a bad guy, and never the twain shall meet, and never shall journalism have any direct implication in the decisions of these values!

> The reporters had described in detail a throat-wound extending from the larynx to the back of the neck, as well as the two stab-wounds in the breast, which had pierced the heart, the two others on the left side of the back, and the cutting off of the breasts, which could almost be detached from the body. They had expressed their abhorrence of it, but they did not leave off until they had counted thirty-five stabs in the abdomen and described the long slash from the navel to the sacrum, which continued up the back in a multitude of smaller slashes, while the throat showed the marks of throttling. From such horrors they could not find their way back to Moosbrugger's kind face, although they themselves were kind men and yet had described what had happened in a matter-of-fact, expert way and obviously breathless with excitement. They made little use even of the most obvious explanation: that here they were confronted with a madman—Moosbrugger had already been in lunatic asylums several times on account of similar crimes. (M.w.Q. 1:75; DMoE, 68)

Already at this stage a certain narrative modulation occurs which challenges the claims of *factuality*, objectivity, and impersonality of journalistic discourse. In the above, the narrator reports a slight contradiction between how (a) the so-called extreme concern over "factuality" encouraged the journalist (b) not to leave out one single "sensational," gruesome detail, while using quantification to lend an impression of exactness. The principle of Objectivity and markers of value come into conflict. What is more, the reporter emphasized the contradiction between the friendly looks of Moosbrugger and his status as a criminal (principle of excluded middle), instead of finding therein a possible uncertainty or "complementarity." The press's theory of explanation seems to be one of relating events either *causally* or *contradictorily* but never complementarily.

Ulrich asks himself a question which places into doubt the claims of complete objectivity and independence from the interests of other discourse, such as, for example, those of the police and that of the public taste for "bloody details." Ulrich asks himself: "Where was the *source of* all of these details reproduced by the news?" a question which is far from innocent. The answer to this question is also suggested: "Perhaps from the discourse of the police, but then again perhaps from other discourses such as *fiction*, the alter ego of journalism": "Where had the reporters got their nimble expertness in describing the work of his knife?" (M.w.Q. 1:139; DMoE, 120–21). As well as being governed by a principle of factuality, the journalistic discourse also operates according to a principle of linearity and causality, a procedure evidenced by the search into the roots of Moosbrugger's life for a *chronologically linear* and *causal* explanation of the "crime." "As a boy Moosbrugger had been a poverty-stricken wretch, a shepherd lad in a hamlet so small that it did not even have a village street; and he was so poor that he never spoke to a girl" (M.w.Q. 1:76; DMoE., 69).

Finally, the narrative commentary which englobes all of this discourse on journalistic discourse completely undermines the principle of factuality and the true vs. false dichotomy, making them categories nonpertinent to explanatory knowledge. In other words, narrative modalization serves to ironize the habits of journalistic discourse by reducing them to the status of probable fiction and arbitrariness, the implicit opposite of factual experience: "The probability of learning something unusual from a newspaper is far greater than that of experiencing it; in other words, it is in the realm of the abstract that the more important things happen in these times, and it is the unimportant that happens in real life" (M.w.Q. 1:76; DMoE, 69).

The play between probability and being, where the latter is found more in writing than in existence, places into doubt the claim of any discourse to "represent the facts." It remains probable.

5.2.2 Psychiatric discourse: Reason's use of madness/madness' irony of Reason

For Michel Foucault, the discourse of madness is an ironic sign-production in that it mixes up any distinction between real and imaginary, between true object and illusion or image: "Madness is here, at the heart of things and of men, an ironic sign that misplaces the guideposts between the real and the chimerical, barely retaining the memory of the great tragic threats—a life in society, the mobility of reason" (our translation).[19]

If the discourse *of* madness is an ironic destructuring of the classical discourse of Reason, what then is psychiatric discourse, the discourse *on* madness? If Moosbrugger's discourse is ironic, what then are the discourses about Moosbrugger? It is perhaps these latter, discourses *on* madness, that the former, discourse *of* madness, ironizes. We may begin by isolating some of the traits of discourse *on* madness, the psychological, medical and psychiatric discourse, all of which assume Moosbrugger's madness as their Object.

Moosbrugger's madness itself, as well as the "voices which Ulrich hears" ("Ulrich hoert Stimmen"), serve to reveal the habits of these various discourses on Moosbrugger and to disturb and disarm them as well as to loosen the constraints they pose.

The psychiatric discourses, whether they absolve or condemn Moosbrugger, function according to the principles of excluded middle and of exclusivity of truth. Moosbrugger is *either* a criminal responsible for his actions *or* insane and hence innocent:" . . . an attitude in keeping with that of the psychiatrists, who had declared him normal quite as often as they had declared him not responsible for his actions" (M.w.Q. 1:75–76; DMoE; 68–69).

Clarisse witnesses the following carnival (à la Bakhtin) of discourses when she visits Moosbrugger in the asylum and witnesses a poker game between Moosbrugger, a priest, and two psychiatrists of opposing schools, Pfeiffer and the assistant. The psychiatrists situate their respective positions at opposite poles of the axis. Pfeiffer, on the one hand, claims that society *needs* "bad people" and hence it should not just declare them insane but rather punish them as evil: "Moosbrugger [ist] zurechnungsfaehig" (DMoE, 1547). On the other hand, he claims equally exclusively and absolutely that anyone who commits a murder is insane and the responsibility of society; hence there are no criminals, only insane people:

> . . . to handle with great skill every criminal whose mental health was in question like a ball that one is supposed to force through the gaps of science to reach the goal of punishment. (DMoE, 1548)

Then the priest is asked to pronounce a judgement, but he refuses to do so, saying that, in the end, God will decide: "It is only religion that insists on personal responsibility for every sin before God, and such questions are, therefore, in the end nothing but a matter of religious conviction. . . . God has the final word" (DMoE, 1549).

The exclusive claim to absolute knowledge of each chapel is evidenced by Friedenthal's introduction of Clarisse in which he says that she had come from Paris to see that: ". . . nowhere in the world are the sick better taken care of than here" (DMoE, 1548). What is more, the mention of God is inserted in order to illustrate that he who has the perfect possession of reason and knowledge (of the discourse on madness from the field of sanity/reason) also has the equivalent of the knowledge of God or at least one which is grounded in God. He is, as Descartes said, "maître et possesseur de l'univers." Indeed, as Foucault's theory would have it, madness is necessary as an affirmation of the absolute power of reason by virtue of the former's submission to the latter. The age of reason absolutely needed madness in order to affirm its own reason relative to what was not reason.[20]

The conflict between the two psychiatrists is a conflict of *classification*, of *division* and of *ordering*, all of which are internal procedures of classical discourse:

One need only think of each of those abbreviations linked up with hundreds, or at least dozens, of printed pages, each page linked up with a man with ten fingers, a man who writes it, and for each of his fingers ten disciples and ten opponents, each disciple and each opponent also with ten fingers, and to each finger the tenth part of a personal idea, and one gets a faint picture of what truth is like. (M.w.Q. 2:28485; DMoE, 534)

With the beginning of positivism, represented in psychiatry by Tuke and Pinel, one of the primary concerns was to order, to classify, to separate, and to hierarchize types of madness and criminality.[21] The bibliography of discourses on madness in *Der Mann ohne Eigenschaften* reflects the way that madness itself is classified, i.e., dependent upon science's labelling and ordering of madness, in this case by means of societies and journals that treat the topic: "AH., AMP., AAC., AKA., AP., ASZ., BKL., BGK., BID., CN., DTJ., DJZ., FBgM., G.A. . . . ZSS., Addickes *ibid*. Aschaffenburg *ibid*., Beling *ibid*. and so on. Or, translated into words: Annales d'hygiène Publique et de Médecine légale, ed. Brouardel, Paris . . ." (M.w.Q. 2:284; DMoE, 533). The object—illness—is discursively constituted by knowledge of it.

However, this positivistic separation of the criminal from various degrees of insanity is shown, in the passage on Clarisse's visit to the asylum, to be more a form of repression or surveillance than a merciful or philanthropic mission. Foucault sees this separation of madness from criminality, and the confinement of madness, as an overcoded form of tyrannical and puritanical surveillance and repression, veiled as humanitarianism and philanthrophy:

Eighteenth-century positivism linked madness more firmly than ever to confinement, and this by a double tie: one which made madness the very symbol of the confining power and its absurd and obsessive representative within the world of confinement; the other which designated madness as the object *par excellence* of all the measures of confinement. Subject and object, image and goal of repression, symbol of its blind arbitrariness and justification of all that could be reasonable and deserved within it; by a paradoxical circle, madness finally appears as the only reason for a confinement whose profound unreason it symbolizes.[22]

Moosbrugger, on the other hand, simply affirms his own responsibility and guilt as though it were merely to escape from these totalitarian categories, which as the Other's discourse, try to possess and reduce him.

Hence too he [Moosbrugger] hated no one as fervently as the psychiatrists who believed they could dispose of his entire difficult personality with a few long Latin or Greek words, as though for them it were an everyday matter. As always happens in such cases, medical opinion as to his mental state fluctuated under pressure from the juristic body of ideas. (M.w.Q. 1:80; DMoE, 72)

This philanthropy of psychiatry is but a panoptic reinforcement of social control via an exclusive discourse of knowledge. In the penal system, Moosbrugger is subjected to a "degradation process" (R. D. Laing), whereas in the asylum, he is not tied; he plays poker freely in the society of other doctor/observers. However, the asylum's discourse is one of therapeutic, monological inequality. Moosbrugger is the Object of the others' discourses; in the end, they do not dialogue "with" Moosbrugger. And, what is more, Moosbrugger has been brainwashed into quietly acquiescing in his role as Object. He is happy to be a curiosity, the center of attention! As Foucault states, the absence of chains is not madness liberated, but rather madness mastered. Moosbrugger is constrained to respect the right of others to speak *about* him without speaking *with* him. And Moosbrugger must acknowledge that they speak the truth: He must judge himself as they judge him: "Something had been born, which was no longer repression, but authority."[23] *Once one party alone has the power to discourse, there can be no interaction, no dialogue, no freedom with and for madness.*

Moosbrugger is made to attest to the fact that words belong to others. He also recognizes and demands the "justice" of the punishment levied upon him by reason, i.e., death. In confinement, Moosbrugger renounces any more conflict with society and welcomes the end. His discourse has been subsumed by all other social discourses. It no longer struggles for a field of its own.

The positivistic discursive categories of psychiatry try to reduce the dynamic form of Moosbrugger's existence to a set of technical terms. Moreover, they force Moosbrugger to revolt and proclaim his own sanity, i.e., his own responsibility for his actions, independent of any social determination. These discourses force Moosbrugger to sign his own death warrant when they force him to cry out in revolt against their classical procedures, as in a sort of "Catch 22" situation: "Justice has been done" (DMoE, 84–85).

The various psychiatric discourses of knowledge merely talk about and over the head of Moosbrugger: "There thus existed between these four men a cordial understanding that Moosbrugger's head was at stake, but that did not bother them" (DMoE, 1549). Their discourse has not arrived at the Freudian stage, a stage where the madman is no longer reduced to silence but where he is encouraged therapeutically to dialogue: ". . . il [Freud] restituait dans la pensée médicale la possibilité d'un dialogue avec la déraison."[24] Although Freud's dialogue was asymmetrically weighted in favour of the thaumaturgical doctor, and although Musil was highly critical of Freud, they were contemporaries in Vienna who both seemed to be proposing, however imperfectly, an interactional alternative to the established discursive power structures so well exemplified by the procedures of the discourses on madness. According to Foucault, it was not until Nietzsche, Dostoyevsky, Artaud, and Van Gogh that madness became an

Interpretant of society, reflecting something about it rather than being reduced to the status of an Object for society's scrutiny. Madness, as an Interpretant for society, forced society to justify itself in the face of the sacrificial victims of its own "reason." Accordingly, Clarisse and Ulrich are forced to wonder if Moosbrugger is not a saviour, the sacrificial one, the hero of their epoch. Moosbrugger becomes an Interpretant for society, but also a Representamen which substitutes for the sign-vehicles "Saviour" and "Anti-Christ": Foucault expresses this triadic shifting excellently when he suggests that, later, reason does not judge madness but madness judges reason:

> What is necessarily profane in a work returns; at the time of the failed work, of madness, society experiences guilt.[25]

> After Port-Royal, men would have to wait two centuries—until Dostoievsky and Nietzsche—for Christ to regain the glory of his madness, for scandal to recover its power as revelation, for unreason to cease being merely the public shame of reason.[26]

The maieutic, and heuristic functions of Musil's irony come to the fore once Moosbrugger is treated not merely as the Object of a sign-function but as a genuine triadic semiosis, as an Interpretant for the society of discourses, which had tried to render him a static Object of society's claims to truth and power (cf. figure 5).

> Let us generalize: in the nineteenth century, psychiatric discourse is characterized not by privileged objects, but by the way in which it forms objects that are in fact highly dispersed. This formation is made possible by a group of relations established between authorities of emergence, delimitation, and specification.[27]

To summarize, we may hierarchize the discourses on madness in *Der Mann ohne Eigenschaften* as follows:
(1) therapeutic versus penal confinement;

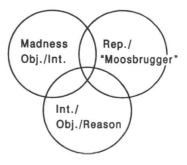

Fig. 5

(2) social versus penal confinement dictated by norms of behavior;

(3) planes of psychological characterization and taxonomy;

(4) relations between authority and medical decisions (Leinsdorf and the juridicial system);

(5) the filters of observation lent by psychiatric, forensic, and juridicial interrogation;

(6) means of communciation between political authority, public opinion (journalism), and medical and juridical authority.

The conflict between hierarchies of power in the relations between medical and juridicial discourses on Moosbrugger, and hence the contextual relativity of what claims to be absolute, should illustrate the ironic result of the juxtaposition of these two discourses on Moosbrugger.

5.2.3 Socrates revisited: Jurisprudence, the great silencer

Jurisprudential discourse, while posing as the source of right judgement, is initially dependent on the filters of the questionnaires of the police and of psychiatry. The court case and convictions are based on a confession that Moosbrugger made to the police in order to "help out the latter's career."

In seeking to establish Moosbrugger's biography, the order of his actions, and the causal relations between his various violent attacks, juridical discourse exemplifies its own concern for the classical scientific procedures of structure, linearity, causality, and hierarchy, just as much as it shows us the journalistic and psychiatric adherence to these same discursive principles: "This judge rolled everything up into one, starting with the police-reports and the vagrancy, and then presented it to Moosbrugger as his guilt" (M.w.Q. 1:84; DMoE, 75).

However, Moosbrugger's own interpretation of his life illustrates that here is indeed a bias in the filters of knowledge of the juridical discourse. Its "objectivity" is questioned by Moosbrugger's impression that the connections made by juridical discourse were of no pertinence to his person at all: "But for Moosbrugger it all consisted of separate incidents that had nothing to do with each other, each of them with a different cause, which lay outside Moosbrugger and somewhere in the world as a whole" (M.w.Q. 1:84; DMoE, 75).

The discourse of jurisprudence does not recognize the ideal communicational postulate of equal access to discourse (as proposed by Habermas). Moosbrugger tries to appropriate the juridical discourse for himself in order to explain his case. However, Moosbrugger does not belong to the juridical society of discourse/field/discipline. Moosbrugger is not in the field of truth and hence his discourse is not accepted as truth nor as powerful: "There were two kinds of tactics fighting each other, two kinds of unity and logical consistency; but Moosbrugger had the less favourable position, for even a cleverer man could not have expressed his strange shadowy agruments" (M.w.Q. 1:84; DMoE, 75).

Instead of listening to Moosbrugger's somewhat hyperbolic or parodistic appropriation of their discourses as defenses of his actions, the members of this professional society of discourse rejected it, merely declaring Moosbrugger to be intelligent, hence meriting a harsher sentence!

Moosbrugger was aware that everything from discourse to women belonged to others. He realized, implicitly, that the exclusivity of their societies of discourse, their claims to know the truth about an object—Moosbrugger—gave them power to reaffirm the socioeconomic order of things, i.e., to condemn Moosbrugger rather than to let him, as Interpretant, cast any aspersions upon their own discourse and conduct:

> Moosbrugger was wrathfully aware that they all talked just as it suited them and that it was this talking that gave them the power to treat him any way they liked. (M.w.Q. 1:279; DMoE, 235)

> All women were already someone else's law, and so were all apples and all beds. And the gendarmes and the magistrates were worse than the dogs. (M.w.Q. 1:281; DMoE, 237)

Foucault points out that the complex of discourses on madness resulted in a submission of the medical discourse to socioeconomic concerns. Men were "cured" either through work camps or through confinement, depending on whether society needed a greater workforce or to rid itself of unemployed vagabonds. The discourse of knowledge, both psychiatric and juridical, was not one of interaction; it was a hierarchically organized strategy to maintain power within the hands of the few who already possessed it.

It has been illustrated above that there are certain recurrent, recalcitrant habits of discourse which are shared by the societies of discourse in power and which, like ideology, propagate a certain false consciousness of the relation of truth to society. Moosbrugger's awareness of the relation of possession of certain fields of discourse to the preservation of power and the socioeconomic status quo serves to demystify the professed objectivity and relativize the absoluteness of these classical discourses.

5.2.4 *"Moosbrugger is the table"*?

When Moosbrugger, instead of being an Object, becomes an Interpretant for himself and for society, several other discursive procedures enter into play in *Der Mann ohne Eigenschaften*. These procedures dislocate those of the discourses of knowledge. Moosbrugger, as vehicled in the discourses of the narrator, Clarisse and Ulrich, becomes an Interpretant-effect of the whole episteme in which he appears: "The gloominess of his mind was connected with the gloominess of the times" (DMoE, 1718).

Moosbrugger's discourse flagrantly defies the classical discursive procedures of excluded middle and of propositional content, as well as that of comprehensibility. His discourse does not conform to the referential, axiological, syntactical norms of human understanding. When asked to add 14 and 14, Moosbrugger replies, "anywhere from 28 to 40, but why stop there?" (DMoE, 240). When shown a picture of a fox, he replies that "it could be a squirrel but then again it could also be a hare" (DMoE, 240). Need we note the potential mode of his thought? Whereas for discourses of knowledge each Object and Representamen has its absolute, established relation, Moosbrugger, on the other hand, feels no remorse at vertiginously substituting one for the other, including other sign-functions for himself, in a passage not unlikenable to Ionesco: "The table was Moosbrugger. The chair was Moosbrugger. The barred window and the bolted door were himself" (M.w.Q. 2:111; DMoE, 395).

At this point we may also recall that we argued earlier that Peirce's own naming, renaming, classification, and reclassification of signs was tantamount to an infinite substitution of one triadic sign-function for another. Moosbrugger's ultimate irony resides in his reduction of the status of the object or act, the crime, the murder, to discourse itself. A harmless discursive symbol, "Rosenmund," is mutated, transformed, substituted for by a monstrous Interpretant-effect. The word becomes a crime and the crime is reduced to the status of the word. The crime is a pure discursive formation, a switch from one commonplace word, "Rosenmund," to a horrendous, metamorphosized witch, and then to the act of slaughter. All this occurs within the new discourse of Moosbrugger, a discourse that constitutes Moosbrugger's "anderer Zustand": " 'Your sweet rose-lips,' but suddenly the words gave way at the seams, and something came about that was very distressing: the face went grey, just like earth under the mist, and at the end of a long stem there was a rose. Then the temptation to take a knife and cut it off . . ." (M.w.Q. 1:285; DMoE, 240).

Moosbrugger's crime becomes what Foucault has referred to as the "discursive formation of the object/event."

5.2.5 Madness versus referentiality

Whereas the discourses of classical science rely upon a distinction of the sign from the referent, of Representamen from Object, regardless of the Interpretant, madness, says Foucault, is a complete confusion and indiscrimination of the difference between the Representamen and the Object, between sign and reality, and between illusory image and truth. The example par excellence is hallucination. The great antiscientific ironist, Kierkegaard, in *Fear and Trembling*, made an ironist's career out of Abraham's inability to know which was which, reality or hallucination. Madness occurs when the images, which are so close to the dream, receive the affirmation or the negation that constitutes such an error.[28] "Before us appears the great theme of a crisis that confronts the madman with his own meaning, reason with unreason, man's lucid ruse with the blindness of the lunatic—a crisis which marks the point at which illusion, turned back upon itself, will open to the dazzlement of truth."[29]

For triadic semiotics and quantum mechanics, the image may become the object reality and yet also turn against itself, declaring itself to be only a created reality, constituted by the image itself. In Peircean semiotics the object, the Representamen and the Interpretant are constantly uncertain, constantly substituting for each other. Is this a semiotics of madness or a mad semiotics? Certainly it is not a semiotics of the Age of Reason.

6.0 Ulrich! Man without Qualities—Discourse without Habits

The ironic relativization of the discourses which claim to know Moosbrugger initially occurs in Ulrich's discourse as a Socratic expression of the complete lack of knowledge and comprehension. Ulrich cannot grasp the relationship of Moosbrugger's discourse to that of jurisprudence. As Moosbrugger leaves the court after being sentenced to death, crying that 'justice has been done,' Ulrich feels completely confused by the "*imbroglio*" of discourses that had led up to the verdict of guilty and to Moosbrugger's reply (DMoE, 84–85).

Apart from this "Socratic ignorance," Ulrich demonstrates several other discursive practices which contribute to habit-breaking and to the ironic interaction of discourses.

6.1 Radical relativization of the discourse of the Other

Ulrich's first technique is to recontextualize all that is said about the Object, Moosbrugger, in relation to the Object, society. For example, for those who take Moosbrugger to be an exceptional case which does not implicate them, Ulrich replies that Moosbrugger constitutes a sort of collective archetype of all mankind, one which is embedded deeply within the subconscious: "Yet somehow Ulrich could not help thinking: if mankind could dream collectively, it would dream Moosbrugger" (M.w.Q. 1:85; DMoE, 76). However, Ulrich does not let the meaning of Moosbrugger rest there. He provokes a radical discursive recontextualization of Moosbrugger.

Ulrich "performs" the same substitution of one sign-function for another, making Moosbrugger a critical Interpretant of elements of society in relation to Bonadea and to the hypocrisy of puritanical mores in Viennese society. He suggests to Bonadea that she always sides with the participant in the act but not with the act itself (which makes her own nymphomanic acts unjustifiable as well): " 'What it comes to, then, Ulrich insisted, 'is that you are for the victim everytime.' . . . . 'But if you so consistently condemn the act,' Ulrich answered. . . . 'how then, Bonadea, are you going to justify your adulteries?' " (M.w.Q. 1:138; DMoE, 120).

In a more global context, the Moosbrugger case is relativized by other statements made by Ulrich regarding values in general: "I believe it can be proved to one a thousand times by all the usual sturdy arguments that something is good or beautiful, and it'll be all the same to me. I shall take my bearings solely from whether its presence makes me feel a rising or a sinking" (M.w.Q. 3:122; DMoE, 770).

Not only do the classical values of good and evil become problematic for Ulrich, but he can also make no absolute distinction between the image of a murderer and the image of the rest of mankind: "The split in him was different; it lay precisely in the fact that he repressed nothing and so could not help seeing that what the murderer's image faced him with was something no stranger, or any less familiar, than any other image in the world" (M.w.Q. 2:439; DMoE, 653).

Elsewhere, Ulrich situates the same Object, rigor, not only in the context of Moosbrugger's methodical stabbing, but also in that of the thinker, the soldier, the politician, etc. In the former, rigor is a sign of guilt or of madness; in the latter series of Interpretant contexts, rigor is a quality to be valued:

> If a murderer proceeds in a matter-of-fact and efficient manner, it will be interpreted as particular brutality. A professor who goes on working out a problem in his wife's arms will be reproached with being a dry-as-dust pedant. A politician who climbs high over the bodies of the slain is described as vile or great according to the degree of his success. Of soldiers, executioners and surgeons, on the other hand, precisely the same cold-bloodedness is demanded as is condemned in others. (M.w.Q. 1:174; DMoE, 149)

At another point, the exclusivity of the Object, Moosbrugger's madness, is threatened by the narratively modulated suggestion that Ulrich (the protagonist) also has certain traits of madness and marginality in relation to society. Not only Moosbrugger has hallucinations, but Ulrich as well "hoert Stimmen" (DMoE, 119).

6.2. Trying on discourses for size

Throughout his discourse on Moosbrugger, Ulrich adopts various other discursive habits, as if experimentally, i.e., "essayistically" trying them on for size, only to cast them away as insufficient and as too partial, while recognizing their value as "Partialloesung." In speaking with Bonadea about Moosbrugger, Ulrich pleads the causes of the law, of social medicine, of frightened society, of psychiatry, of "humanism," etc.

Having adopted no one point of view, no one discourse with which to sum up Moosbrugger, Ulrich reflects upon himself with dissatisfaction, but in a way which reveals completely his attitude toward all discursive habits and fields of habits. The only habit that Ulrich possesses is that he does not fix any habit at all! His only perspective is to be perspectivist! But even this habit is "perspectivized" by Ulrich in a supreme gesture of discursive metaperspectivism.

Urlich's discursive practice proceeds by using temporary pockets of established habits and then by juxtaposing them, a procedure which places in relief the incompatibility of so many absolutist discourses. The political discourse, the scientific, the military, etc., all claim to have exclusive mastery of logical rigor, and yet they have no comprehension of the "rigor" of Moosbrugger's murder:

> "What is there left of me?" Ulrich thought with bitterness. "A man, perhaps, who is brave and incorruptible and imagines that for the sake of inner freedom he respects only a few external laws. But this inner freedom consists in being able to think everything, in knowing—in every human situation—why one need not bind oneself to it, and in never knowing what one would wish to be bound by!" (M.w.Q. 1:314; DMoE, 265)

6.3 Radical auto-relativization of relativization

Ulrich becomes an Interpretant not only for other discourses about Moosbrugger but also of his own discourse about Moosbrugger and for his own discourse about other discourses. He becomes a voice which simultaneously points out its own limitations, which consist in never being able to decide upon a particular discursive practice and, correspondingly, upon a praxis in the social or ethical arena. Ulrich criticizes himself for possessing only the capacity: ". . . for discovering two sides to everything—the moral ambivalence that characterised almost all his contemporaries and was the disposition of his generation, or, one might even say, its fate. . . . What right had he to treat Bonadea badly?" (M.w.Q. 1:314; DMoE, 265).

The problem of discourse's relation to values reemerges when Ulrich reproaches himself for being so critical toward the discursive habits of others, especially Bonadea's, when he himself is not capable of any discursive praxis whatsoever, merely of temporarily borrowing them in order to criticize them.

However, while Ulrich points out that his tendency of discarding discursive habits does destroy ideology in society, he also indicates a further advantage of his discursive process. If one recalls that, for Bateson and Eco, the overcoding of society's discourses is tantamount to neurosis and ideology, whereas the overcoding of the psyche is madness, Ulrich is quite correct to distinguish himself from the madman. For Ulrich, the madman has only certain limited, fixed, entrenched, imprisoning habits; the sane man has every discursive possibility since he is not predetermined by specific habits: "A person who is responsible for his actions can always do the other thing, too, but a person who is not *never* can!" (M.w.Q. 1:315; DMoE, 265). Could this imply that it is precisely this communicational irony taken as a disruption and shifting of discursive practices which safeguards man's sanity. Insanity is not unreason but rather an overcoding or a severe limitation of possibilities. Habit breaking is freedom.

Briefly, there are several habits which Ulrich refuses to overcode. These habits may be treated as postulates of communicational praxis or as discursive procedures.

(1) The postulate of *propositional content* or of *representation* of something true about the world is openly violated by Ulrich when he speaks with Agathe: ". . . and the reality of it was really quite great! . . . What reality am I talking about? Is there another?" (DMoE, 1084). It will be recalled that Musil defines the *plurality* of the *objects of observation*, which depend on the multiplicity of contexts of experimentation, as irony: "Where there are fewer external objects, extend the irony also to the situation of a person like Ulrich" (DMoE, 1841). The constant changing of the Object of discourse, with no pretension to fix the Object (in this case Moosbrugger), makes it impossible to hold a postulate of referentiality: ". . . but his thoughts were still far from inclined to be tied down, and so instead of speaking out immediately, he preferred to change the subject" (DMoE, 1254).

(2) The *postulate of sincerity* is also disregarded by Ulrich with the added twist of uncertainty that Ulrich himself does not know whether he is lying or not: "Ich weiss nicht einmal selbst, ob ich luege" (DMoE, 216). Ulrich's violation of this postulate is related by the narrator to the violation of the same postulate for narrativity. The narrator admits of the impossibility of narrating without lying, when he speaks of the drive to confabulate, "Lust zu fabulieren."

(3) All that Ulrich says is without the *conviction lent by the postulate of sincerity*. In the most complex of discursive investigations, Ulrich maintains the distance of an experimenter who is not really involved in what he is saying.

(4) The violation of another postulate, *the postulate of the author as subject of enunciation*, also contributes to the detachment of Ulrich from any particular discursive field of habits. Ulrich does not identity himself as the sole source or unique place of the practice of any one discourse. Rather, the words speak Ulrich! The habits adopt Ulrich temporarily until yet other habits displace them: "Ulrich felt the probe. It was as though he were speaking in some strange language in which he could go on talking fluently, but only externally, without the words having any roots in him" (M.w.Q. 2:316; DMoE, 558).

At one point, Ulrich is astounded (yet he sees it as an aspect of the discursive process) to find that Diotima is using his "own" discursive techniques; they are the exclusive property of no one: " 'So it's come to this, has it,' he said to himself, 'that this giant hen has begun talking exactly like me?' " (M.w.Q. 2:327; DMoE, 566).

(5) The final trait of discourse which Ulrich refuses to observe is *that of linear, causal, continuous development of argument and reference*. Each time that Ulrich begins to define or explain an object, his discourse breaks off, or else he displaces the field of reference from one triadic field to

another without arriving at a conclusion in the previous triadic relation. Ulrich dialogues with himself in his journal as he tries to define "love," "necessity," "possibility," or "motivation," all of which are interconnected in the triadic expansion of the discourse fields. He shifts from trying to define "love" to trying to define "motivation" and then moves on to a definition of "necessity" etc., in an attempt to circumscribe some more firm or stable system of meaning and belief:

> I have just said "the hands of the binder," and have given myself over to the rocking sensation of a metaphor, as if this woman could never be a corpulent, elderly person. That is moonlight of the wrong kind! . . . In the middle there is something that I have called motivation. In life we do not usually act according to motivation, but according to necessity, in a chain of cause and effect. (DMoE, 1421)

The flux and nonalliance of Ulrich's own discourse with any particular standpoint is indicated by Ulrich's own realization that "in this perspective his standpoint, that divided himself off from others, was neither here nor there" (DMoE, 247ff.).

The *lack of totality or continuous development* of any particular sign-relation is evidenced by the constant *breaking-off* that Ulrich's discourse undergoes when he is trying to describe a delicate and difficult phenomenon, i.e., his very inability to fix a discourse practice and hence to engage continuously and with commitment in any singular praxis at all. The inability to decide upon any discourse or upon any action is what seems to distinguish Ulrich from all of the rest of the characters in *Der Mann ohne Eigenschaften* with the exception of Agathe:

> Lucky the man who can say 'when,' 'before' and 'after'! . . . In their basic relation to themselves most people are narrators. They do not like the lyrical, or at best they like it only for moments at a time. And even if a little 'because' and 'in order that' may get knotted into the thread of life, still, they abhor all cogitation that reaches out beyond that. What they like is the orderly sequence of facts, because it has the look of a necessity, and by means of the impression that their life has a 'course' they manage to feel somehow sheltered in the midst of chaos. And now Ulrich observed that he seemed to have lost this elementary narrative element to which private life still holds fast, although in public life everything has now become non-narrative, no longer following a 'thread', but spreading out as an infinitely interwoven surface. (M.w.Q. 2:436; DMoE, 650)

> "And now I will tell you all about why I don't do anything," . . . "One can't do anything, because—but you won't understand this anyway—" he began, going right to the beginning, but then he took out a cigarette and devoted himself to lighting it. (M.w.Q. 2:64; DMoE, 357)

To summarize, Ulrich not only relativizes and disrupts discursive habits by placing them into relation with each other, but he is a man without qualities and a man of possibilities precisely because he is a man without fixed discursive habits, a man of all possible discourses, unconstrained by any particular postulates of communication. This, of course, is the discursively manifest phenomenon of the "experimental life" and of Ulrich's perspectivist predisposition for essayism as a mode of expression. The drawback lies in the inability to act as long as no habit is pragmatically proposed as leading to or justifying a particular action.

It is this, Ulrich's incapacity to fix discursive habits, which makes him incapable of laying claim to any specific qualities and of undertaking any action of life:

> An unpractical man—and he not only appears to be so, but actually is—will always be unreliable and incalculable in his intercourse with other people. He will perform actions that mean something different to him from what they mean to others, but is reassured about everything as soon as it can be summed up in an extraordinary idea. . . . And since the possession of qualities presupposes that one takes a certain pleasure in their reality, all this gives us a glimpse of how it may all of a sudden happen to someone who cannot summon up any sense of reality—even in relation to himself— that one day he appears to himself as a man without qualities. (M.w.Q. 1:13–14; DMoE, 17–18)

However, as will be seen, this inability to fix a discursive habit becomes itself a severe constraint. Later, in dealing with the question of discourse, epistemology, and *interest/values*, this problem will be seen to resurface even more acutely. How can one remain discursively, epistemologically consistent, as Ulrich tries to do by not accepting as total any limited field or practice of discourse, and yet summon the conviction in certain values which is necessary to make choices that lead to PRAXIS?

7.0 Quasi-direct Discourse—the Impersonality of Irony

Throughout *Der Mann ohne Eigenschaften* neither Ulrich nor the narrator (not to mention Musil), acts (functions) as authorial, controlling voice, i.e., as the subject of enunciation. No single, exclusive, anthropomorphic source of discourse can be isolated for the context of the *whole* novel.

What Volochinov/Bakhtin refer to as the relativity of voices in quasi-direct discourse best explains the constant production of signs and their constant contextual interaction, independent of any single controlling voice or of any frontiers of discourse. Other terms that Bakhtin uses to describe this new narrative phenomenon are "dialogism" and "polyphony."

The extent of this interactional production of discourses is so vast that, in *Der Mann ohne Eigenschaften*, one cannot speak of a *narrated* or even of narrative any more. All that we have in *Der Mann ohne Eigenschaften* is constant narration, a constant production of discourse. This makes *Der Mann ohne Eigenschaften* an innovative practice of the novel were it not that, potentially, one should recognize all discourse as merely a constant production of signs. In this case, what singles out *Der Mann ohne Eigenschaften* is its self-recognition as a failed narrative and as a constant narration (7.3).

7.1 Sharing words

In the opening books of *Der Mann ohne Eigenschaften* one might disagree with the above argument that the narrator seems to situate the discourses of others in a form of free indirect discourse centered around his own and Ulrich's voices and foci. An example of the controlling frontiers of the narrator's reporting voice in relation to the reported voice occurs in the narrator's relativization and criticism of Ulrich's indecisiveness:

> "Why," Ulrich suddenly thought, "why didn't I become a pilgrim?" . . . Why did he live so vaguely and undecidedly? Undoubtedly—he said to himself—what kept him, as under a spell, in this aloof and anonymous form of existence was nothing but the compulsion to that loosing and binding of the world that is known by a word one does not like to encounter alone: spirit. And though he himself did not now why, Ulrich suddenly felt sad and thought: "It's simply that I'm not fond of myself." (M.w.Q. 1:178; DMoE, 153)

The quotation marks, the punctuation, the switching of pronouns, the adjectives in the narrative discourse, all are opposed to or separated off from Ulrich's own discursive expressions. There is no infiltration or interaction between these delineated discursive fields. Ulrich is a character whose voice the narrator reports, a narrator who may once have had something in common with, or have been identical to Ulrich, but who now takes his distance from him in the form of discursive barriers. He cannot assume his own discourse, as he says, because he does not love himself.

Bakhtin argues that free, indirect discourse sets up boundaries between the speech that is doing the reporting and the reported speech. It retains its own contractual and semantic autonomy, while leaving the speech texture of the context perfectly intact.[30] He states that, although the reporting and the reported discourses interrelate with each other, they do so as structures closed off from one another. In other words, there is no triadic overlapping and interlocking of semiotic fields or contexts.

However, as the novel progresses the tables turn on the dominance of any reporting voice over the reported voice. Ulrich's voice, for example, is so much infiltrated by other discourses and vice versa, that he asks himself: " 'So it's come to this, has it,' he said to himself, 'that this giant hen has begun talking exactly like me?'" (M.w.Q. 2:327; DMoE, 566). The infiltration of the reporting with the reported discourse, to the degree that they are no longer discernible one from the other, and the subsequent relativization of values amount to what Bakhtin calls "quasi-direct discourse." For Bakhtin, quasi-direct discourse exhibits far more social interaction and receptivity to the discourses of the Other than does free indirect discourse. Quasi-direct discourse is the *active* relation of one discourse to another within the mobile, constructional activity of language itself. *Language is no longer subsumed under authorial authority.* Quasi-direct discourse is a sort of "steeping" of the reporting context within the reported context and vice versa. They begin to sound like each other, and it becomes impossible to situate a particular sign-function exclusively within the context of one or the other. There is a mixture of the contextual time and space frames as well as of the respective style and tone dimensions. This is true to the degree that any sign may apply equally well to various fields of frames.[31] Quasi-direct discourse derives its tone and word-choice from direct discourse; its verbal tenses and persons are derived from indirect discourse.[32]

The following example is simultaneously a thematization and a performance of quasi-direct discursive infiltration. It shows most clearly how the various sign-functions dialogically "go both or many ways," so to speak:

> Today, when everything under the sun is talked about in the same breath with everything else, when prophets and charlatans make use of the same phrases except for shades of difference that no busy person has time to track down, [. . .], it is very difficult to assess the value of a man or an idea correctly. [. . .]
> But it [the great writer] must be someone whose importance is already an established fact, so that the words can intelligibly be pinned on to him, though it does not in the least matter where. And such a man was Arnheim. (M.w.Q. 2:25–26)

One might suppose that the reporting voice is uniquely that of the narrator, were it not that in the choice of nouns—"Charlatan"—the expressed distaste for Arnheim already implicates a penetration of the reported voice of Ulrich. There are also sign-functions which indicate the infiltration of the context of the "high-society of Diotima's parlour," as for example, "no busy person has time," "great writer," "shades of difference." There are also overtones of the context of pseudoscientificity in the syntagms "to assess the value of" and "established fact." Nevertheless, the authorial voice also uses all of these phrases as one could equally well imagine Ulrich doing. The fact of the matter is, as is so well stated in the above quotation, that 'it becomes impossible intelligibly to pin words onto particular speakers.'

Quasi-direct discourse explains more fully the interaction of discourses in *Der Mann ohne Eigenschaften* that Krysinski refers to as "le discours quasi-citationnel"[33] or Hochstaetter as the "Zitatcharakter,"[34] both with reference to *Der Mann ohne Eigenschaften*. There certainly do exist certain consensual overlappings in what is meant by these terms. There are no discernible boundaries between quoted and quoting discourses; there is no controlling, quoting voice. One can only speak of discursive interaction and interpenetration in these cases.

Another example of the interaction and infiltration of one discourse by another is the penetration of Agathe's discourse by Lindner's discourse. The cliché sign-functions of Lindner, the moralist, undergo a radical semantic transformation once they interact within the context of a character who is fundamentally "socially irresponsible" (according to Ulrich): "Had she followed him with her eyes, she would have been struck by this man's stiff, skipping gait as he went down the rocky path, for it was cheerful, proud, and yet, nervous, gait" (DMoE, 1045).

Throughout the novel such an infiltration of discursive fields occurs intertextually per se. Clarisse's discourse is inflected with Nietzsche's discourse, Diotima's with Maeterlinck's discourse of the "silent language of love," and Arnheim's with the discourse of Rathenau.[35]

The dominance of quasi-direct discourse necessitates a reexamination of the status of the source of discourse and of the referential properties of verbal and pronominal deictics. *Who is the speaking subject or author?* No one in particular and potentially everyone in general. Musil's writing dispenses with the assumption that there is an isolatable, fixed, anthropomorphic subject of discourse; he speaks rather of a collective "we" subject of enunciation: "Things which lay claim to objective validity, not just subjective. Perhaps as a criterion: statements to which one can prefix the pronoun 'we'" (Tbg., 239).

One could not find a more succinct expression of the epistemological criterion of validity elaborated in Part One under the rubric of "public objectivity."

Elsewhere, Musil describes his role as simply that of a "Beobachter"—an observer—as opposed to that of some sort of emanator of discourse (Tgb., 817).

It is Blanchot who best describes the innovative formula of enunciation in *Der Mann ohne Eigenschaften* as "impersonal," where no single, personal voice controls either discourse or knowledge. Rather, some deindividualized interactive collectivity of voices or even discourse itself, independent of any person, is responsible for sign-production:

> . . . where "I" would refer neither to the character of the novel, nor to the author, but to the relationship between the two, the "I" which is not an "I" that the author must become by depersonalizing himself through art—which is essentially impersonal—and by this character who accepts the fate of impersonality. . . . But by the end he feels even more drawn to third-person narration and hesitates continually in accepting the perhaps unbearable obligation.[36]

Such also is the way that Foucault describes the new conception of discourse, in which its authorial source[37] is not considered to be any single, anthropomorphic subject.

Rather than originating from a single point of origin, discourses circulate within certain romanesque boundaries, subsumed under the deictic "Robert Musil." Quasi-direct discourse in *Der Mann ohne Eigenschaften* marks a radical extension of the individualization and dispersion of the subject of enunciation. Just as in paradise Agathe and Ulrich had the feeling that *words were choosing them*, so too does Musil when he states: "I strive to create a situation that lies outside myself . . . I am then not the one who speaks; rather, the sentences exist outside myself, like some material that I must manipulate" (Tgb., 682). The author is a manipulator and a facilitator of discourse rather than its source. The following words from Karl Kraus indicate that such a dispersion of the subject of enunciation in a host of other discourses was common to the language philosophy of Musil's Vienna: "I command the language of others. Mine does what it wants with me."[38]

"Le discourse *se* pratique" says Foucault, a reflexive expression which indicates that discourses generate themselves and interact within variously circumscribed fields independent of any subject of enunciation. The ontological status of the subject of enunciation falls into doubt in this case, as opposed to a situation where discourse ontologically founds the subject and vice versa (Benveniste).

All that we may assume is the ontological status of discourse itself, as opposed to that of any subject. This is Louis Marin's revolutionary view of deictics, which he regards as revealing merely the "pure being in its extreme generality"[39]: "the Verb has become the thing itself, invisibly present within it, and the thing, itself absent, thus makes the Verb visible";[40] ". . . the thing stated becomes by the act of speech the act itself, the body-subject."[41]

Marin insists that it is the use of neutral deictics, such as "il," "est," and "on," which accentuates the dethroning of the subject of enunciation:

> By eliminating the personal subject of enunciation, confinement to the third person authorizes the ontological advent of the representations of the world of things. . . . "It," subject of the verb "to be," is the authentic neuter which indicates the indescribable emergence of being and thing and excludes any reference to a subject of representation and discourse. . . . "It is" refers to being in general, to the beginning of its emergence.[42]

Such also is the function of the extensive use of the *impersonal* and the *passive modes of* discourse in *Der Mann ohne Eigenschaften*: "Against his will, thinking went on in him" (M.w.Q. 1:284; DMoE, 240). "It is life that thinks around man and dancingly creates for him the connections that he himself, when he makes use of his reasoning power for the same purpose, can only laboriously glean together and never to such kaleidoscopic effect" (M.w.Q. 1:284; DMoE, 409). The "es" and the "er" displace the "Ich," to which Musil attributes no psychological, anthropomorphic, ontological status; "Ich" exists in the same way as discourse exists: "I tell a story. This 'I,' however, is not a fictitious person but the novelist. An informed, bitter, disappointed human being. 'I' . . . But also what I have encountered in the other characters in the novel" (Tgb., 579).

The impersonal—deindividualized, interactive—status of discourse in *Der Mann ohne Eigenschaften* is the crowning of our whole argument regarding the relation of the subject to discourse. Both knowledge and discourse are impersonal in modern discourse and hence fundamentally uncertain. "The impersonality of knowledge, of the scholar, discloses an obligation it [modern discourse] perilously consents to and whose changes to reality it looks for, if the reality of the times were not a century behind the knowledge of the times."[43]

Frier, also, draws the connection between the use of the impersonal and the ontological, between representational and epistemological uncertainty:

> One notices that the "es" [it] and the "etwas" [something] work together in the representation of uncertainty and produce a context of their own. The special characteristics of "etwas" are its function as a very indefinite indication of quantity (semantic level) and its declarative function (synactic level).[44]

7.2 Dialogism and polyphony

Musil describes his narrative in terms of the dialogical tension established between various positions of discourse and the fluctuating reality that results from the lack of any governing, dominant, authorial position: "What I say will contain my mistakes and, to the extent that I am no fool, my virtues; but what matters is not this personal variation, but rather the objective context" (Tgb. 664–65).

One may also recall that Musil describes his work as "work simultaneously irradiating each other" "sich gegenseitig bestrahlende Worte" (G.W. II, 1147). In this regard, it seems fair to equate irony and the quasi-direct narrative as the absence of a dominant voice, with what Bakhtin calls "dialogism" and "polyphony."

> The plurality of independent and unmerged voices and consciousness and the genuine polyphony of full-valued voices are in fact characteristics of Dostoevsky's novels. It is not a multitude of characters and fates within a unified objective world, illuminated by the author's unified consciousness that unfolds in his works, but precisely *the plurality of equal consciousnesses and their worlds*, which are combined here into the unity of a given event, while at the same time retaining their unmergedness. In the author's creative plan, Dostoevsky's principal heroes are indeed *not only objects of the author's word, but subjects of their own directly significant*

word (neposredstvenno znachashchee solvo) as well. . . . the task of constructing a polyphonic world and destroying the established forms of the basically monological (homophonic) European novel. (Bakhtin's emphasis).[45]

For Bakhtin, the basic unit of all discourse is dialogical interaction:

Any enunciation belonging to a discontinuous communicational process is a feature of dialogue, in the broad sense of the term thus including written works. Enunciation, understood as part of the social dialogue, is the basic unit of language . . .[46]

At one point, dialogism is described in the same way that Peirce describes signs, i.e., as continuously interacting with and substituting for each other:

The understanding of a sign is, after all, a set of references between the sign apprehended and other, already known signs; in other words, understanding is a response to a sign with signs. And this chain of ideological creativity and understanding, moving from sign to sign and then to a new sign, is perfectly consistent and continuous: from one link of a semiotic nature . . .[47]

The roots of dialogism and polyphony were found, by Bakhtin, to lie not only in the Menippean Satires, but also in Socratic dialogues, whose links to irony are historically self-evident.[48]

What is more, for Bakhtin, polyphony, dialogism, quasi-direct discourse, all have very significant axiological, epistemological and social implications in relation to other more classical forms of discourse: "The menippea is characterized by extraordinary freedom of philosophical invention and invention within the plot."[49]

For Bakhtin, the vicissitudes of the utterance and the speaking personality in language reflect the vicissitudes of verbal and ideological interaction.[50] Bakhtin suggests that free-indirect discourse belongs to an episteme of the "classical inviolabilities of the boundaries of an authorial dominance." He describes this discourse as a linear style, as an ideological assurance, and as dogmatism where there are clear-cut external contours for the speech of the other. The internal individuality of the other is minimized in favor of the dominance of the privileged reporting position. Bakhtin associates this discourse with the "authoritarian dogmatism of the Middle Ages," and with the "rationalistic dogmatism of the Seventeenth and Eighteenth Centuries."[51]

On the other hand, quasi-direct discourse is a plethora and flux of types and levels of discourse. All intonations are dispersed and are no longer summed up by one voice or person. All speech and values flow freely into one another in an open field or circuit. The difference is ideological. Bakhtin relates this discursive episteme to what he calls the "realistic and critical individualism in its pictorial style and tendency to permeate reported speech," and with "relativistic individualism beginning with the development of this interaction and its decomposition of the absoluteness of the authorial context."[52] We wish to suggest here that the dominant discursive function of the modern episteme is quasi-direct, polyphonic, dialogical, discursive production and interaction. This interactional view and practice of discourse contributes to the freedom and the relativity of this episteme; such also is the *"Geistige Bewaeltigung"* toward which Musil confessed to be striving in and through his discursive production of *Der Mann ohne Eigenschaften.*

7.3 Narration in the impossibility of narrative

At the opening of *Der Mann ohne Eigenschaften* a man and a woman are presented. They are then introduced as *possibly* being Arnheim and Ermelinda Tuzzi. Finally, they are left unidentified since these two latter characters 'could not possibly' have been in the streets of Vienna at the time.

At the end of Ulrich's bewildering and not quite registered experience of being mobbed, rescued, and seduced, the narrative voice intervenes saying: "That was what happened" ("So hatte es sich ereignet") (DMoE, 30). However, Ulrich did not quite know what it was that had happened.

Later, as much discourse circulates around the sign-function "Collateral Campaign," one finds the following chapter titles, despite the fact that nothing happens because of all the talk around the Campaign. Events are always pending but nothing ever actually occurs in the Campaign:

> A great event is on the way. Count Leinsdorf and the river Inn. (M.w.Q. 3:388; Chapter 34, DMoE, 994)

> A great event is on the way. Meseritscher of the press. (M.w.Q. 3:391; Chapter 35, DMoE, 996)

> A great event is on the way. Bringing a meeting with some old acquaintances. (M.w.Q. 3:399; Chapter 36, DMoE, 1002)

> A great event is on the way. But nobody has noticed it. (M.w.Q. 3:423; Chapter 38, DMoE, 1022)

In *Der Mann ohne Eigenschaften,* the status of the event, especially of the represented event, is very problematic. The crisis of referentiality is responsible for this problematic status. What occurs in *Der Mann ohne Eigenschaften* is a divesting of the act/event of its ontological status within representation:

> There was a great deal going on, and one was aware of it. One thought well of what was done by oneself, and thought the same thing dubious if it was done by others. Every schoolboy could understand the details of what was

going on, but as regards the whole there was nobody who quite knew what was really happening, except a few persons, and even they were not sure whether they knew. Only a short time later it might all just as well have happened in a different order or the other way around. . . . (M.w.Q. 2:179; DMoE, 449)

All that occurs in the plans for the "Parallelaktion" is the action of discourse, the event in Diotima's salon where discourse upon discourse is produced and interacts with its counterparts: "The Collateral Campaign paraded in all its glory and brilliance: eyes beamed, jewels glittered, wits flashed" (M.w.Q. 3:388; DMoE, 994).

Moreover, *due precisely to this problematic status of the event, events are often* represented in the subjunctive mode of possibility (potentia) in *Der Mann ohne Eigenschaften.*[53] They could always have been otherwise:

. . . even God probably preferred to speak of His world in the subjunctive of potentiality (*huc dixerit quispiam*—here it might be objected. . .), for God makes the world and while doing so thinks that it could just as easily be some other way. (M.w.Q. 1:15; DMoE, 19)

It might even be asserted that they have been cheated, for one can nowhere discover any sufficient reason for everything's having come about as it has. It might just as well have turned out differently. (M.w.Q. 1:151; DMoE, 131)

In the "Parallelaktion" things "may" happen, that is to say, "possibly," but, what is more, they happen only as discursive (as opposed to empirically "real") events: "it had not been anything real" ("nichts Wirkliches gewesen") (DMoE, 34); "the esoteric idea of an event without anything actually happening" ("geheimssinnigen Vorstellung eines Geschehens ohne dass etwas geschieht") (DMoE, 1237); ". . . as if one were not a human being at all, but merely a figure in a book" ("als waere man kein Mensch, sondern bloss eine Gestalt in einem Buch, . . .") (DMoE, 592).

One example of the problematic status of the event is Ulrich's experience of the "Major's wife," with whom he had a passionate affair, whereby the reality of the event is no longer retrievable or representable: "Ihre welt war ihm in zwischen so fremd geworden, dass ihn die Aussage, sie sei die Frau eines majors gewesen ergoetzlich unglaubhaft anmutete" (DMoE, 123).

It is the problematic and de-ontological status of the event, as opposed to a representation of the "real" events, which interests Musil. "I am not interested in real explanations of real events. My memory is bad. Besides, the facts are always exchangeable. What interests me is the spiritually typical, I might even say the ghostliness of the event" (G.W. II, 939).

Finally, it is due to the ghostliness of events, i.e., the dubious status outside of discourse, that both Ulrich and Musil consider the event to be unnarratable and unrepresentable:

> And now Ulrich observed that he seemed to have lost this elementary narrative element to which private life still holds fast, although in public life everything has now become non-narrative, no longer following a 'thread,' but spreading out as an infinitely interwoven surface. (M.w.Q. 2:436; DMoE, 650)

> Although they could not have said what exactly had taken place. (DMoE, 1083)

The fact that the event could not be represented, that reality could never be presented as anything more than a likeness ("ein Gleichnis") leads to a new kind of discursive practice, a practice of narration as infinite discursive presentation (Darstellung) instead of a narrative as representation (Vorstellung) of some extradiscursive act or object: "The point of the story in this novel is that the story the novel is supposed to tell is not told" (DMoE, 1937). Representation is impossible, hence abandoned by Musil. Presentation is all there is. Not only does the communicational episteme give rise to an alternative to representational narrative; it also presents an alternative to the referential epistemology of the classical episteme—we arrive at a pragmatic, interactional epistemology.

As Blanchot explains, Musil derives this technique from his *inability and refusal simply to represent a story: . . . his refusal of narrative which is at the origin of his narratives.*[54] Musil himself at one point states that he derives a narrative technique from his *inability to represent a period of duration,* a remark which reinforces the temporal dislocations irony. Musil is quite unable to adhere to the referential episteme. It is in crisis!

The "narrating of unnarratability," "the ghostlines of events," the "enclosure within the discursive event alone," all these phrases point to Musil's trade-off of narrative representation in favor of infinite discursive, communicational, narrational, interactional praxis. Musil's insistence upon the relativity of events, their possibility (and hence their dependence upon hazard and their status as pure materiality of discourse), all bring him close to positioning and practicing a discourse like the *new discourse* that Foucault says we should work toward:

> In the sense that this slender wedge I intend to slip into the history of ideas consists not in dealing with meanings possibly lying behind this or that discourse, but with discourse as regular series and distinct event, I fear I recognise in this wedge a tiny (odious, too, perhaps) device permitting the introduction, into the very roots of thought, of notions of *chance, discontinuity, and materiality.*[55]

Somewhat by chance, somewhat discontinuously, Musil's *Der Mann ohne Eigenschaften* is the discursive practice which is, par excellence, built up of the pragmatic material interaction of infinitely expanding fields of other discursive practices. *Der Mann ohne Eigenschaften* is not narrative; it is a constant narration made up of other narrations, a discourse of and with other discourses.

Herein lies the major transformation that Musil's discursive practice effects on the procedures of the classical episteme, thus heralding the opening of the modern episteme. We cannot but strike a consensus with Krysinski, who placed the following remark from Klebnikov at the head of his article on Musil: "Narrative is architecture built on words. Architecture built on narratives is the master narrative."[56] In *Der Mann ohne Eigenschaften*, discourse, by virtue of its theorization and its praxis of opening up its own narration or discourse to other narrations and discourses, becomes the "surrécit," thus championing communicational interaction and heralding the end of referentiality and anthropocentrism in discourse.

CONCLUSION

PRAXIS
ABDUCTION IN HUMAN INTEREST

> His [the theoretician's] presentation of societal contradictions is not merely an expression of the concrete historical situation, but also a force within it, to stimulate a change; then his real function emerges.
>
> (Horkheimer, *Critical Theory*)

0.0 Knowledge and Human Interest

Kant divided theory and praxis. Practical reason, governing morality, expressed the ought of existence. Pure, theoretical reason was disinterested judgement, based on the "is" of existence. At least since that moment classical science has claimed to be value-free, neutral, and objective. It claims simply to state the facts without predictions for action. Critical philosophy's main concern is often described as that of pointing out the discrepancy between "is" and "ought." The apparent ethical concerns of Socrates, Kierkegaard, and Jankélévitch[1] would situate irony in the camp of a critical theory such as that espoused by the Frankfurt School, that is to say, in a field where the question of the reconciliation of theory and praxis is crucial and where the knowledge interest is not only one of understanding but also of critique.

The modern theories of discourse of Peirce, Bateson, Foucault, and Habermas, as well as Musil's narrative praxis, all exhibit a renewal of the concern for the relationship between discursive theory and practice, on the one hand, and for a social praxis which aims at a utopian society and at a utopian knowledge, on the other hand. Foucault's entire intellectual project, for example, shows the relation of discourse of knowledge to practices of power. Habermas's theory of communication, which tries to ground a critical interest, stems from the critical philosophy of the Frankfurt School. Nevertheless, as will be shown, this renewed concern for interest seems to be more than an isolated phenomenon, but rather a growing discursive regularity that may characterize the modern episteme as opposed to the postmodern episteme's denial of the historical project (Habermas versus Lyotard).

1.0 Musil: Theory and Praxis

For Musil, the natural laws of science and moral laws were inseparable:

> He was of course aware of the distinction drawn between laws of Nature and moral laws, the former being the outcome of observing Nature, which is amoral, the latter having to be imposed on human nature, which is not so stubborn. Yet it seemed to him something in this distinction was no longer valid, and what he had actually meant to say was that this left morals in a state that was intellectually a hundred years behind the times, which was why it was so difficult to apply them to present-day needs. (M.w.Q. 3:95; DMoE, 747)

At every step in Ulrich's predicament, the question of how to reconcile theory with life, or intellect with action, is repeatedly posed: "What attitude should a spiritual human being take to reality?" (G.W. II, 940). And of how to legitimate action.

> People expect Ulrich to do something in the second volume. And they know what he should do. How to do it: I'll give no advice to the K.P.D. [Communist Party of Germany], etc. Active spirit and spirit of action. (DMoE, 1939)

> And Ulrich felt that now at last he must either live for an attainable goal like anyone else, or get seriously to grips with these 'impossibilities'.(M.w.Q. 2:440; DMoE, 653)

In *Power/Knowledge* Foucault states that it is the duty of the intellectual to seek an alternative less hegemonic politics of knowledge. Not only in the thematic field of Ulrich's dilemmas, but also in Musil's own narrative and metanarrative discursive production, the question of theory and praxis, of narration and ethics, is omnipresent: "Ever since my youth I have considered the aesthetic to be an ethical matter" (Tgb., 777). For Musil, writing sought: ". . . the true (not just psychological but ethical) determinants of the action" (Tgb., 232). "The problem of how to go about telling a story is both *my stylistic problem and the main character's life-problem*."[2]

However, practice does not necessarily indicate something which surpasses writing or discourse altogether. Musil, in the above quotation, saw an important aspect of praxis to lie in poetic praxis *per se*, which replaced a critical theory of the novel with a romanesque practice of narrative theory. For him, (as for Friedrich Schlegel) the best theory of the novel would be a practice of the novel: "[Theory of the novel is] not exclusively theory about the novel—the novel itself is the presentation of a theory: the detailed exposition of the relationship between the theory of cognition, the theory of literature and *The Man without Qualities*."[3]

The necessity of arriving at an action on the basis of semiotized knowledge, or of theory, is also suggested by Bateson as the next step in questioning the relation between map and territory: "I receive various sorts of

mappings which I call data or information—upon receipt of these I act."[4]
For Peirce, action is an integral part and cornerstone of the definition of
pragmatic truth. In this way habit is inextricably connected with impend-
ing action, but it is also preconditioned by other discursive habits. Habit
is: "readiness to action in a certain way under given circumstances and
when actuated by a given motive . . ." (5.517).

> By a conditional habit I mean a determination of man's occult nature
> tending to cause him to act in a certain general way in case certain general
> circumstances should arise and in case he should be animated by certain
> purposes. (5.517)
>
> How otherwise can a habit be described than by a description of the kind of
> action to which it gives rise with the specification of the conditions and of
> the motive. (5.491)
>
> The modification of a person's tendencies toward action as habit-chang-
> ing . . . (5.467)
>
> The identity of habit depends on how it might lead us to act. (5.491)

Indeed, the definition of pragmatic truth itself is not only oriented to the
Interpretant-effect, but also toward the effect in the sense of the action or
conduct that the sign-relation could possibly lead us to: "Consider what
effect, that might conceivably have *practical bearings*, we conceive the
object of our conception to have. Then, our conception of these effects is
the whole of our conception of the object." (5.402)
What is more, action is related to the satisfaction of desire; hence the
whole issue of value or will is at the heart of modern epistemology:

> For truth is neither more nor less than that character of a proposition which
> consists in this, that belief in the proposition would, with sufficient experi-
> ence and reflection, lead us to such conduct as would tend to satisfy the
> desires we should then have. To say that truth means more than this is to say
> that it has no meaning at all. (5.373)

2.0 The Ethics of a Quest for Utopia: Practical Experiments in Utopianism

While the Vienna Circle is often interpreted as ignoring or rejecting
problems of value, Toulmin and Janik's reading of Wittgenstein argues
that, contrary to the Cambridge School's Russelian, positivistic reading,
even in the *Tractatus* the problem of values, inherited mostly from
thinkers such as Kierkegaard, who was the most popular philosopher in
Vienna at the time, hovers over the whole work.
The ethical quest in *Der Mann ohne Eigenschaften* is one for a utopian
existence which would be an alternative to "Seinesgleichen,"[5] i.e., earlier

defined as a confidence that sense experience reveals of Reality. Utopia in
Der Mann ohne Eigenschaften has three dimensions. "Die drei Utopien"
are: (1) utopia as a new way of living, (2) utopia as a new way of reasoning,
of perceiving Reality, and (3) utopia as a new discourse or a new way of
communicating (DMoE, 1925):

> The utopia of inductive reasoning.
> The utopia of alternative (not rational, motivated, etc.) life in love.
> Also the utopia of essayism. The utopia of the pure "other condition"
> [anderer Zustand] with its opening or branching off to God—Mysticism
> without occultism . . .
> Even though utopias they still have different degrees of reality. (DMoE,
> 1881–82)

In this formulation, Utopia is certainly *not* classical science with its
true/false distinctions. Utopia would be a *new discourse, a perfect communication.*

All three aspects of the utopian quest tie directly into the quest for a
new discourse, one where reference is not the central function: ". . . how
does *that* find its way into morality? . . . you'd already be across the
frontiers of the lunatic realm! But that's just the way every word needs to
be taken, literally, otherwise it rots away into a lie. Yet one mustn't take
any word literally, else the world turns into a madhouse!" (M.w.Q. 3:96;
DMoE, 748–49).

2.1 Utopia as total/perfect communication

The first experiment that Ulrich made with utopia was that of the exact
life, which he later found to prove inadequate. Subsequently he sought
utopia in an experiment with mysticism and the "other State" ("anderer
Zustand") which led to the incestuous experiment with Agathe in the
"voyage to paradise" ("Reise in Paradies"). The journey to paradise, under-
taken by Ulrich and Agathe, as the title indicates, was a search for utopia.
However, this search was a very special one. It was a quest for a perfect
discourse, one which would unite both beings in perfect, ecstatic, communication with each other, a creation of the "anderer Zustand." To a
degree, i.e., in a closed, temporally limited field or context, this perfect
very areferential yet fully communicational discourse *was* realized: ". . .
words do not cut it in such circumstances, and the fruit remains on the
branch, even though one expects to bite into it immediately: this is un-
doubtedly the first secret of daylight mysticism" (DMoE, 1088–89).

Maurice Blanchot perhaps best describes the transformation of discourse in the utopian experiment of the "anderer Zustand" by saying that
language is transformed, that the primordial antithetical schism is bridged
and that communication ensues even in silence. The mystical experience
of love entails a very new type of discourse:

Reality does not suffice. He who opens the way to the imaginary gives to the impossible an almost material existence where brother and sister unite one with the other. *Language and Love are bound in one.* In order to appreciate the change undergone by abstract language in contact with the "limitless, marvelous, amazing and unforgettable state in which everything would be united by a single "Yes," one must look to the common ground shared by the intoxication of feelings and the mastery of words which would transform the two, making dry abstraction into a new kind of passion and the transports of feeling more clear-headed. Words which are in great need of silence.[6]

Nevertheless, the utopian experiment still failed. Two explanations are given for this failure of the "journey to paradise." The first problem was that of making the intensity of the ecstatic moment last in time: "Mystische[s] Gefuehl [. . .], das [. . .] niemals zur 'vollen Wirklichkeit' gelangt!" (DMoE, 1243).[7]

The second difficulty, and the one which interests us most here, is *isolation from the community* and the sense that Ulrich and Agathe had of wasting their lives while the world continued to evolve regardless of them: "Er sieht, wie ihr Leben sich verliert und auch seines" (G.W. II 941). The "anderer Zustand" was realized as a communicational practice that had completely isolated itself from the world: "But brother and twin sister, the 'I' and the 'not-I,' feel the inner conflict of their commonness; they fall into ruin together with the world and flee" (G.W. II, 940).

It was due precisely to this isolation from society that the utopian could not be found in the journey to "paradise": "But the attempt to fix and hold on to the experience fails. The absolute cannot be maintained" (G.W. II, 940).

Elsewhere, Agathe had asked Ulrich if, in succumbing completely to the dictates of desire one did not give way to frivolity, capriciousness, and snobbism. Ulrich replied: "Yes!" The signal of the failure of the utopian experiment was not only *Ulrich's need to act,* but also *Agathe's compulsion to begin to "socialize"* with the other guests at the hotel. In short, the failure of their utopian experiment proved that one could not simply neglect the need for praxis in the social arena and flee into a dyadic monad closed off from the world.

The quest for utopia in the "andere Zustand," then, was rejected by both Ulrich and Musil due to its impotence to extend perfect communication in society, i.e., in the public sphere: "The utopias did not yield any practical results. The 'other condition' [anderer Zustand] is no prescription for practical life" (DMoE, 1905).

Blanchot points out one very key factor when he says that, despite the failure of the communication of the "anderer Zustand" to come to terms with the demands of the community, *the book continues:* ". . . perhaps by establishing an ethics capable of opening up the world community to a liberation movement, forever uncommon, renewed and pure. A failure which however does not end the book."[8]

3.0 Utopian Moment versus Utopian Process

The book does not end with this failure of the other state. If the utopian experiment failed, then where does the continuation of Musil's discursive practice lead? It leads to two propositions: The first argument is connected to the observation that, in direct relation to the failure of the various utopian experiments (including the utopia of "exactness," of the collateral campaign, and of the "anderer Zustand"), there was an increase in violence resulting finally in the outbreak of the war. All of these experiments led to war. And war reopened the question of the value and possibility of praxis in society: "All lines end in war." "The like of it [Seinesgleichen] leads to war" (DMoE, 1902). "The man who blends brutality with humane phrases a foreshadow of the future" (DMoE, 1927). It is as though there were for Musil a direct relation between "War" and the inability of any theoretical experiment including Ulrich's (but not exclusively) to lead to a *socially integrated utopian praxis*. This failure results in the outbreak of the war: War is the same as the "other condition" [anderer Zustand] (DMoE, 1932). "I find myself in a completely defenseless position. [The] irresolvable situation of the theoretician. . . . If one does not have the practical energy (talent) for it, one simply goes to war" (DMoE, 1933).

To rephrase more succinctly, and more colloquially, while Ulrich is still "pussy-footing it around" in his hermetic and discursively solipsistic utopian experiments on the social front, war is about to break out. These two events are not unrelated. In the vein of Habermas, the failure to practice an ideal communication socially leads to a breakdown of dialogue and to strategic action, i.e., war.

Nevertheless, it would be a mistake to argue that, because of the outbreak of the war, Musil's novel, and consequently his irony, are fundamentally distopian and pessimistic. Musil insists that *his novel is utopian*, that it continuously seeks the intellectual/spiritual conquest of the world and its accompanying new morality:

> The interviewer: Although your novel gives the characters no way out other than the plunge into mobilization, I do not believe it is to be taken pessimistically?
> Musil: You are right about that. On the contrary, I make fun of the decline of the West and its prophets. What we need is a new morality. Our old one is insufficient. My book might be able to provide material for such a morality. It is an attempt at dissolution and the suggestion of a synthesis. How do I categorize my novel? I would like to contribute to the spiritual overcoming of the world. Also by means of the novel. (G.W. II, p. 941)

What is more, Musil does not say that the utopian aspect of his novel is realized in any particular moment. On the contrary, he describes his discursive practice as one which is infinitely utopian. "What I offer in the novel will forever remain a utopia; it is not 'tomorrow's reality'" (Tgb., 862). With the failure of one particular utopian experience the novel itself does not become distopian. To understand the "process" of utopia is to understand the nature of irony's utopia as process. Utopia is not fixed; it is not a pocket of habits nor an absolute field of truth. "A utopia is not a goal but a direction."[9] Utopia is not an end but a direction or a vector: one which is both portrayed and produced by the infinite production of narration in *Der Mann ohne Eigenschaften*.

4.0 A Normative Discourse and Utopian Discursive Praxis

How is it that discourse can play a utopian role in history? According to Allemann, for example, the discursive irony in *Der Mann ohne Eigenschaften* has absolutely no utopian function. Allemann qualifies irony as the opposite of utopia, speaking of the "absolut(e) gegenironisches Prinzip der Utopie."[10] On the other hand, Arntzen relates Musil's irony/satire directly to utopia, saying that "Satire ist Utopie ex negativo."[11]

At this stage, it might be useful to recall a similar difference of opinion regarding the utopian function of romantic irony. Here Peter Szondi contradicts Friedrich Schlegel himself. Schlegel insists that the qualities of discourse which were earlier identified with irony lead to a new, utopian world. Szondi, on the other hand, argues in a somewhat Hegelian vein that irony remains a negativity which does not accept its transgression toward future utopia:

> Consequently, negativity, irony, thought of as surpassing the former, itself becomes negativity. It attains its ends either in the past, or the future, ... In such a manner, it shuts itself off from the road to perfection which, in its own way, proves to be intolerable, and the fact that it [irony] leads in the end to emptiness is the real tragedy.[12]

For Szondi the view of irony which refuses utopia altogether is indeed a tragic view, *tragic, that is, as opposed to ironic.* If Szondi allows for any utopian moment in irony, it is only a negative dialectical moment. Ironic utopia, for Szondi, is what aims at utopia by virtue of its criticism of what is not utopia: "Everlasting agility characterizes modern man who lives in class. To become aware of one's chaotic existence, to experience it on a conscious level, is to adopt an ironic attitude towards it. But this idea also leads to utopia—'From this confusion and chaos, a world can spring forth.'"[13]

4.1 The negative dialectics of utopia as ironic critical discursive praxis

This negative dialectical view of discursive irony is the only type of utopia that many of Musil's critics find in *Der Mann ohne Eigenschaften*. In general the only discursive utopia is grasped as a sort of *negative theology*, whereby utopia is defined only by virtue of all that irony contrafactually shows not to be in existence. This is what Krysinski refers to as the *"apophatic function"* of irony in Musil.[14] "There's some great intoxication emanating from the Word, an obscure memory, and sometimes one wonders if everything we experience isn't just scraps of some ancient wholeness of things destroyed long ago, shreds that we once fixed together into one piece and got it all wrong" (M.w.Q. 3:96; DMoE, 749).

Such an apophatic view is easy to speak about in discursive terms. One may define this first stage of the utopian function of alternative discourse as that which breaks up fixed habits or fields of discourse. These fixed habits are distopian by virtue of their partiality and their ideological overcoding, as well as their false pretense of totality and of utopian identity. To paraphrase Adorno as earlier cited, a critical discourse is utopian to the degree that it shows that "Das Ganze ist das Unwahre," and that "despair was given to us for the sake of hope." However, we should not forget that Adorno's own followers turned against him in the end for having gone no further towards utopia than a theoretical critique of distopia. There was no affirmative moment in critical theory, something that we will see Habermas set out to rectify.

4.2 The ultimate interpretant

In terms of Peircean semiotics, the positive as opposed to utopian tendency of discourse may be discussed in relation to what Peirce calls the "ultimate interpretant." Is the "ultimate interpretant" the end of the semiotic process where one arrives at a perfect, utopian, socially just, legitimate knowledge? Or is the "ultimate interpretant" that which destroys any fixed pockets of habits of knowledge that purport to be total knowledge? At this point Peirce defines the "ultimate interpretant" as the fully rational, absolutely systematized, or habit-formed universe, i.e., the final knowledge of all things: "an element of pure chance survives and will remain until the world becomes an absolutely perfect, rational, and symmetrical system, in which mind is at last crystallized in the infinitely distant future" (6.33).

What should be noted here, though, is that such an ultimate interpretant never really occurs—rather it is a counterfactual possibility for the infinitely distant future (except in the death of the entire community).

At another point, Peirce simply defines "ultimate interpretant" as "self-conscious habit." This will be seen to approximate Habermas' insistence on the liberating capacity of the *self-reflective* process:

The habit conjoined with the motive and the conditions has the action for its energetic interpretant; but action cannot be a logical interpretant, because it lacks generality. . . . It somewhat partakes of the nature of a verbal definition, and is as inferior to the habit, and much in the same way, as a verbal definition is inferior to the real definition. The deliberately formed, self-analyzing habit—self-analyzing because formed by the aid of analysis of the exercises that nourished it—is the living definition, the veritable and final logical interpretant. (5.491)

Musil, in places, describes his discursive production, and more specifically his irony, as that which does battle against falsehood and distopia in quest of, or in preparation for, the utopian:

A basic ironic attitude, which, I hasten to add, does not mean for me a gesture of superiority, but rather a form of struggle. (G.W. II, 941)

Fiction is in essence the struggle for a higher human nature. (G.W. II, 1021)

In a note for the end of Der Mann ohne Eigenschaften, Musil states that all ideology leads to war, and in this case, the role of alternative ironic discourse is simply to destroy ideology. Irony would be a negative force which would keep us "pure" in expectation of utopia: "But for the sake of a world that may yet come one should keep oneself pure" (DMoE, 957).

Burton Pike is another critic who describes the utopian function of Musil's irony only in terms of what we earlier called clearing the way in the sense of a destruction of, or distanciation from, the nonutopian, in preparation for what is utopian: "Irony is the way to myth and utopia, for only a person who is detached from life and able to weigh its possibilities in expectation of an ultimate ideal is aware of the value of myth and utopia."[15]

But it is Mueller who best illustrates the negative dialectics of Musil's irony with regard to utopia. Mueller says that Musil poses the problem of "substantielle Sittlichkeit ohne diese im Hegelschen Sinne aufzuheben." In other words, Musil poses the problem of theoretical and ethical knowledge, while refusing to synthesize, in false totality, the antitheses of the "ought" and "is" of theory and world history, even though they "ought" to be synthesized. This is an alternative discourse's utopian role as negative dialectics,[16] and irony is one such discourse.

An example of negative dialectical utopianism in Der Mann ohne Eigenschaften would be the transcendence of fixed pockets of morals, i.e., of validity claims, whereby Ulrich's constant recontextualization shows that "Every morality has a limit, a point beyond which it ceases to function" (DMoE, 1862). An alternative discourse imposes a practice of the transmutation of values such that any ethical, moral, or practical judgment is shown to be a partial one and not the total one, as classical scientific discourses would proclaim. Alternative discourse, in the form of common infinite semiosis, transcends all partial pockets of sign-relations and consequently the limitations of the actions based upon them. Such a discourse would go beyond the doxa of "good" in search of an ethical expansion of the field to include the "good bad": "Ironic defense against the objection that only bad people are portrayed: The good people are for the war. The bad against it! In general the novel must discover and represent the 'good bad,' since the world needs it more than the 'good good'" (DMoE, 921).

The possibility of utopia in the form of progressive social action does, however, presuppose that certain value positions have been legitimated as a basis for praxis. In other words, if, as in instrumentalist, control-oriented discourse, good is the false good, then alternative discourse as negative utopian force must become the good bad. As J. F. Lyotard once said of Adorno, where evil is on the side of God then good has no choice but to side with the devil.[17]

4.3 The possibilities of alternative discourse as constructive utopia: Affirmation of value and interest

Nevertheless, besides this negative utopia, Musil's alternative discourse goes beyond a mere apophatic function and toward positing an alternative in the positive or constructive sense. Poetry is a battle, but a battle for a higher human existence: "um eine hoehere menschliche Artung" (G.W. II, 1021). For Musil, alternative discourse not only exposes and destroys distopia, but also, irony is constructive of utopia ("Konstruktive Ironie"). Here alternative discourse not only holds out for utopia as constructive irony, it also presents its potential "*possibilities*": "Utopias are pretty well the same as possibilities" (DMoE, 246). But what, then, is the nature of this constructive, possible utopia which would go beyond a negative dialectic? Alternative discourse moves away from an epistemology based on facticity (empiricism) and toward an episteme of the possible, the potential realm where choice and value are not excluded but avowed.

In order to grasp a utopian function of constructive irony, two other notions must be considered, that of the *difference established by Bateson between codification and value*, and that of *emancipatory interest in communicational interaction for Habermas.*

In the framework of the theory of communication, Gregory Bateson differentiates between codification and value in order later to show that, although classical, occidental, (i.e., positivist scientificist) thought makes this separation, it is really epistemologically quite impossible to do so. Epistemology and ideology are two sides of the same coin. The notion of a system of codification is meant to refer to the process through which the individual, seeking to reconcile incoherencies and hence obstacles to decoding the world, tries to "achieve a congruence between something in his head and the external world." He does this by "altering what is in his head."[18]

The system of values, on the other hand, is meant to refer to the reverse process, where "the individual attempts to achieve a coincidence of the external and the internal by altering the external to fit his internal model, i.e., according to a configuration of his value system."[19]

According to Bateson, occidental, classical, scientific thought has long held that it can separate value from codification and as such objectively know its object. This discourse of knowledge claims to be completely free from the subject's values, biases, or prejudices of knowledge: "Human beings in occidental cultures do really talk and act as though these processes were separable."[20]

Contrary to classical scientificist occidental thought, ecological thought would recognize and accept, as do perturbation theory and Peircean interactional semiotics, that the subject's values are in operation during all types of knowing, whereby the subject merely adjusts its knowing apparatus to the object. In other words, in a modern, postclassical episteme, the discourse of science would no longer be able to occult its value judgments. These latter are fully active in any and every process of knowing. What is more, somewhere between the processes of knowing and evaluating there is *action*, the middle term: ". . . he [the observer] begins to form an image such that, acting in terms of that image, he will achieve his goal. It is also evident that perception determines values as we see things, so we act. . . . Action would seem to be the middle term in which perception and value meet."[21]

Value applies not only to the process of information-gathering, but also to negative entropy in the sense of biological and informational survival, i.e., in the sense of defying the second principle of thermodynamics: "Negative entropy, value, and information are, in fact, alike insofar as the system to which these notions refer is the man plus environment and insofar as, both in seeking information and in seeking values, the man is trying to establish an otherwise improbable congruence between ideas and events."[22]

Now, says Bateson, referring to none other than Freud, the presence of value in determining knowledge is nothing new and is not necessarily pejorative:

> it is well known that *wish and perception partially coincide*. Indeed this discovery is one of *Freud's* greatest contributions. [. . .] he [the person] must act in terms of what he knows—good or evil—and when he acts he will meet with frustration and pain if things are not as he "knows" them to be. Therefore he must, in a certain sense, *wish them to be as he "knows" they are.*[23]

4.4 Affirmation of value—liberation from repression

This affirmation of value is quite comparable, in both its Freudian and self-reflexive epistemological overtones, to the following remark made by

Peirce: "To negate our inherent prejudices in pretending to liberate ourselves from universal doubt is nothing more than a form of repression" (1.109). And although it cannot be discussed at length here, not only Habermas' *Knowledge and Human Interests*, but the whole enterprise of Critical Philosophy is a discourse levelled against the positivist, scientificist assumption that knowledge is objective and divorced of all "interest."

Both Habermas and Bateson suggest that, due to the impossibility of exorcising value from scientific discourse, rather than pretending to be objective while simultaneously using the accompanying power to reinforce certain interests (such as technocratic interests), an alternative discourse would acknowledge its values or interests as science and include in our calculations those values which would fulfill certain social requirements: "We must introduce moral and ethical considerations to our relation with nature and reevaluate the way advanced technology arrogates nature, [or] we will destroy our environment which is part of our circuit of survival."[24] This ecological-cybernetic alternative, suggests Bateson, depends upon a flexible interaction with other ideas/signs: "But the survival of an idea is also determined by its relation with other ideas. Ideas may support or contradict each other; they may combine more or less readily. They may influence each other in complex, unknown ways or in polarized systems."[25]

Bateson insists that both information and the environment become ecologically entropic (he equates this state to neurosis at the individual level) when limited, restricted, and strategically controlled: "Some ideas become pathogenic when implemented with modern technology." Employing cybernetic "lingo," Bateson equates *over-habit-forming with nonflexible, noninteractive, "hard-programming,"* the ideological implications of which are present everywhere: "The variable which does not change its value becomes ipso facto hard-programmed: [. . .] another way of describing habit-formation."[26]

Based on the above considerations Bateson suggests a new science with a new, international interest or value-system. This new interest is *itself based on "interactionality,"* whereby one *interactionally* studies the *interactions* of man and the environment, the latter of which is itself a huge *interaction*. The ideal of an ecology is based on the ideal of free interaction. Of course, when Bateson describes the *environment* in this way, one cannot resist relating it to Peirce's notion of the ever-expanding, triadically interactive semiotic field: "Ecology, in the widest sense, turns out to be the study of the interaction and survival of ideas and programs (i.e., differences, complexes of differences, etc.) in circuits."[27]

Before embarking upon the investigation of the type of utopian international interests that Bateson, Habermas, and Bakhtin suggest and beginning the search for the relation of alternative discourse to utopian communication, one remark from Musil serves to illustrate that wish and value were also very high on his scale of priorities: "I would be very grateful to the public if it paid less attention to my aesthetic qualities and more to my will" (G.W. II, 942).

What then are these interests of science? In keeping with the Frankfurt School and Critical Philosophy Habermas would argue for the impossibility of classical, positivist science and proposes as its replacement an advancing of *emancipatory interests* proper to *all* types of human interaction. Habermas suggests that the mechanical Marxists have interpreted Marx as restricting the demands for emancipation to the activity of *work, the economic sphere.* Habermas himself applies these interests to various levels of power in all spheres and types of human interaction, especially those of the activity of communication. Just as Foucault refuses to restrict his analysis of discourse and power to the economic or state spheres of society, so too does Habermas: "*social interaction,* which includes communicative activity, the struggle for recognition and class antagonisms, that is, ethical and political praxis. . . ."[28]

For Habermas, the emancipatory interest has historical grounds that posit it as emerging out of cognitive dissonance. Science cannot be objective, and thus it should defend certain interests of society and the community (the *polis*), the interests that have been proposed since the beginnings of Greek philosophy and which have persevered throughout the whole of Judeo-Christian thought. These interests are those of *equal opportunity, emancipation, self-development, autonomy* ("Muendigkeit"), *free, unconstrained interaction of citizens, etc.*[29]

The utopian interest that Habermas is advocating is a practice of all types of communication which would follow certain emancipatory and freely interactional procedures. First the mutations of any ideal communication are exposed as they occur in reality and then the utopian alternative is proposed "*counterfactually.*" By "counterfactual" Habermas means the opposite of the fact, yet affirmed as a negation of that fact. The mutations of an ideal communication are overtly identified by Habermas with the strategic, compulsory action of both forms of totalitarian discourse, e.g., Stalinism and capitalism: "capitalism as an individual strategic action oriented towards controlled social organization."[30] The interactional interest acts as the alternative form of reasoning and social organization to Weber's concept of Western bureaucratic rationality based on purposive, rational, instrumental action.

Habermas' distinction is between the ideal communicational interaction and the reality from which the former is, so to speak, counterfactually "extrapolated." A discourse, such as Agathe's and Ulrich's violation of pragmatic universals, which exposes the mutations of an ideological discursive habit or a pragmatic validity claim, posits and defines in one and the same stroke *the counterfactual possibility of the ideal undistorted* discourse. The quasi-ideal discourse would be the opposite or the absence of the factual permutations. According to K. O. Apel, pragmatics links with the question of value in that these interests in communicational interaction comprise a *"universal ethics of speech"* based on the: ". . . symmetrical distribution of opportunities for the selection and execution of speech-acts that relate to propositions as propositions, to the relation of the speaker to his utterances, and to the observance of the rules."[31]

Ideal communicational competencies must not be thought of either as real objects or as transcendental structures in the Kantian sense. Their ontological status is one of possibility, "potentia." It is one of an ideal based on the counterfactual extrapolation from the particular, individual speech-acts. The ideal speech situation is not a real universal, merely a quasi-universal in that it exists merely as potentia:

> The last and the most important structural condition of possible conversation is that of the speaker's act, contrafactually, i.e., as if the conditions outlined above were actually realized. Hence the concept of an ideal speech situation is not merely regulative (as in Kant) nor existential (as in Hegel) because *no society as yet allows these conditions to be met.*
>
> Hence, the ideal speech situation may be compared with a transcendental illusion, but not so in the sense of being a metaphorical extension of a category of Reason, rather as a *constitutive condition of possible conversation.* Hence it is a constitutive appearance, and a pre-appearance, *a utopian moment.*
>
> It cannot be determined a priori whether this pre-appearance is merely an illusion or is an empirical condition for the (even if only asymptomatic) realization of its utopian moment. Hence it contains a practical hypothesis. From that hypothesis—the critical theory of society takes its departure.[32]

Kortian, writing about Habermas, elucidates quite clearly the "nontranscendental" implications of counterfactuality: "Counterfactual qualifies the norm in its relation to the facts that it is supposed to measure. To speak of distorted communication in effect presupposes reference to an ideal of ̦successful communication. The function of such an ideal is critical or 'counterfactual.' "[33]

The difference between counterfactual utopia and the utopia that arises out of the negative dialectical discourse might be exemplified by the difference between Habermas' and Adorno's social theories. Whereas Adorno only managed to criticize what was not utopia, Habermas went one step further in using the failings of reality as a basis upon which to propose possible solutions in the sense of a *contextually but partially realizable potential,* i.e., as something toward which the pragmatics of discourse should tend. Rather than remaining within complete negativity, Habermas surpasses Adorno and dares to posit certain traits of (positive) utopia beyond a negative dialectic. What is more, these traits are properly pragmatic, discursive traits. This potential for utopia would then be the *ideal speech situation* toward which discursive pragmatics must strive.

4.5 Irony → discourse; discourse → utopia; irony → utopia

To return briefly to the problematics of irony as alternative discourse, it remains to be shown that the discursive traits counterfactually suggested by Habermas as a "universal pragmatics" correspond to the radical definition which we gave at the end of Part One to the discursive procedures of the interactional episteme as infinite, free, interaction of discourse-production, above and beyond various pockets of habits. Of course, we are far from suggesting that anyone has ever realized such a utopia, merely that some discourses have come closer or have tended toward it more than others; Musil's ironic narration is one of them.

Earlier it was seen that Habermas had defined intentionally distorted communication as a distortion of validity claims of communication once the consensual legitimation of those rules had broken down. Both the understanding of communication and the legitimation of action are dependent upon an acceptance of these claims by participants. Once their validity is questioned, new communicational postulates must be found if the rules of the language game are to be consensually legitimated rather than strategically enforced (i.e., by forceful and repressive action of all sorts). Therefore, the first utopian role of an alternative discourse is the "liberation of speech acts from the imperative network of interactions [which] expresses itself in the differentiation between speech and its concomitant normative background."[34] In other words, alternative discourse's first degree utopian function is a norm-breaking function, only this time the norms are communicational constraints.

The question posed by Habermas, then, is the following: Once these validity claims are no longer accepted by the participants, such as Ulrich and Agathe in the utopian experiment, as the "good" validity claims, i.e., as claims which serve the interest of all speech users and legitimate practical decision-making, how do we decide upon new ones? It is here that the second, constructive definition of discourse as utopia enters into play. Once it has delegitimized the laws of communicational competency, utopian or emancipatory discourse must move to the plane of discursive interaction, i.e., discussion free from constraint and infinitely expanding. Discourse must make this shift in order eventually to arrive at a new temporary set of constraints upon which to legitimate purposive action. However, this discursive interaction is no less a praxis than is communicational practice.

Habermas, unlike Foucault, distinguishes "discourse" from "communication" in that the latter obeys certain constraints and the former is a free interaction in the absence of such constraints: at a self-reflective level pertaining to communication, discourse is where we discuss the rules we will follow by a consensus which is to be constructed in free and open communication:

> . . . "discourse" as that form of communication which is free from the constraints of the very process of action and experience, and which allows

for an exchange of arguments on hypothetical validity claims, (whereby
truth and legitimacy may count as discursively redeemable validity claims,
while veracity can only be subject to a test of consistency over a period of
continued interactions).[35]

As opposed to communication based on validity claims and rules
which serve as the normative background in the former definition of irony
as a norm-breaking function, discourse is a continuous production of
signs "liberated from the imperative network of interactions" and hence
discourse "expresses itself in the differentiation between speech and its
concomitant normative background." It is in "discourse" that the rules of
interaction can be abandoned in favor of an interaction which explicitly
questions and thematizes these very constraints: "It is only with the
transition to 'discourse' that the validity claim of an assertion or the claim
for the legitimacy of a command, viz. the underlying norm, can explicitly
be questioned and topicalized in speech itself."[36]

For Habermas, freedom implies this right to question and change the
rules or norms of communication. This notion is very much akin to
Peirce's earlier discussed concept of the self-reflective habit. For Habermas, there is a transcendental, emancipatory moment in the reflection
upon discursive constraint, a reflection necessary for these constraints to
be loosened or dispensed with. The metadiscursive moment is emancipatory for Habermas, although one might argue that it adheres to the
same episteme that it comments on.[37]

To carry this argumentation one step further, it may be recalled that at
the end of Part One, modern discourse was identified with pure, infinite,
interactive discourse production, i.e., with semiosis. Secondly, for Habermas, free, emancipated interaction is the utopian form of communication.
It therefore follows that modern or alternative discourse in its most far-
reaching and radical sense, i.e., as the practice of discourse pure and
simple, is precisely the interested, utopian, emancipatory interaction that
discursive practice is considered to be. In order to appreciate the impact of
this "deduction," it cannot be overemphasized that discursive interaction
is a form of social praxis. As far as Habermas is concerned, communicational interaction is the basis for social praxis which may be either
utopian or distopian. Alternative discourse is simply infinite semiosis,
unconstrained by procedures and epistemological assumptions of classical discourse. Discourse as infinite interaction is utopian, emancipatory
interaction. Therefore, such an alternative discourse is utopian praxis!

Habermas' theory of discourse corresponds to Peircean semiotics and
Foucauldian theory of discursive constraint. We argue that they are not
incompatible. First of all, K. O. Apel reads a utopian summum bonum into
Peirce's theory of discourse, whereby:

Just as Kant, as an analyst of consciousness, had to postulate as a presup-
position of epistemology, that by cognition something like the synthetic

unity of consciousness has to be reached, in just the same way modern logicians of science starting from a semiotic basis of analysis, could, or rather should, postulate that it must be possible, for something like the unity of intersubjective interpretation of the world to be reached by the way of interpretation of signs.[38]

However, Peirce, just like Musil's Toerless, could not accept Kant's occult transcendentalism, i.e., the problem of explaining the necessity of our ideas being determined by categories. What Peirce replaced this transcendental justification with was a *consensual legitimation within the community*, arrived at *through semiosis*, i.e., infinite triadic interaction. This is Peirce's summum bonum, one which is a *utopian, social, semiotic ideal* based on unlimited interaction within the community:

> The real [. . .] is that (more exactly: the object of opinion) which, sooner or later, *information and reasoning would finally result in* and which is therefore independent of the vagaries of me and you. Thus, the very origin of the conception of reality shows that this conception essentially involves *the notion of a community, without definite limits, and capable of a definite increase of knowledge*. (5.322, emphasis added)

Apel argues that "the highest point of Peirce's transformation of Kant's transcendental logic is the 'ultimate opinion' of the indefinite community of investigators."[39] However, we must not be led into assuming that one day all semiosis will stop once it has arrived at the truth. One word from the above quotation alerts the reader to the opposite of closure: "indefinite." An "indefinite community" is one which is constantly interacting and expanding. The only way for the community to expand indefinitely is in and through discourse. Hence, for Peirce, truth is dependent upon infinite semiosis. Truth *is* infinite semiosis, a semiosis which is nevertheless firmly anchored in the community, hence in communication. Because the community is indefinite, truth is always a possibility ("potentia") realized only as contrafactually limited but ever expanding interaction. Peirce's renowned definition of pragmatic truth also emphasizes possibility in the subjunctive mode, something which is often ignored in favor of an emphasis on practical outcome. "Consider what effects, *that might conceivably* have practical bearings, we conceive the object of our conception to have" (5.402, emphasis added).

The "self-analyzing habit," which is akin to what Habermas calls the self-reflective moment in analytical discourse, is for Peirce the "final opinion" associated with the "ultimate Interpretant." The "ultimate Interpretant" may be just the very knowledge of the conditional possibility and interactional relativity of truth and meaning based upon all possible, conceivable circumstances which can never be finalized or arrested. A utopian version of truth, which might be better termed "validity," may be the acceptance and practice of semiosis as infinite interaction and production of discourse within the community. As such, the community's and

truth's indefiniteness would be recognized and respected. The social consequences of such a recognition are not slight. Where interaction and
emancipation are the guidelines of truth (though it means that truth is
indefinite and divested of any absolute power), then the distopian, repressive forces of unilateral, absolute discourse of knowledge will also
lose their power:

> Truth is that concordance of an abstract proposition with an ideal limit
> towards which the investigation would tend to lead to scientific belief; the
> abstract proposition may possess this concordance in virtue of its avowal of
> its inexactness and of its unilaterality, and this avowal is an essential
> ingredient of truth. (5.565)

Musil, in a key passage, expresses the role of the author in terms almost
exactly similar to those which define infinite semiosis. The writer seeks
the unknown, the analogical, the possible solution. This quest is without
end. The duty of the writer is constantly to invent new solutions, new
interrelations, new constellations, new variables, and new prototypes:

> This is the native territory of the writer, the domain of his reason. Whereas
> his opponent seeks the stationary and is content if he can construct accord-
> ing to his calculations as many equations as there are unknowns, for the
> writer there is from the outset no end to the number of unknowns, equa-
> tions, and possible solutions. The task is: to discover every new solution,
> connection, constellation and variable, to produce prototypes of oc-
> curences, enticing models of human existence, to discover the inner man.
> (G.W. II, 1029)

Musil's practice of narration never ceases to do this except perhaps in
death, death being the only point for Peirce where semiosis ends, although
of course his readers carry on the process. What is more, Musil explicitly
states the necessity of reinserting the search for utopia into the community, and hence the necessity of rejecting the "anderer Zustand." "It is
not a question of making the "other condition" [anderer Zustand] the
bearer of social life. It is much too fleeting" (Tgb., 660). Utopia must relate
theory and society: "Utopia of the age of experience. Through the creation
of a society oriented towards spirit" (DMoE, 1916).

What Musil calls "new irony" or "constructive irony," which we would
associate with an alternative discourse of knowledge and praxis, is
strongly tied to the social: "New irony. Forms of society, moralities, etc. are
wholes in which the particulars appear to be determined" (Tgb., 631).
"New irony" is a moral affirmation and a form of society/community! As
such, new, "modern" discourse based on interaction is the discursive
practice which, for critical thought, reinserts the individual back into the
social and makes his interactive practice a condition of knowledge, i.e., a
central feature of an episteme alternative to instrumental positivistic
science:

. . . speech is accepted as the organ of the community. Critical thinking is a function neither of the isolated individual nor of a sum-total of individuals. Its subject is rather a definite individual in his real relation to other individuals and groups, in his conflict with a particular class, and, finally, in the resultant web of relationships with the social totality and with nature. . . . Furthermore, the thinking subject is not the place where knowledge and object coincide nor consequently the starting point for attaining absolute knowledge.[40]

5.0 "Induktive Gesinnung" and "Abduction"

Finally, above and beyond Tyche, how does this potential of modern discourse explain the emergence of alternative or new possibilities? This new type of discourse, taken as unconstrained, utopian interaction and which can only be spoken of counterfactually, would have to involve a new type of reasoning. Curiously enough, both Peirce and Musil began to formulate such a *new type of reasoning* in relation to a new type of discourse and a new logical space. However, neither got much further than naming and vaguely describing it, a major limitation of their work, we would contend.

In the notes for the completion of *Der Mann ohne Eigenschaften*, Musil suggests that the only alternative utopia to be experimented with, as both an ethical and practical solution for living, is what he calls "induktive Gesinnung":

> The utopia of the "other condition" [anderer Zustand] is superseded by inductive reasoning. (DMoE, 1860)

> Perhaps make the "idea of the inductive age" the main point after all. Induction requires presuppositions, but these must only be used heuristically and must not be considered unchangeable. The weakness of democracy was the lack of any basis for deduction; it was an induction that did not correspond to the underlying spiritual standpoint. (DMoE, 1860)

Beyond these rare hopeful politically oriented remarks, Musil says little about inductive reasoning. This last possible salvation, an alternative to traditional classical deductive reasoning, is perhaps also a counterfactual ideal (Musil calls it "heuristisch") which cannot as yet be positively realized, but merely posited as possibility. Musil gives some indication as to what "induktive Gesinnung" could be, but he puts it forward only as a "direction." "Induktive Gesinnungen" at least allows the direction to be known.

"Induktive Gesinnung" reaffirms the importance of a democratic community of interacting investigators in their quest for truth, as opposed to that of the absolute individualist truth of classical science. This new reasoning is ". . . [an] attempt at a natural morality of inductive cooperation" (DMoE, 1930). Inductive reasoning does not ignore the necessity of finding a reasoning which is applicable not only to mathematical or theoretical problems but also to ethical problems of value and praxis in society. Inductive reasoning is described as a "complicated moral mathematics" ("komplizierte moralische Mathematik") (G.W. II, 1080) and as an inductive moral ("die selbst den Kriterien genuegt, die sie auferlegt . . ." (DMoE, 1864). Nevertheless, the type of ethic sought in this new reasoning is not absolute; rather it is a "dynamische Ethik" (Tgb., 552). "Induktive Gesinnung" is the only alternative left for legitimation of motivation for life's actions: "The utopia of motivated life and the utopia of the 'other condition' (anderer Zustand) will be dealt with starting in the journal group of chapters. All that will remain—in a reversal of the order—will be the utopia of inductive reasoning. With this the book will end" (DMoE, 1887).

Finally, Musil equates "induktive Gesinnung" with the givens of the community taken as the social state of affairs. The knowledge yielded by "induktive Gesinnung," just as the Peircean summum bonum, is completely, socially interactional: "The utopia of inductive reasoning or of the given social condition" (DMoE, 1885).

Peirce names his alternative form of knowledge "Abduction." This alternative is for Peirce the only logical operation which introduces any new ideas and hence the possibility of getting out of an old logical space of tired habits (8.388). Peirce's notion of abduction, which he also refers to as "hypothesis," and earlier in his career as "induction," is even terminologically quite closely related to Musil's notion of "induktive Gesinnung." Just as by "induction" Musil did not mean the same as J. S. Mill's definition of "induction," but rather pointed to a new way of reasoning, so too Peirce saw the need to expand the meaning of this term and hence eventually changed it to "abduction." Later in his work, Peirce said that most of what he had previously called induction was really "abduction" (8.227). As did Musil, Peirce sought, in abduction, some new way of reasoning that could go beyond observable facts and the limitations of distopian reality:

> By induction, we conclude that facts, similar to observed facts, are in cases not examined. By hypothesis, we conclude the existence of a fact quite different from anything observed, . . . (2.636)

> Abduction supposes something of a different kind from what we have already observed, and frequently something which it would be impossible for us to observe directly. (2.640)

Although abduction is tied to the process of habit formation, it is supposed to describe *how it is that we form new habits or new hypotheses to explain certain habit phenomena* (6.144, 2.711, 6.286).[41]

What is more, abduction is not merely a method: it is the search for *a new method of methods* (i.e., a whole new episteme?), one which would guide all sciences in the attempt to transcend distopian reality via social praxis (where, by praxis, we mean the union of theory and practice).

"The producing of a method for the discovery of methods is one of the main problems of logic" (3.364). This notion also corresponds to the earlier-mentioned suggestion that utopian discourse is free, unconstrained interaction, whereby various methods would *lend* aspects to each other, rather than exclusively isolating themselves within their own, privatized realms of truth.

One is justified in saying that, for Peirce, the utopian possibility of going beyond the established facts of a method and finding a new method which would be not only *counterfactual* but also *suprafactual* lies in abduction. By suprafactual we mean based on possibility rather than on factuality. Abduction is the possibility of a new "Zusammenhang," a new metaphorical relationship or analogical relation (as Musil and Peirce respectively phrase and practice it).[42] For Peirce, abduction is never what reasoning *is*, rather what "reasoning *ought to be*" (2.7). Both abduction and inductive reasoning are potential reasonings of the future, as well as being possible reasonings: "Abduction merely suggests that something *may be*" (5.17), (6.475), (8.238).

However, while simultaneously remaining in the realm of the possible, abduction also should ultimately reach utopian truth (2.781). What can this truth possibly be?

We might suggest, from what Peirce says below and from the fact that Musil himself continuously substituted new utopian suggestions for old ones, that *abduction is a utopian kind of reasoning which grows out of itself and surpasses itself*. For example, Peirce says that abduction is the essence of pragmatism (5.196, 6.469, 6.606), and hence may be seen to have grown out of Peirce's pragmatic thought. He then says that abduction goes beyond the logic of pragmatism: "Pragmatics is not the whole of logic of abduction" (5.196). Without belaboring the point, alternative discourse, taken as a specific form of reasoning within the logical space of classical discourse though opposed to it in modern discourse, seems to have grown beyond the very type of reasoning from which it had arisen. The utopian potential of modern discursive practices is to transcend the conditions of possibility of the classical episteme against which they arose.

What is abduction or "induktive Gesinnung?" Are we justified in talking about such sketchy utopian suggestions? How do these new types of reasoning, left by their authors in the embryonic stage, relate social communication to progressive political action? Is there a chance of ever realizing such a discourse or will it remain always in the realm of the counterfactual?

One could in good faith answer all of these questions only with a remark from Peirce and another from Foucault, two pioneers in the search for a new discourse. These remarks apply equally well to induction and abduction as they do to this present discourse on an alternative to referential discourses of knowledge:

> "We must not make hypotheses that will absolutely stop inquiry." (7.480)

> I believe we must resolve ourselves to accept three decisions which our current thinking rather tends to resist, and which belong to the three groups of function I have just mentioned: to question our will to truth; to restore to discourse its character as an event; to abolish the sovereignty of the signifier (our translation).[43]

Whence the potential non-ending of narration in the middle of a sentence with three suspension points . . .

NOTES

Introduction: Epistemic Croquet

1. Juergen Habermas, "Modernity versus Postmodernity," *New German Critique*, no. 22 (Winter 1981), pp. 3–15. Jean François Lyotard, *La Condition postmoderne*, Paris: Minuit, 1979.

2. English versions of citations from *Die Verwirrungen des Zöglings Toerless* and from Books One and Two of *Der Mann ohne Eigenschaften* are from the English translation of these works by Eithne Wilkins and Ernst Kaiser: *Young Toerless* (New York, 1955); and *The Man without Qualities*, 3 vols. (London, 1953–1960). Hereafter all references to these works will follow the quotations directly in the text, e.g. (M.w.Q., 25), (Y.T., 123). Translations of citations from the *Nachlass* and from Musil's journals and essays, as well as from secondary sources in German, have been made by William Lee.

3. Robert Merril, ed., "Introduction," *Ethics/Aesthetics Post-Modern Positions* (Washington: Maisonneuve Press 1988), p. vii.

4. I deal with this transdisciplinarity and the politicization of science that it implies in "La Scientization de la politique/La Politicization de la science," in *Le Tiers Communicationnel*, ed. G. H. Brunel, Pierre Boudon, and Marike Finlay, Montreal: Editions Preambule, 1989.

5. Robert Musil, *Der Mann ohne Eigenschaften* in *Gesammelte Werke*, ed. A. Frisé (Hamburg, 1978), vol. 1. Hereafter all references to this work will follow the quotation directly in the text, e.g. (DMoE, 35). It should be noted that there are several earlier cloth and paperback editions of *Der Mann ohne Eigenschaften* and that there is no consistency in the pagination among any of the various editions. It should also be noted that there is much argumentation about the reconstitution of the last volume of *Der Mann ohne Eigenschaften*. Frisé and Philippe Jaccottet, the French translator of Musil's novel, believe in the fidelity of Musil's earlier sketches and later notes for the completion of *Der Mann ohne Eigenschaften*. However, Kaiser and Wilkins, the English translators, for somewhat "moralistic" reasons, did not translate any of the last volume, saying that Musil's notes could not be depended upon and that he had really not intended to have the incestuous experiment realized. We have to admit that we find this argument irresolvable on grounds of intentionality, nor do we see it as particularly pertinent to exclude any of Musil's writing from the field of discourse which we consider to be his own. Therefore, in citing *Der Mann ohne Eigenschaften* we treat the last volume as an integral part of the text. However, we had to be content with translating it ourselves and citing only the German original.

6. I wish to acknowledge my debt to Timothy J. Reiss, who as my teacher impressed me with his reading of Peirce, which informs this work throughout.

7. Michel Foucault, *L'Ordre du discours* (Paris, 1971), p. 49; *The Archaeology of Knowledge and The Discourse on Language*, trans. A. M. Sheridan Smith (New York: Harper and Row, 1976), p. 228.

8. Foucault, *L'Ordre du discours*, pp. 50–51.

9. Ibid., p. 49. See also Emile Benveniste, *Problèmes de linguistique générale*, vol. 1 (Paris, 1966), p. 260: "La langue n'est pas possible que parce que chaque sujet se pose comme "je.""

157

10. Timothy J. Reiss, "Cartesian Discourse and Classical Ideology," *Diacritics* (Winter 1976), pp. 19–27.

11. Michel Foucault, "What Is an Author?" in Donald Bouchard, ed., *Language, Countermemory, Practice* (Ithaca: Cornell University Press, 1977), pp. 113–138.

12. Habermas, "Modernity versus Postmodernity," p. 3.

13. Fritz Mauthner, *Woerterbuch der Philosophie: neue Beitraege zu einer Kritik der Sprache*, in Alan Janik and Stephen Toulmin, *Wittgenstein's Vienna* (New York, 1973), pp. 127–128 (emphasis added).

14. See Karl Kraus, *Die Letzten Tage der Menschheit*, in *Werke*, ed., Heinrich Fischer (Munich: Koesel Verlag, 1952–1966), 14 vols. See also Toulmin and Janik's excellent account of the epoch in *Wittgenstein's Vienna*.

15. Robert Musil, "Beitrag zur Beurteilung der Lehren Machs," Dissertation zur Erlangung der Doktorwuerde (Berlin: 1908).

16. Patrick Heelan, *Quantum Mechanics and Objectivity* (The Hague, 1965), p. 95.

17. Marike Finlay, *Dialogical Strategies/Strategic Dialogues: A Discursive Analysis of Psychotherapeutic Interaction*, New York: Ablex, forthcoming.

18. Robert Musil, "Interview with Oscar Fontana, 'Was arbeiten Sie?'" (April, 1926), in Musil, *Prosa und Stuecke, Kleine Prosa, Aphorismen, Autobiographisches, Essays und Reden, Kritik*, in *Gesammelte Werke*, vol. II (Hamburg, 1978), p. 942. Hereafter all references to this volume will follow directly in the text, e.g. (G.W. II, 942).

19. Robert Musil, *Tagebuecher*, in *Gesammelte Werke*; Robert Musil, *Prosa, Dramen, Spaete Briefe* (Hamburg, 1952), p. 722. Hereafter all references to this work will follow the quotation directly in the text, e.g. (Tgb., 384).

20. Dietrich Hochstaetter, *Sprache des Moeglichen: Stilistischer Perspektivismus in Robert Musils "Mann ohne Eigenschaften"* (Frankfurt, 1972), p. 107.

21. Dietrich Hochstaetter and Helmut Arntzen, *Satirischer Stil. Zur Satire Robert Musils im Mann ohne Eigenschaften* (Bonn: Bouvier, 1970), p. 39.

22. Beda Allemann, *Ironie und Dichtung* (Pfullinger, 1956–1969), p. 211.

23. Candace Lang, *Irony/Humor*, (Baltimore and London: The Johns Hopkins University Press, 1987).

24. Linda Hutcheon, *Theory of Parody: The Teaching of Twentieth Century Art Forms* (New York: Methuen, 1985).

25. Hutcheon, "A Postmodern Problematics," in Merril, ed., pp. 1–10.

26. Michel Foucault, *Les Mots et les choses* (Paris, 1966), p. 62. See also Leo Spitzer, "Linguistic Perspectivism in Don Quixote," in *Linguistics and Literary History* (Princeton: Princeton University Press, 1976), p. 41: "It is as if language in general was seen by Cervantes from the angle of perspectivism. . . . Perspectivism informs the structure of the novel as a whole: we find it in Cervantes' treatment of the plot, of ideological themes as well as in his attitude of distantiation toward the reader."

27. Juergen Habermas, "Neoconservative Culture Criticism in the United States and West Germany," in *Habermas and Modernity*, ed. R. Bernstein (Cambridge: MIT Press, 78–94).

28. Frederich G. Peters, *Robert Musil: Master of the Hovering Life* (New York, 1978), p. 15. A single quotation from Peters' hermeneutic approach will mark off his hermeneutics as compared to our own aims in this section: "Musil believed that the universe was without inherent meaning and that beneath man's feet there yawned a dizzying abyss. Having now considered some of Musil's intentions, we may with some curiosity examine the nature of Musil's literary style, the form of expression chosen by this self-declared moralist, rationalist, mystic and nihilist."

29. Toulmin, From *Logical Analysis to Conceptual History*, quoted in *Wittgenstein's Vienna*, p. 166.

I. The Potential Habit of Many Realities

1. Immanuel Kant, *Critique of Pure Reason*, trans. Norman Kemp Smith (London, 1963), pp. 194–256, quoted in Heelan, p. 81.

2. Heelan, p. 81.

3. Robert Musil, *Die Verwirrungen des Zoeglings Toerless*, in *Gesammelte Werke*, vol. II, pp. 77–80.

4. Ludwig Wittgenstein, *Tractatus logico-philosophicus* (Frankfurt, 1921–1964), p. 115.

5. Peter Nuesser, *Musils Romantheorie* (The Hague, 1967), pp. 13ff. Johannes Loebenstein, "Das Problem der Erkenntnis in Musils kuenstlerische Werk," in *Robert Musil, Leben, Werk, Wirkung*, ed. Karl Dinklage (Vienna, 1960), pp. 77–131.

6. Ernst Mach, *The Analysis of Sensations*, p. 12, quoted in Janik and Toulmin, p. 81. See also Einstein, in Holton, "Mach, Einstein, and the Search for Reality," *Daedalus* 97 (Spring, 1968): 662. Einstein is quoted in Holton as saying that the positivists, namely Mach, were wrong in thinking that they could do without a real world in the sense that Einstein later in his life insisted upon, a Spinozian, Leibnizean sense of the universal laws underlying the ordering and construction of the universe. "It is the postulation of a 'real world' which so to speak liberates the 'world' from the thinking and experiencing subject. The extreme positivists think they can do without it; this seems to me to be an illusion, if they are not willing to renounce thought itself".

7. Juergen Habermas, "Comte and Mach: The Intention of Early Positivism," in *Knowledge and Human Interests*, trans. Jeremy Shapiro (Boston, 1968–71), p. 81.

8. Musil, *Beitrag*, p. 33.

9. Ibid.

10. Habermas, *Knowledge and Human Interests*, p. 87: "Although the concept of fact is elucidated by means of the doctrine of elements, the function of knowledge itself remains in obscurity. . . . Mach only undertakes reflection in order to direct it against itself, dissolve the subjective conditions of metaphysics, and destroy prescientific schematizations. . . ."

11. Ibid., p. 82.

12. Ibid., p. 87.

13. Ibid.

14. Allemann, p. 198.

15. Mauthner, *Woerterbuch*, in Toulmin and Janik, p. 128.

16. Max Planck, "The Unity of the Scientific World Picture," in *Physical Reality*, in Holton, p. 662.

17. Musil, *Beitrag*, pp. 5 and 15.

18. Mach, in Musil, *Beitrag*, p. 53.

19. S. G. B. Brush, "Mach and Atomism," *Synthèse* 18, 2/3 (April, 1968): 192–216.

20. Capek, Milic, "Ernest Mach's Biological Theory of Knowledge," *Synthèse* 18, 2/3 (April, 1968): 177.

21. Heelan, p. 31.

22. Hans Reichenbach, *The Rise of Scientific Philosophy* (Berkeley, 1962), pp. 175–176.

23. Heelan, pp. 174–175: "Colors, sounds, etc., which constituted the World-for-us, took on a new symbolic character and became a 'language' which 'spoke' of

the physical structure and intrusions behind them. . . . The 'language' appropriate to an instrument when it 'speaks' is 'physicalist language' insofar as it 'translates' the hidden state of the object into a uniquely determined sensible sign."

24. Heelan, pp. 175–176.

25. Ibid., p. xii.

26. Ibid., p. 184: "The reduction of the wave packet then is nothing more than the expression of the scientist's choice of a measuring process which is different from the means used to prepare the pure state."

27. Habermas, *Knowledge*, pp. 89–90.

28. Gregory Bateson, *Steps to an Ecology of Mind* (New York, 1972), p. 64.

29. Ibid., pp. 454–455.

30. Charles S. Peirce, *Collected Papers of C. S. Peirce*, ed. Charles Hartshorne and Paul Weiss (vols. 7 and 8 ed. Arthur Burks) (Cambridge, Mass., 1931–58). Unless otherwise specified, subsequent references to Peirce's writings will be placed within the body of the text directly following the quotation in the following form, which indicates the volume and the number of the section in this edition, e.g. (5.257).

31. Regarding the "transmutation of values" see Gilles Deleuze, *Nietzsche et la philosophie* (Paris, 1973), pp. 127ff. "Musilkritik" generally recognizes Musil's debt to Nietzsche. However, the fact that it is Clarisse who is the "Nietzsche-junkie" in *Der Mann ohne Eigenschaften*, and that Ulrich and the narrator constantly take a narrative distance from Clarisse, as well as the fact of Clarisse's ensuing madness, indicate a more problematic relation between Musil and Nietzsche than one of direct influence. We will try to show that Musil, while acknowledging the critique which Nietzsche makes of theories of knowledge and values, as well as of discourse, seeks another solution to the dilemma than the one Nietzsche proposed, this latter having ended in madness.

32. Friederich Nietzsche, *Gesammelte Werke*, vol. 3 (Leipzig, 1900–1915), pp. 903 and 440: "If all objective knowledge (cognition) is declared to be merely [knowledge of] appearances, then there is no longer any possibility of a synthesis: Our cognitive apparatus is not designed for 'cognition.' In as much as the word 'knowledge' has any meaning at all, the world is knowable: but it can be *interpreted* differently; there is not a single meaning lying behind the world, rather countless meanings. Perspectivism. We analyse the world according to our needs, our drives and the for and against."

33. Heelan, p. 177.

34. Ulrich Karthaus, *Der andere Zustand: Zeitstrukturen im Werke Robert Musils* (Berlin, 1965), p. 69.

35. Maurice Blanchot, *Le Livre à venir* (Paris, 1959), p. 203.

36. Heelan, p. 42.

37. Helmut Arntzen, *Satirischer Stil bei Robert Musil* (Bonn, 1970), p. 64.

38. Mach, in Musil, *Beitrag*, p. 53.

39. Musil, *Der Mann ohne Eigenschaften*, p. 1929:

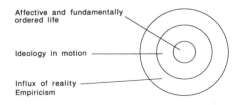

40. C. S. Peirce, "Letter to Lady Welby," (Oct. 12, 1904), in Thomas Olshewsky, ed., *Problems in the Philosophy of Language* (New York, 1969), pp. 22–30.

41. *C. S. Peirce's Letters to Lady Welby*, vol. I., ed. Irwin Lieb (New Haven, Conn.: 1953), p. 32, in David Savan, *An Introduction to C. S. Peirce's Semiotics* (Toronto, 1976), p. 1.

42. T. J. Reiss, "Archéologie du discours et critique épistémique: Projet pour une critique discursive," in *Philosophie et littérature*, ed. Pierre Gravel (Montreal, 1979), pp. 143–189: "If experiment is included in nomothetic representation which presents as well the process of observation, if the process of observation necessarily and always changes that observation—then the laws of discourse which account for it must be in a dialectical relation."

43. Heelan, p. 175: "Of itself, the instrument is 'dumb,' it waits to be questioned by the scientist, and the form of the question structures its response. For example, . . . the data may evoke a mere description of its material reality (a bubble chamber track) or an explanation of its intentional reality (a signature of an Omega-minus particle)—or an assertion or denial of a hypothesis (the Eightfold Way). The instrument responds to the noetic intention of the scientist; it does not create it. It 'speaks' only if 'questioned'; and the structure of its response mirrors the structure of the 'question asked' of it."

44. Weyl, *Philosophy of Mathematics and Natural Sciences*, quoted in Heelan, p. 108. "We have observational or operational concepts—things-for-us."
"The human way of discerning the presence of this activity then, is to study, to recognize its effects on other things . . ." For the importance that Peirce attaches to the notion of Interpretant, see Savan, pp. 29ff.

45. Peirce, "Letter to Lady Welby," (1908), in Charles Ogden and I. A. Richards, *The Meaning of Meaning* (New York, 1927), p. 288: "Now the problem of what the 'meaning' of an intellectual concept is can only be solved by study of the interpretants or proper significate effects, of signs. . . . some important subdivisions. The first proper significate effect of a sign is a *feeling* produced by it. This 'emotional interpretant' . . . it will always involve an effort. . . . it will always do so through the mediation of the emotional interpretant. I call it the *energetic interpretant*. . . . But what further kind of effort can there be?" (5.475–6) ". . . I will call it the *logical interpretant*, without as yet determining whether this term shall extend to anything besides the meaning of a general concept." (5.476)

46. Gregory Bateson, "Information, Codification, and Metacommunication," in Bateson and Jurgen Reusch, *Communication: The Social Matrix of Psychiatry* (New York, 1951–68), p. 419.

47. Michel Foucault, *L'Archéologie du savoir* (Paris, 1969), pp. 117ff.

48. Bateson, *Ecology*, p. 275.

49. Ibid., p. 338.

50. Juergen Habermas, *Communication and the Evolution of Society*, trans. Thomas McCarthy (Boston, 1979), p. 30.

51. Ernst Mach, *The Structure of Mechanics*, 5th ed., trans. T. J. McCormack (Lasalle, Ill.: Open Court, 1945), p. 580, in R. S. Cohen, p. 137.

52. Habermas, *Knowledge*, p. 85: "Mach's shallow materialism blocks off epistemological inquiry into the subjective conditions of the objectivity of possible knowledge. The only reflection admissible serves the self-abolition of reflecting on the knowing subject. The doctrine of elements justifies the strategy of 'thinking nothing of one's ego; and resolving it into a transitory combination of changing elements.'"

53. Peirce (5.314): ". . . there is no element whatever of man's consciousness that had not something corresponding to it in the word; and the reason is obvious. It is that the word or sign that man uses *is* the man himself. For as the fact that every thought is a sign, taken in conjunction with the fact that life is a train of thought, proves that man is an external sign; that is to say, the man and the external sign are identical, in the same sense in which the words homo and man are identical. Thus my language is the sum total of myself; for the man is the thought."

54. Foucault, *L'Archéologie*, p. 67; *Archaeology*, p. 49.

55. Foucault, *L'Archéologie*, 61; *Archaeology*, p. 45.

56. Foucault, *L'Archéologie*, p. 63; *Archaeology*, p. 46.

57. Foucault, *L'Archéologie*, p. 59.

58. Ibid.

59. Mikhail Bakhtin and V. N. Volochinov, *Le Marxisme et la Philosophie du Langage* (Paris, 1977), pp. 27–28; M. Bakhtin and V. N. Volochinov, *Marxism and the Philosophy of Language*, trans. L. Matejka and I. R. Titunik (New York: Seminar Press, 1973), p. 11.

60. Jerzy Pelc, "On the Concept of Narration," *Semiotica* 1 (1971).

61. Oskar Marius Fontana, "Erinnerungen an Robert Musil," in Karl Dinklage, ed., *Robert Musil, Leben, Werk, Wirkung* (Wien, 1960), pp. 336ff. In 1942, at the age of 62, Musil died leaving his novel unfinished. There remained no neat scheme waiting to be rounded off. In the unfinished fragments for a continuation of *Der Mann ohne Eigenschaften*, one may discern a certain uncertainty, a lost direction with several alternatives posed for a solution to Ulrich's life and his epoch, none of which are definitively decided upon. In Part Two, I will try to illustrate that Musil's practice of process and incompleteness is the type that Lyotard describes below, i.e., a "continuous destruction of bourgeois institutions" as opposed to the false ideology of progress which is merely 'trompe l'oeil'.

Jean-François Lyotard, *Dérivé à partir de Marx et de Freud* (Paris, 1973), p. 40. ". . . the incompletion of a work is theoretically the subterraneous guarantor of the continual creation and destruction of institutions that the bourgeoisie calls 'progress'. But it is the very opposite, really an incompletion, while capitalist progress and mobility are illusions, mobility in a system itself static that book I of *The Capital* will give its canonical expression."

62. Burton Pike, *Robert Musil: An Introduction to his Work* (New York, 1969), p. 158.

63. Hermann Pongs, *Romanschaffen im Umbruch der Zeit. Eine Chronik von 1952–1962*, vol. 4 (Tuebingen: Verlag der Deutschen Hochschuhlererzeitung, 1963), pp. 330–345.

64. Peirce (6.07).

65. T. J. Reiss, "Peirce, Frege, la vérité, le tiers inclus et le champ pratique," *Langages* (1980), p. 123.

66. Mauthner, *Beitrage*, vol. 1, p. 92, in Janik and Toulmin, p. 129.

67. Bateson, *Ecology*, p. 410.

68. Ibid., p. 393.

69. Ibid., p.396. Bateson is also very careful to define message as a relationship. (p. 275).

70. Ibid., p. 289. ". . . all perception and all response, all behaviour and all classes of behaviour—. . . must be regarded as communicational in nature."

71. Ibid., pp. 484ff.

72. Heelan, p. 5. "A World is also intersubjective. . . . This overlapping of Worlds is a condition *sine qua non* of communication between people."

73. Foucault, *L'Archéologie*, pp. 161–163, and 41; *Archaeology*, p. 29.

74. Garbis Kortian, *Métacritique* (Paris, 1979), pp. 115–116; *Metacritique: the Philosophical Argument of Jürgen Habermas*, trans. John Raffan (Cambridge: Cambridge University Press, 1980), pp. 120–121.

75. Ernst Kaiser and Eithne Wilkins, "Musil und die Quadratwurzel," in Dinklage, ed., p. 169. Musil admits the uncertainty of his own judgments and the necessity of allowing for their surpassability when he speaks of the number of times he has changed his view of Rilke and Hoffmannsthal, concluding that "there is no objective judgment but only a 'living one'" (Tgb., 865, my paraphrase). "Musil's method is in fact the provisional method of a believer who simply

believes in nothing and therefore must always be 'exact' in order that he does not accidentally accept something which he has not yet verified. He himself called this method—presumably in reference to Cusanus' 'De Docta Ignorantia'—the 'methodology of unknowing.'"

76. George Gentry, "Habit and Logical Interpretant," in *Studies of the Philosophy of Charles Sanders Peirce,* ed. Philip Wiener and Frederick Young (Cambridge, Mass.: Harvard University Press, 1952).

77. Werner Heisenberg, "Remarks on the Origin of the Relations of Uncertainty," in *The Uncertainty Principle and Foundations of Quantum Mechanics: A Fifty Year Survey,* ed. William C. Price and Seymour S. Chessick (New York, 1977), p. 6. The concept of indeterminacy does not signify a causality but indicates a change in the mode of expression and grasping of "that" which has been called "knowledge."

78. Heelan, p. 90.

79. Heelan, p. 154. "On the one hand, the elementary particle is not phenomenally real; for it has 'no colour, no smell, no taste; . . . and the concepts of geometry and kinematics, like shape or motion in space, cannot be applied to it consistently.' On the other hand, it is not a pure (inhaltsleer) idea, for it can be 'converted from potency to act,' by the process of measurement and observation. Heisenberg called it real but potential."

Werner Heisenberg, *Physics and Philosophy,* p. 186, in Heelan, p. 154: "In experiments about atomic events we have to do with things and facts, with phenomena that are just as real as any phenomena of daily life. But the atoms or elementary particles themselves are not as real: they form a world of potentialities and possibilities rather than one of things and facts."

80. Heelan, pp. 153ff.

81. Werner Heisenberg, *Martin Heidegger Festschrift,* (1959), p. 291, in Heelan, p. 151.

82. Heisenberg, *The Physicist's Conception of Nature,* p. 15, in Heelan, p. 152.

83. Heisenberg, *The Physicist's Conception of Nature,* p. 291, in Heelan, p. 152.

84. Heelan, p. 54.

85. Ibid., p. 82.

86. It was Baumann who first pointed out the close similarity between Musil's theory of possibility and partial solution, on the one hand, and the principle of uncertainty on the other hand.

Werner Heisenberg, *Physik und Philosophie,* 1959, p. 37, in Gerhart Baumann, *Robert Musil, Zur Erkenntnis der Dichtung* (Bern, 1965), p. 173: ". . . as a rule we can only predict probability. No longer can objective phenomena be determined by mathematical formulas, but only the probabilities of the occurrence of certain phenomena. It is no longer the . . . occurrence, but rather the possibility of occurrence . . . that is subject to strict natural laws. . . . The probability function, unlike the mathematical model of Newtonian mechanics, does not describe a definite occurrence, rather, at least in regard to the process of observation, an aggregate of possible occurrences."

87. Albrecht Schoene, "Zum Gebrauch des Konjunktivs bei Robert Musil," in *Deutsche Romane von Grimmelshausen bis Musil,* ed. Jost Schillemeit (Frankfurt, 1966–1974), pp. 290–318.

88. Reiss, "Archéologie du discours," pp. 177ff.

89. Ibid., p. 185.

90. Umberto Eco, *L'Oeuvre ouverte* (Paris, 1965), pp. 17ff.

91. One might, contrary to the interpretation that Russell gives to the *Tractatus,* interpret Wittgenstein's definition of a "Bild" as a definition of potentia, in that it is both contextually situated and only possible:

"2.202 Das Bild stellt eine moegliche Sachlage im logischen Raume dar.

2.203 Das Bild enthaelt Moeglichkeit der Sachlage, die es darstellt." Wittgenstein, *Tractatus*, p. 18.

92. Emile Benveniste, "Sémiologie de la langue," *Semiotica* 1 (1969).

93. Capek, p. 177. "Anticipating Peirce and Dewey, he [Mach] defines any problem which man faces as a result of conflict between an established mental *habit* and a widened field of observation; when our thought becomes adjusted to this widened field of experience, the problem disappears or using the words of C. S. Peirce, 'the doubt is appeased.' The adjustment of our thoughts to experience is, according to Mach, quite analogous to the adjustment of physical organs to their environment; in fact, this change in thoughts (Gedankenumwandlung) which we observe in ourselves is merely a part of a wider evolutionary process."

94. Mach, *Analyse der Empfindungen*, p. 294, in R. S. Cohen, pp. 139ff: "The same elements are related to the self through many points of connection. The points of connection, however are not permanent. They are constantly arising, vanishing, and changing. Nor does the association of "Verknuepfungspunkten" with the self contradict a Peircean semiotics, since this would amount to saying that the self is a collection of pockets of habits, a paraphrase of the Peircean phrase that "matter is mind hide-bound with habit."

95. Bateson, *Ecology*, pp. 131–132.

96. Peirce (5.295–97). "[. . .] attention is the power by which thought at one time is connected with and made to relate to thought at another time; or, to apply the conception of thought as a sign, that it is the pure demonstrative application of a thought-sign. [. . .] Attention produces effects [interpretants] upon the nervous system. These effects are habits, or nervous associations. [. . .] Thus the formation of a habit is an induction and is therefore necessarily connected with attention or abstraction."

97. Peirce (5.295). ". . . since an act cannot be supposed to determine that which precedes it in time, this act can consist only in the capacity that the cognition emphasized has for producing an effect (interpretant) upon memory, or otherwise influencing subsequent thought."

98. Mach, *Conservation*, p. 49, in R. S. Cohen p. 139. Mach, as well, insists upon the mnemonic aspect of coded representation: "What we 'represent' . . . behind the appearances (has) only the value of a memoria technica, or formula whose form, because it is arbitrary and irrelevant, varies very easily with the standpoint of our culture."

99. Bateson, *Ecology*, p. 501. "The phenomenon of habit formation sorts out the ideas which survive repeated use and puts them in a more or less separate category. These *trusted* ideas then become available for immediate use without thoughtful inspection, while the more flexible parts of the mind can be saved for use on newer matters. . . . frequency of use of a given idea becomes a determinant of its survival in that ecology of ideas which we call Mind; and beyond that survival of a frequently used idea is further promoted by the fact that habit formation tends to remove the idea from the field of critical inspection."

100. Peirce (6.58–59). ". . . there is probably in nature some agency by which the complexity and diversity of things can be increased; and that consequently the rule of mechanical necessity meets in some way with interference.

"By thus admitting pure spontaneity or life as a character of the universe, acting always and everywhere though restrained within narrow bounds by law, producing the infinitesimal departures from law continually, and great ones with infinite infrequency."

See, regarding stochastics, Michel Serres, *La Naissance de la physique dans le texte de Lucrèce: Fleuves et turbulences* (Paris: Minuit, 1977). The "Clinamen" for Serres is one of the first elaborations of a theory of change via stochastics.

101. Bateson, *Ecology*, p. 381.

102. Ibid., p. 497.

103. Ibid., p. 500.

104. Heelan, p. 43. "Heisenberg's insistence on 'observable quantities' was a return to the individual and empirical manifestations of reality which, as such, to our way of knowing, are penetrated with a certain quality."

105. Theodor Wiessengrund Adorno, *Philosophie der neuen Musik* (Frankfurt, 1958). Interestingly enough, another type of sign-production noted for breaking with habits is that of modern music, referred to by Adorno as fracturing the norm, and by Brelet as contradicting determinacy by means of chance and discontinuity.

G. Brelet, "L'Esthétique du discontinu dans la musique nouvelle," in *Musiques nouvelles* (Paris: Klinsieck, 1968), p. 266: "Discontinuity is an open gap in determinism through which the contingency of chance and freedom can penetrate; the unforeseeable."

106. Musil, "Tagebuecher," in Kaiser and Wilkins, "Musil in die Quadratwurzel," in Dinklage, *Leben, Werke und Wirkung*, p. 157.

107. In relativity physics, as well, field replaced the classical notion of ontological substance, as Einstein explains: "A new concept appeared in physics, the most important invention since Newton, the 'field' (p. 142). The acknowledgement of the new concepts gained more ground and the "field" eventually eclipsed the substance. . . . a new reality was created, a new concept for which there was no place in Newtonian mechanics. Slowly and by a constant struggle, the notion of 'field' succeeded in occupying the first place in physics and is among the fundamental concepts of this science" (p. 230).

Albert Einstein and L. Infeld, *L'Evolution des idées en physique* (Paris: Payot, 1978), pp. 142 and 230. It is as field that energy may be conceived as potentially realizing both waves and particles.

108. Bateson, *Ecology*, p. 188.

109. Ibid., pp. 265–268. "Does the older materialist thesis really depend upon the premise that contexts are isolable? Or is our view of the world changed when we admit an infinite regress of contexts linked to each other in a complex work of meta-relations? . . . Does the possibility that the separate levels of stochastic change [in phenotype and genotype] may be connected in the larger context of the ecological system alter our allegiance in the battle?"

110. Foucault, *L'Ordre du discourse*, p. 32; *Discourse on Language*, p. 222.

111. Foucault, *L'Archéologie*, p. 39; *Archaeology*, p. 27.

112. Cohen, pp. 133 and 142.

113. Heisenberg, in Heelan, p. 150.

114. See also Peirce (8.012) and (7.319).

115. Peirce (5.316–17): "Finally, as what anything really is, *is* what it may finally come to be known in the ideal state of complete information, so that reality depends on the ultimate decision of the community; so thought is what it is, only by virtue of its addressing a future thought which is in its value as thought identical with it, though more developed. In this way, the existence of thought now depends on what is to be hereafter; so that it has only a potential existence, dependent on the future thought of the community. [. . .] The individual man, since his separate existence is manifested only by ignorance and error, so far as he is anything apart from his fellows, and from what he and they are to be, is only a negation." There is some argument among Peirce scholars as to whether the knowledge of the community ultimately leads to the complete and total field of truth. The case of the ultimate interpretant is posed once again. Habermas describes Peirce's notion of the community as an epistemological ideal of the same nature as the categorical imperative: "The structure of scientific method guarantees both the revisability of all individual statements and the possibility in princi-

ple of an ultimate answer to every emerging scientific question" (Habermas, *Knowledge*, p. 92).

116. It is on the basis of the Peircean notion of consensus of the community that both Apel and Habermas will be seen to posit a consensus of communicational norms or postulates of validity, which will be seen to be essential to any theory of utopian, communicational interaction: "The illocutionary force of a speech act, which brings about an interpersonal relationship between consensually interacting participants, arises from the binding force of acknowledged norms of action: to the extent that a speech act is part of consensual interaction it actualizes an already established value-pattern" (Habermas, "Some Distinctions in Universal Pragmatics," in *Theory and Society* 3, No. 2 (Summer 1976), p. 158). In other words Habermas and Apel avoid speaking of referentiality and of empirical objectivity by placing truth at the level of intersubjectivity, where interaction should bring about a mutual understanding. The level of objects in the world, or states of affairs, have their status and meaning as a consensus derived through communicative interaction: "In none of these dimensions, however, are we able to name a criterion which would allow an independent judgement on the competence of possible judges, that is, independently of a consensus achieved in a discourse" (Kortian, *Métacritique*, p. 120; *Metacritique*, p. 125).

117. Foucault, *L'Archéologie*, pp. 250ff; *Archaeology*, p. 191.

118. Umberto Eco, *A Theory of Semiotics* (Bloomington, 1976), p. 290.

119. Foucault, *L'Archéologie*, pp. 242 and 243.

120. Bateson, *Ecology*, p. 263.

121. Ibid., p. 254.

122. Ibid., p. 244.

123. Foucault, *L'Ordre du discours*, pp. 22–23.

124. Habermas, *Communication*, p. 5 (my emphasis).

125. Habermas, *Communication*, p. 35.

126. Ibid., p. 23.

127. Ibid., p. 158.

128. Habermas, "Some Distinctions," p. 156.

129. Ibid., p. 165.

130. Ibid., p. 167.

131. Habermas, *Communication*, pp. 1–69.

132. Eco, *A Theory of Semiotics*, pp. 151ff.

133. Ibid., pp. 128–129. "A semiotics of code is an operational device in the service of a semiotics of sign-production. A semiotics of code can be established—if only partially—when the existence of a message postulates it as an explanatory condition. Semiotics must proceed to isolate structures as if a definitive general structure existed; but to be able to do this one might assume that this global structure is a simply regulative hypothesis and that every time a structure is described something occurs within the universe of signification which no longer makes it completely reliable."

134. Ibid., p. 128.

II. The Ghostliness of Narrative

1. Maurice Blanchot, *Le Livre à venir* (Paris, 1959), pp. 217ff.

2. Wladimir Krysinski, "Musil vs. Scarron ou l'indétermination du romanesque," *The Canadian Journal of Research in Semotics*, No. 1 (1981), pp. 15ff.

3. Mikhail Bakhtin, *Problèmes de la Poétique de Dostoievski* (Lausanne, 1929–1970), pp. 211ff.

4. Foucault, *L'Archéologie*, p. 71.

5. Foucault, *L'Ordre du discours*, pp. 9–10; *Discourse on Language*, p. 216.

6. Gilles Deleuze and Félix Guattari, *L'Anti-Oedipe* (Paris, 1976), pp. 244–247.

7. Mach, *Die Analyse der Empfindungen und des Verhaeltnisses des Physischen zum Psychologischen* (Jena, 1911), p. 199.

8. Henri Bergson, *Le Rire: Essai sur la signification du comique* (Paris, 1940–1972), p. 113. "Raidure, automatisme, distraction, insociabilité, tout cela se pénètre et c'est de tout cela qu'est fait le comique de caractère."

9. Bakhtin and Volochinov, *Le Marxisme et la philosophie du langage*, p. 15.

10. Habermas, "Some Distinctions," p. 165.

11. Very briefly, a word of warning is due here. First of all, one might object that what I am doing is merely to postulate structures of communication instead of those of narrativity, making for an equally abstract, absolute system. I hope that the comparisons that I have made between codes in linguistic semiotics and codes in communicational semiotics will serve to outline the advantages of postulates of communication over those of "langue." However, the risk still exists that one may pose absolute categories as a filter for all communication, at the expense of the specificity of the actual practices of discourse. The cautions of indeterminacy and relationality theories of discourse which I have worked around to in the preceding chapter should illustrate the difference and epistemological advantages which set a theory of communicational postulates off from a theory of codes, as leading to a theory of discourse production. Eco reiterates these epistemological reservations when he states that some contexts cannot be coded: "Other contexts which can be seen but cannot be coded and possible circumstances which are either unforeseeable or excessively complex and which make up a cluster of different extra-semiotic factors . . ." (Eco, *A Theory of Semiotics*, p. 130).

Basically, what a communicationally oriented theory of discursive habits recognizes that a linguistico-semiotic theory does not is that, due to the very relational, interactional nature of all communication, including the dialogue between the text and the critic within a context, every critical category and result is a product of a communicational relation, hence is relative, biased, and partial: "A semantic system or subsystem is one possibility of giving form to the world. As such, it constitutes a *partial* interpretation of the world and can theoretically be revised every time new messages which semantically restructure the code introduce new position values. . . . But in general, any addressee will turn to his own particular world vision, in order to choose the *subcodes* that he wishes to apply to the message. To define this partial world vision, this prospective segmentation of reality entails a Marxist notion of ideology as "false conscience." Ideology is therefore a message which starts with a factual description and then tries to justify it theoretically, gradually being accepted by society through a process of overcoding" (Eco, *A Theory of Semiotics*, p. 31).

It now remains to be seen what kinds of communicational, semiotic habits could possibly be produced in an analysis of *Der Mann ohne Eigenschaften*, as well as broken by ironic interaction.

12. Habermas, *Communication*, p. 29.

13. Ibid., p. 29.

14. Ibid., p. 29.

15. Ibid., p. 67.

16. Ibid., pp. 63–64.

17. Soren Kierkegaard, *Concluding Unscientific Postscript* (Princeton, 1941–1971), p. 182.

18. Foucault, *L'Ordre du discours*, p. 41; *Discourse on Language*, p. 225.

19. Michel Foucault, *Histoire de la folie* (Paris, 1961), p. 53; *Madness and Civilization*, trans. Richard Howard (New York: Vintage, 1973), p. 37.

20. Foucault, *Folie*, p. 98. Regarding the principle of exclusion, Foucault, *L'Ordre du discours*, p. 11.

21. Foucault, *L'Ordre du discours*, p. 23.
22. Foucault, *Folie*, p. 233; *Madness*, p. 227.
23. Foucault, *Folie*, p. 260; *Madness*, p. 251.
24. Ibid., p. 200.
25. Ibid., p. 99.
26. Ibid., p. 99; *Madness*, p. 79.
27. Foucault, *L'Archéologie*, p. 60; *Archaeology*, p. 44.
28. Foucault, *Folie*, p. 107.
29. Foucault, p. 189; *Madness*, p. 189.
30. Bakhtin and Volochinov, pp. 115–116.
31. Ibid., p. 146.
32. Ibid., p. 9.
33. Krysinski, "Musil vs Scarron," pp. 15ff.
34. Hochstaetter, p. 17.
35. Goetz Mueller, *Ideologie Kritik und Metasprache* (Munich, 1972), p. 2.
36. Blanchot, p. 219.
37. Foucault, *L'Archéologie*, p. 160.
38. Karl Kraus, *Werke*, vol. III, p. 329, in Janik and Toulmin, p. 89.
39. Louis Marin, *La Critique du discours* (Paris, 1975), p. 285.
40. Ibid., p. 298.
41. Ibid., p. 33.
42. Ibid., p. 288.
43. Blanchot, p. 202.
44. Wolfgang Frier, *Die Sprache der Emotionalitaet in den "Verwirrungen des Zoeglings Toerless" von Robert Musil* (Bonn, 1976), p. 168.
45. Mikhail Bakhtin, *Problèmes de la poétique de Dostoyevski* (Lausanne, 1929–70, pp. 10–12; *Problems of Dostoyevsky's Poetics*, trans. R. W. Rotsel (Ann Arbor: Ardis, 1973), p. 4–5.
46. Bakhtin and Volochinov, pp. 14–15.
47. Ibid., p. 28; *Marxism*, p. 11.
48. Bakhtin, *Dostoievski*, p. 38 and pp. 134ff.
49. Ibid., p. 134; *Dostoyevsky*, p. 93.
50. Bakhtin and Volochinov, p. 146.
51. Ibid., pp. 127ff.
52. Ibid., pp. 127ff.
53. Schoene, pp. 290–318.
54. Blanchot, p. 271.
55. Foucault, *L'Ordre du discours*, p. 61; *Discourse on Language*, p. 231.
56. Vélimir Klebnikov, *Zanguesi*, "Introduction," in Krysinski, "Musil vs. Scarron," p. 24.

Conclusion

1. Wladimir Jankélévitch, *L'Ironie* (Paris, 1964). The original edition of this work bore the subtitle "ou la bonne conscience." Irony, for Jankélévitch, is defined in relation to a play on the double meaning of "conscience" in French. Irony is a form of consciousness, i.e., a theory of knowledge. But irony is also a form of conscience, in the sense of moral or ethical presentiment of what "ought" to be.
2. Musil, *Prosa, Dramen, Spaete Briefe*, p. 726.
3. Nuesser, *Musil's Romantheorie*, p. 12.
4. Bateson, *Ecology*, p. 455.
5. It is observed that this (utopian) man as a man of action is already present today; but exact people do not concern themselves with the utopias latent within them. In this connection the essence of utopia is described as an experiment in

which the possible variations of an element of life and its effects are observed, a possibility freed from and developed out of the constraining binds of reality. The utopia of exactitude produces a man in whom can be found a paradoxical combination of exactness and indeterminateness. Beyond the temperament of exactitude everything in him is indeterminate. He attaches little value to morality, since his imagination is focused on changes and, as is shown, his passions disappear and there appears in their place a goodness with something like primal fire about it (DMoE, 1878).

We must emphasize that we are not even beginning to take into account the vast literature on utopia. Our aim here is to present a very limited argument, namely that irony realizes the discursive utopia as emancipatory interaction. This theory of utopia stems directly from the Frankfurt School and matures in its relation to communication in Habermas and Apel. Of course there would need to be a development of this notion of utopia in relation to many other theories of utopia. This is a task which remains for the future.

6. Blanchot, pp. 212–213.

7. William James, *The Varieties of Religious Experience: A Study in Human Nature* (London: Longmans and Green, 1908), pp. 381–425.

William James, in a study on mystical, ecstatic experiences in various ethnic societies finds a common obstacle in all cases, namely that of making the mystical state last. "Mystical states cannot be sustained for long. Except in rare instances, half an hour, or at most an hour or two, seems to be the limit beyond which they fall into the light of the common day" (p. 381).

8. Blanchot, p. 215.

9. Musil, *Der Mann ohne Eigenschaften* (Hamburg, 1957), p. 1594.

10. Allemann, p. 183.

11. Arntzen, in Manfred Sera, *Utopie und Parodie bei Musil, Broch, und Thomas Mann* (Bonn, 1969), p. 3.

12. Peter Szondi, *Poésie et poétique de l'idéalisme Allemand*, trans. Jean Bollack (Paris: Minuit, 1975), p. 109.

13. Ibid., p. 109.

14. Krysinski, "Musil vs Scarron", m.s., p. 3.

15. Pike, p. 160. Although we agree with Pike's qualification here regarding irony, we do not accept what he says about myth, since we give to the notion of myth the same interpretation as do Adorno and Horkheimer in the *Dialectic of Enlightenment*, trans. John Cumming (New York: Seabury Press, 1944–1972), pp. 43ff. For Horkheimer and Adorno, myth is the reification, the false purporting to truth, and the systematization of what was earlier an emancipatory, non-totalitarian moment of reason.

16. Goetz Mueller, *Ideologie und Metasprache* (Muenchen, 1972), pp. 152ff.

17. Jean-François Lyotard, "Adorno come diavolo," in *Des Dispositifs pulsionnels* (Paris: Union Général d'Editions, 1973), pp. 115ff.

18. Bateson, "Information, Codification and Meta-communication," pp. 418–422.

19. Ibid., pp. 418–423.

20. Ibid., p. 423.

21. Ibid., p. 418.

22. Ibid., p. 420.

23. Ibid., p. 420, my emphasis.

24. Bateson, *Ecology*, p. 63.

25. Ibid., p. 502.

26. Ibid., pp. 502–503.

27. Ibid., p. 483.

28. Kortian, *Métacritique*, p. 91; *Metacritique*, p. 97. For Habermas' argument

that emancipation must apply to all types of communicational interaction and not merely to an economic base-structure, which is the particular interest of orthodox Marxism, see Habermas, *Communication*, pp. 97–98.

29. Kortian, *Métacritique*, p. 71; *Metacritique*, p. 78–79. "In its prospective and normative moment, this reflection unites critique with the emancipatory cognitive interest by adumbrating the objective conditions of the context of application of the theory. This leads Habermas to elaborate a theory of communication centred on the concept of a universal pragmatics . . . The task of universal pragmatics is to set out the necessary and sufficient conditions of a possible communication which operates counterfactually, to diagnose the splitting of symbols produced in speech subjected to systematic distortions, and to attempt in this way to create the regulative canons of a constraint-free communication which has recognised normative force."

30. Habermas, *Communication*, p. 114.

31. K. O. Apel, in Habermas, *Communication*, p. 205. See also Juergen Habermas, "Preparatory Remarks to a Theory of Communicative Competence," in Habermas-Luhman, *Theorie der Gesellschaft oder Sozialtechnologie* (Frankfurt, 1971), pp. 101–141, my translation.

32. Habermas, "Some Distinctions," p. 165.

33. Kortian, *Métacritique*, p. 71; *Metacritique*, p. 78.

34. Habermas, "Some Distinctions," p. 163.

35. Ibid., p. 163.

36. Ibid., p. 163.

37. Ibid., p. 164.

38. Karl Otto Apel, "From Kant to Peirce", *Proceedings from the Third International Kant Congress* (1970), p. 92.

39. Ibid., p. 100.

40. Horkheimer, *Critical Theory* (New York, 1972), p. 211.

41. For an excellent discussion of Peirce's notion of abduction and its relation to the formation of new habits, see K. T. Fann, *Peirce's Theory of Abduction* (The Hague, 1970), pp. 28ff.

42. Peirce equates abduction with analogy in the following article: C. S. Peirce, *The Lowell Lectures*, vol. 1, no. 8 (1903), p. 61, cited in, Fann, p. 15.

43. Foucault, *L'Ordre du discours*, p. 53; *Discourse on Language*, p. 229.

BIBLIOGRAPHY

Adorno, Theodor Wiessengrund. *Aesthetische Theorie*. Frankfurt: Suhrkamp, 1970.
———. *Negative Dialectics*. Trans. E. B. Ashton. New York: Seabury Press, 1973.
———. *Philosophie der neuen Musik*. Frankfurt: Europaische Verlagsanstalt, 1958.
———. *Philosophy of Modern Music*. Trans. A. G. Mitchell and Wesley Blomster. New York: Seabury Press, 1973.
Albertson, Elizabeth. *"Ratio und Mystik" im Werk Robert Musils*. Munich: Nymphenburger Verlag, 1968.
Allemann, Beda. *Ironie und Dichtung*. Pfullingen: Neske, 1956–1969, pp. 177–220.
Apel, Karl-Otto. "From Kant to Peirce: The Semiotical Transformation of Transcendental Logic." *Proc. from the Third International Kant Congress*. Ed. Lewis, White, Beck, 1970.
———. "The Transcendental Conception of Language Communication and the Ideal of a First Philosophy." In *History of Linguistic Thought and Contemporary Linguistics*. Ed. Hermann Parret. Berlin: de Gruyter, 1976.
Aristotle. *Poetics*. Trans. and intr. by G. F. Else. Ann Arbor: University of Michigan Press, 1967–77.
Austin, J. L. *How to Do Things with Words*. Ed. J. O. Urmson. Cambridge: Harvard University Press, 1962.
Bachmann, Ingeborg. "Zu Robert Musil's 'DMoE,' Ins tausendjaehrige Reich." *Akzente* I (1954): 50–53.
Bakhtin, Mikhail. *Problèmes de la poétique de Dostoievski*. Trans. Guy Verret. Lausanne: Edition l'Age d'Homme, 1929–1970.
Bakhtin, Mikhail, and V. N. Volochinov. *Le Marxisme et la philosophie du langage: Essai d'application de la méthode sociologique en linguistique*. Trans. and intr. Marina Yaguello. Paris: Minuit, 1977.
Banfield, Ann. "Narrative Style and Indirect Speech." *Foundations of Language: International Journal of Language and Philosophy* 10 (1973).
Bange, Pierre. *Ironie et dialogisme dans les romans de Fontane*. Grenoble: Presses Universitaires de Grenoble, 1974.
Barthes, Roland. "L'Ancienne rhétorique: Aide-mémoire." *Communications* 16 (1970): 172–229.
———. "Introduction à l'analyse structurale des récrits." *Communications* 8 (1966): 1–27.
———. *S/Z*. Paris: Seuil, 1970.
Bateston, Gregory. *Steps to an Ecology of Mind*. New York: Ballantine Books, 1972.
Bateson, Gregory, and Jurgen Reusch. *Communication: The Social Matrix of Psychiatry*. New York: W. W. Norton and Co., 1951–1968.
Bauer, Gerhart. "Die Aufloesung des anthropozentrischen Verhaltens im modernen Roman, dargestellt an Musils 'MoE'," *Deutsche Vierteljahrsschrift* 42 (1968): 677–701.
Bauer, Sophie, et al. *Studien zu Robert Musil*. Koeln: Graz, 1966.
Baumann, Gerhart. "Robert Musil, Eine Vorstudie." *Germanisch-Romantische Monatschrift* 34 (1953): 292–316.

────. "Robert Musil, Die Struktur des Geistes oder der Geist der Struktur."
    Germanisch-Romantische Monatschrift 41 (1960): 420–442.
────. Robert Musil: Zur Erkenntnis der Dichtung. Bern: Francke, 1965.
Bausinger, Hermann. Studien zu einer historisch-kritischen Ausgabe von Robert
    Musils Roman "DMoE." Hamburg: Rowohlt, 1964.
Baxter, Charles. "The Escape from Irony: 'Under the Volcano' and the Aesthetics of
    Arson." Novel 18 (Winter 1977): 114–126.
Benveniste, Emile. Problèmes de linguistique générale. Paris: Gallimard, 1966 and
    1977, 2 vols.
────. "Sémiologie de la lange." Semiotica 1 (1969).
Berghahn, Wilfred. "Die essayistische Erzaehltechnik Robert Musils." Diss. Bonn:
    1956.
Bergson, Henri. Le Rire: Essai sur la signification du comique. Paris: P.U.F., 1940–
    1972.
Blakney, Raymond B. Meister Eckhart: A Modern Translation. New York: Harper
    and Row, 1941.
Blanchot, Maurice. Le Livre à venir. Paris: Gallimard, 1959.
Boehlich, Walter. "Kontroversen ueber den 'MoE'." Die Welt 22 (1963): 6ff.
────. "Untergang und Erloesung." Akzente I (1954).
Booth, Wayne C. The Rhetoric of Fiction. Chicago: University of Chicago Press,
    1961.
────. The Rhetoric of Irony. Chicago: University of Chicago Press, 1975.
Boucher, Maurice. "Ironie romantique." Cahiers du Sud 41 (1937): 29–32.
Bové, Paul A. "Cleanth Brooks and Modern Irony: A Kierkegaardian Critique."
    Boundary II 4, No. 3 (Spring 1976): 727–759.
Braun, Wilhelm. "Musil and the Pendulum of the Intellect." Monatshefte fuer
    deutschen Unterricht 49 (1957): 109–119.
────. "Musil's Siamese Twins." Germanic Review 33 (1958): 41–52.
────. "Musil's Erdensekretariat der Genauigkeituund Seele; a Clue to the Phi-
    losophy of the Hero of 'DMoE'." Monatshefte fuer deutsche Unterricht 46
    (1954): 305–316.
Brelet, Georges. "L'Esthétique du discontinu dans la musique nouvelle." In Musi-
    ques nouvelles. Paris: Klincksieck, 1968.
Brooks, Cleanth. "Irony as a Principle of Structure." In Literary Opinion in Amer-
    ica. Ed. Morton Dawen Zabel. New York: Harper and Brothers, 1949–1951,
    pp. 729–741, vol. II.
────. The Well Wrought Urn. New York: Harcourt, Brace and World, Inc., 1947.
Brosthaus, Herbert. "Struktur und Entwicklung des andere Zustands' in Robert
    Musils 'DMoE'." Deutsche Vierteljahrsschrift 39 (1965): 338–440.
Brush, S. G. B. "Mach and Atomism." Synthèse 18, 2/3 (April 1968): pp. 192–216.
Capek, Milic. "Ernst Mach's Biological Theory of Knowledge." Synthèse 18, 2/3
    (April 1968): pp. 171–191.
────. The Philosophical Impact of Contemporary Physics. New York: Van
    Nostrand, 1961.
Chabrol, Claude, ed. Sémiotique narrative et textuelle. Paris: Larousse, 1973.
Cherry, Colin. On Human Communication. Cambridge, Mass.: MIT Press, 1957–
    1966.
Chomsky, Noam. "Recent Contributions to the Theory of Innate Ideas." In The
    Philosophy of Language. Ed. J. R. Searle. Oxford: Oxford University Press,
    1971, pp. 126ff.
Clough, Wilson O. "Irony: A French Approach." Review of L'Ironie, by Wladimir
    Jankélévitch. Sewanee Review 47, No. 2 (April–June 1939): 175–183.
Cohen, Jean. Structure du langage poétique. Paris: Flammarion, 1966.
────. "Théorie de la figure." Communications 16 (1970): 3–25.

Cohen, Robert S. "Ernst Mach: Physics, Percept and the Philosophy of Science."
    Synthèse 18, No. 2/3 (April, 1968): 132–170.
Cohn, Dorrit. "Psyche and Space in Musil's 'Die Vollendung der Liebe'." Germanic
    Studies, 154–168.
Cook, Albert. "Stendhal and the Discovery of Ironic Interplay." Novel 9 (Fall 1975):
    4–54.
Crane, R. S. "The Critical Monism of Cleanth Brooks." In Critics and Criticism.
    Chicago: University of Chicago Press, 1952.
Culler, Jonathan. Structuralist Poetics: Structuralism, Linguistics and the Study of
    Literature. London: Routledge and Kegan Paul, 1975.
Deleuze, Gilles. Présentation de Sacher Masoch. Paris: Union Générale d'Editions,
    1967.
———. Nietzsche et la philosophie. Paris: P.U.F., 1973.
———. Rhizômes. Paris: Minuit, 1976.
Deleuze, Gilles, and Félix Guattari. L'Anti-Oedipe. Paris: Minuit, 1976.
Derrida, Jacques. L'Ecriture et la différence. Paris: Seuil, 1967.
Dinklage, Karl, ed. Robert Musil, Leben, Werk, Wirkung. Vienna: Auftrage des
    Landes Kärnten und der Stadt Klagenfurt, 1960.
Dinklage, Karl, et al., ed. Robert Musil; Studien zu seinem Werk. Hamburg:
    Rowohlt, 1970. Vol. I–V.
"Le Discours ironique." Proc. of a Conference on Ironic Discourse. July 23–29,
    1979. Urbino: The International Center for Research in Semiotics, to appear.
Doeblin, Alfred. "Ueber Robert Musil." In Aufsaetze zu Literatur. Olten: Walter,
    1963.
Dolezel, Lubomèir. "A Scheme of Narrative Time." In Semiotics of Art. Ed.
    Ladislav Matejka and Irwin Titunik. Cambridge, Mass.: M.I.T. Press, 1976,
    pp. 209ff.
Domic, René. "Les Inconvènients de l'ironie." In La Vie, les moeurs. Paris: Librarie
    Académique Didier, 1895.
Duwe, Wilhelm. Ausdrucksformen deutscher Dichtung, vom Naturalismus bis zur
    Gegenwart, Eine Stilgeschichte der Moderne. Berlin: E. Schmidt, 1965, pp.
    46–49.
Dyson, A. E. The Crazy Fabric. London: Macmillan, 1965.
Eco, Umberto. L'Oeuvre ouverte. Trans. C. Roux de Bezieux. Paris: Seuil, 1965.
———. La Structure absente. Trans. Uccio Esposito Torrigianis. Paris: Mercure de
    France, 1972.
———. A Theory of Semiotics. Bloomington: Indiana University Press, 1976.
Ehrmann, Jacques, ed. Structuralism. New York: Doubleday, 1970.
Empson, William. Seven Types of Ambiguity. London: Pelican, 1930.
Fachenheim, Emil. Metaphysics and History. Milwaukee: Marquette University
    Press, 1961.
Fann, K. T. Peirce's Theory of Abduction. The Hague: Nijhoff, 1970.
Finlay, Marike. "The Potential of Irony: From a Semiotics of Irony Towards an
    Epistemology of Communicational Praxis: Friedrich Schlegel and Robert
    Musil." Diss., Université de Montréal, 1981.
———. "Semiotics or History: From content analysis to contextualized discursive
    praxis." Semiotica 40, No. 3/4 (Fall/Winter 1982): 230–266.
———. "Pour une épistémologie de la communication: Au-delà de la représenta-
    tion et vers la pratique." Communication/Information, Vol. V, No. 2/3
    (Hiver/Eté 1983).
———. "Perspectives of Irony and Irony of Perspectives: A Review." The Canadian
    Journal of Research in Semiotics 5, No. 3 (Spring 1978): 3–51.
———. Powermatics: A Discursive Critique of New Communications Technology.
    London: Routledge and Kegan Paul, 1987.

————. *The Romantic Irony of Semiotics: Friedrich Schlegel and the Crisis of Representation.* Berlin: Mouton de Gruyter, 1988.

Fischer, Ernst. "Das Werk Robert Musils." *Sinn und Form* 9 (1957): 851–861.

Fontanier, Pierre. *Les Figures du discours.* Intr. Gérard Genette. Paris: Flammarion, 1977.

Foucault, Michel. *L'Archéologie du savoir.* Paris: Gallimard, 1969.

————. *Histoire de la folie.* Paris: Union Générale d'Editions, 1961.

————. *Les Mots et les choses.* Paris: Gallimard, 1966.

————. *L'Ordre du discours.* Paris: Gallimard, 1971.

Frier, Wolfgang. *Die Sprache der Emotionalitaet in den "Verwirrungen des Zoeglings Toerless" von Robert Musil: Ein Beitrag zur angewandten Textlinguistik.* Bonn: Bouvier, 1976.

Frye, Northrop. *The Anatomy of Criticism.* Princeton: Princeton University Press, 1957.

Gans, Eric. "Hyperbole et ironie." *Poétique* 24 (1975): 488–494.

Gardner, Martin. "Can Time Go Backward?" *Scientific American* 216 (January 1967): 98–108.

————. "On the Contradictions of Time Travel." *Scientific American* 230 (May 1974): 120–213.

Genette, Gérard. *Figures II.* Paris: Seuil, 1969.

————. *Figures III.* Paris: Seuil, 1972.

————. "Frontières du récit." *Communications* 8 (1966): 152–163.

————. *Mimologiques: Voyage en Cratylie.* Paris: Seuil, 1976.

————. "La Rhétorique restreinte." *Communications* 16 (1970): 158–171.

Glicksberg, Charles I. *The Ironic Vision in Modern Literature.* The Hague: Martinus Nijhoff, 1969.

Gottschnigg, Dietmar. "Die Bedeutung der Formel 'Mann ohne Eigenschaften'." In *Musil Studien.* Ed. U. Bauer. Munich: Wlm. Fink, 1973. Vol. IV.

————. *Mystische Tradition im Rome Robert Musils.* Heidelberg: Stiehm, 1974.

Graf, Gunter. *Studien zur Funktion des ersten Kapitels vom Robert Musils Roman "DMoE": Ein Beitrag zur Unwahrhaftigkeits—Typik der Gestalten.* Göppingen: Alfred Kummerle Verlag, 1969.

Greimas, Algirdas Julien. *Du Sens.* Paris: Seuil, 1970.

————. "L'Enonciation." *Signicaçao: Revista Brasileira de Semiotica* 1 (1974): 1–26.

————. *Essais de sémiotique poétique.* Paris: Larousse, 1972.

————. *Maupassant: La Sémiotique du texte.* Paris: Seuil, 1976.

————. *Sémantique structurale.* Paris: Larousse, 1966.

————. *Sémiotique et sciences sociales.* Paris: Seuil, 1976.

Habermas, Juergen. *Communication and the Evolution of Society.* Trans. Thomas McCarthy. Boston: Beacon Press, 1979.

————. *Knowledge and Human Interests.* Trans. Jeremy Shapiro. Boston: Beacon Press, 1968–71.

————. *Legitimation Crisis.* Trans. Thomas McCarthy. Boston: Beacon Press, 1973–1975.

————. "Some Distinctions in Universal Pragmatics." *Theory and Society* 3, No. 2 (Summer 1976): pp. 156–167.

————. *Theory and Practice.* Trans. John Viertel. Boston: Beacon Press, 1971–1973.

————. *Theorie des kommunikativen Handelns,* vol. I & II. Frankfurt: Suhrkamp, 1981.

Habermas, Juergen, and Niklas Luhmann. *Theorie der Gesellschaft oder Sozialtechnologie.* Frankfurt: Suhrkamp, 1971.

Haidu, Peter. *Aesthetic Distance in Chrétien de Troyes: Irony and Comedy in "Cliges" and "Perceval."* Geneva: Droz, 1968.

Hall, Stuart. "The Determinations of News Photographs," in *The Manufacture of News.* Stanley Cohen and Jock Young. London: Constable, 1973. pp. 176–190.

Hallays, André. "L'Ironie." *Revue Politique et Littéraire* 9, No. 17 (April 1898): 515–521.

Hamon, Philippe, ed. *Poétique de récit.* Paris: Seuil, 1977.

Hartzell, Richard, E. "The Three Approaches to the 'Other State' in Musil's 'MoE'." *Colloquia Germanica* 10, No. 3 (1976–1977): 204–219.

Hass, Hans-Egon and Gustav-Adolf Mohrlueder, eds. *Ironie als literarisches Phanomen.* Koln: Kiepenheuer and Witsch, 1973.

Heelan, Patrick. *Quantum Mechanics and Objectivity.* The Hague: Martinus Nijhoff, 1965.

Heintel, Erich. " 'DMoE' und die Tradition." *Wissenschaft und Weltbild* 13 (1960): 179–194.

Herrenius. *Rhetorica ad Herrenium.* Ed. and trans. Harry Caplan. Cambridge, Mass.: Harvard, 1954.

Hirsch, E. D., Jr. *The Aims of Interpretation.* Chicago: University of Chicago Press, 1976.

Hjelmslev, Louis. *Prolègomènes à une théorie du langage.* Trans. Una Canger. Paris: Minuit, 1968–1971.

Hochstaetter, Dietrich. *Sprache des Moeglichen: Stilistischer Perspektivismus in Robert Musils "MoE."* Frankfurt: Athenaeum Verlag, 1972.

Hochstaetter, Dietrich, and Helmut Arntzen. *Satirischer Stil. Zur Satire Robert Musils im Mann ohne Eigenschaften.* Bonn: H. Bouvier u. Co. Verlag, 1970.

Hoehn, Gerhart. "Une Logique de la décomposition." *Esthétique* I (1975): 97–139.

Hoffrichter, Werner. *Studien zur erlebten Rede bei Thomas Mann und Robert Musil.* Hague: Mouton and Co., 1965.

Holton, Gerald. "Mach, Einstein, and the Search for Reality." *Daedalus* 97 (Spring 1968): 636–673.

Honig, Christoph. "Die Dialektik von Ironie und Utopie und Ihre Entwicklung Robert Musils Reflexionen: Ein Beitrag zur Deutung des Romans 'DMoE'. Diss. Berlin: 1970.

Honold, Helga. "Die Funktion des Paradoxen bei Robert Musil, dargestellt am 'MoE'." Diss. Tuebingen: 1963.

Hooker, Ward. "Irony and Absurdity in the Avant-Garde Theatre." *Kenyon Review* (Summer 1960): 436–454.

Horkheimer, Max. *Critical Theory.* Trans. John O'Connell. New York: Herder and Herder, 1972.

Hutchens, Eleanor N. "The Identification of Irony." *ELH* 28 (December 1969): 352–363.

L'Ironie: Linguistique et sémiologie: Travaux du Centre de Recherches Linguistiques et Sémiologiques de L'Université de Lyon II 2 (1976).

Jaessel, Geroff. "Mathematik und Mystik in Robert Musils Roman 'DMoE': eine Untersuchung ueber das Weltbild Ulrichs." Diss. Munich: 1963.

Jakobson, Roman. *Essais de linguistique générale.* Trans. Nicholas Ruwet. Paris: Minuit, 1963.

———. "Linguistics and Communication." In *Structure of Language and Its Mathematical Aspects. Proceedings of Symposia in Applied Mathematics* 12 (1961): 247ff.

Janik, Allan, and Stephen Toulmin. *Wittgenstein's Vienna.* New York: Simon and Schuster, 1973.

Jankélévitch, Vladimir. L'Ironie. Paris: Flammarion, 1964.

Jauss, Hans-Robert. Literaturgeschichte als Provokation. Frankfurt: Suhrkamp, 1970.

―――. "Zum Problem der Granzziehung zwischen dem Laecherlichen und dem Komischen," and "Ueber den Grund des Vergnuegens am komischen Helden." In Das Komische. Ed. W. Preisendanz and R. Warning. Muenchen: 1976, pp. 36–384 and 103–132.

Jay, Martin. The Dialectical Imagination. Boston: Little, Brown, 1973.

Kaiser, Ernst. " 'DMoE', ein Problem der Wirklichkeit." Merkur 11 (1957): 669–687.

Kaiser, Ernst, and Eithne Wilkins. Robert Musil, Eine Einfuehrung in das Werk. Stuttgart: W. Kohlhammer, 1962.

Kalow, Gert. "Robert Musil." In Deutsche Literatur im 20. Jahrhundert, Strukturen und Gestalten. Ed. H. Frieckmann. Heidelberg: O. Mann, 1959. Vol. III., pp. 304–319.

Kant, Immanuel. Critique of Pure Reason. Trans. Norman Kemp Smith. London: Macmillan, 1963.

Karthaus, Ulrich. Der andere Zustand: Zeitstrukturen im Werke Robert Musils. Berlin: Eric Schmidt Verlag, 1965.

Keil, Heinrich, ed. Grammatici Latici. Leipzig: Treubner, 1875–1880, 5 vols.

Kemper, Claudette. "Irony: A New Approach with Occasional Reference to Byron and Browning." Studies in English Literature 7 (1967): 709–719.

Kierkegaard, Soren. The Concept of Irony. Trans. Lee M. Capel. London: Harper and Row, 1956.

―――. Concluding Unscientific Postscript. Trans. D. Swenson and Walter Lowrie. Princeton: Princeton University Press, 1941–1971.

―――. Either/Or. Trans. D. Swenson and L. Swenson, with revision by H. Johnson. Princeton: Princeton University Press, 1944–1971.

Kimpel, Dieter. " 'Beitraege zur geistigen Bewaeltigung der Welt . . .' Ueber den Romanbegriff Robert Musils." In Deutsche Roman-theorie, Beitraege zu einer historischen Poetik des Romans in Deutschland. Ed. Reinhold Grimm. Frankfurt: Grimm, 1968, pp. 371–396.

Kortian, Garbis. Métacritique. Paris: Minuit, 1979.

Krieger, Murray. "An Apology for Poetics." In Ira Konigsberg, ed. American Criticism in the Poststructuralist Age. Ed. Ira Konigsberg. Ann Arbor: University of Michigan Press, 1981, pp, 87–101.

Kristeva, Julia. Polylogue. Paris: Seuil, 1977.

―――. Semiotike: Recherches pour une sémanalyse. Paris: Seuil, 1969.

Krysinski, Wladimir. "Isotopie et dislocation des codes dans 'Six personnages en quête d'auteur,' de Luigi Pirandello." Proc. of the First Congress of the International Association of Semiotics. Milan: 1974.

―――. "Musil vs. Scarron ou l'indétermination du romanesque." Canadian Journal of Research in Semiotics. No. 1, 1981.

Kuehn, Dieter. Analogie und Variation: Zur Analyse von Robert Musils Roman "DMoE." Bonn: B. v. Wiese, 1965.

Kuehne, Joerg. Das Gleichnis; Studien zur inneren Form von Robert Musils Roman, "DMoE." Tuebingen: Niemeyer, 1968.

Lacan, Jacques. Ecrits. Paris: Seuil, 1966.

Lalande, André. Vocabulaire technique et critique de la philosophie. Paris: P.U.F., 1926–1976.

Lange, Victor. "Musils 'Das Fliegenpapier'." Colloquia Germanica 10, No. 3 (1976–77): 193–203.

Lausberg, Heinrich. Elemente der Literarischen Rhetorik. Munich: Hueber, 1963.

Lukàcs, George. The Theory of the Novel: A Historico-Philosophical Essay on the

Forms of Great Epic Literature. Trans. Anna Bostock. Cambridge, Mass.: MIT Press, 1971–1975.

Lyotard, Jean-François. *Dérivé à partir de Marx et de Freud.* Paris: Union Générale d'Editions, 1973.

———. *Des Dispositifs pulsionnels.* Paris: Union Générale d'Editions, 1973.

Mach, Ernst. *The Structure of Mechanics.* Trans. T. J. McCormack, Lasalle, Ill.: Open Court, 1945, 5th ed.

Marin, Louis. *La Critique du discours: sur la "Logique de 'Port-Royal' et les Pensées" de Pascal.* Paris: Minuit, 1975.

———. *Le récit est un piège.* Paris: Minuit, 1978.

———. *Utopiques: Jeux d'espaces.* Paris: Minuit, 1978.

Metz, Christian. "La grande syntagmatique du film narratif." *Communications* 8 (1966): 122–123.

Michel, Karl Markus. "Die Utopie der Sprache." *Akzente* 1 (1954).

Monod, Jacques. *Chance and Necessity.* Trans. Austin Wainhous. New York: Vintage, 1972.

Morris, Charles. "Foundations of the Theory of Signs." In *Foundations of the Unity of Science Encyclopaedia* 1, no. 2 Chicago: University of Chicago Press, 1938.

Muecke, D. C. *The Compass of Irony.* London: Methuen, 1969.

———. *Irony: The Critical Idiom.* Fakenham: Methuen and Co., Ltd., 1970.

Mueller, Goetz. *Ideologie Kritik und Metasprache.* Munich: Wlm. Fink Verlag, 1972.

Mueller, Guenther, "Erzaehlzeit und erzaehlte Zeit." *Morphologische Poetik.* Tubingen: 1948–1968.

Murillo, Louis Andrew. *The Cyclical Night: Irony in James Joyce and Jorge Luis Borges.* Cambridge, Mass.: Harvard University Press, 1968.

Musil, Robert. *Gesammelte Werke.* Ed. Adolf Frisé. Hamburg: Rowohlt, 1978. Vols. I and II.

———. *Der Mann ohne Eigenschaften.* Hamburg: Rowohlt, 1957.

———. *Prosa, Dramen, Spaete Briefe.* Ed. Adolf Frisé. Hamburg: Rowohlt, 1952.

———. "Tagebuecher, Aphorismen, Essays und Reden." In *Gesammelte Werke,* vol. II. Ed. Adolf Frisé. Hamburg: Rowohlt, 1955.

———. "Beitrag zur Beurteilung der lehren Machs." Diss. Berlin: 1908.

———. *The Man without Qualities.* Trans. Eithne Wilkins and Ernst Kaiser. London: Secker and Warburg, 1953–60.

———. *Young Toerless.* Trans. Eithne Wilkins and Ernst Kaiser. New York: Pantheon, 1955.

———. *L'Homme sans qualités.* Trans. Philippe Jaccottet. Paris: Seuil, 1957, 4 vols.

Nelson, Robert J. *Play within a Play.* New Haven: Yale University Press, 1958.

Neveux, Jean, B. "Robert Musil Jugendstil et Sezession." *Etudes Germaniques* 4 (1968): 582–599.

Nietzsche, F. W. *Gesammelte Werke.* Leipzig: C. G. Neumann, 1900–1915, 19 vols.

Nuesser, Peter. *Musils Romantheorie.* The Hague: Mouton, 1967.

Ogden, Charles, and I. A. Richards. *The Meaning of Meaning.* New York: Harcourt Brace Inc., 1927.

Olshewsky, Thomas, ed. *Problems in the Philosophy of Language.* New York: Holt, Rinehart and Winston, Inc., 1969.

Ortega Y Gasset, José. *The Dehumanization of Art, and Other Essays on Art, Culture and Literature.* Trans. Helene Weyl. Princeton: Princeton University Press, 1948–1968.

———. *Meditations on Quixote.* Trans. Evelyn Rugg and Diego Marin. New York: W. W. Norton and Co., Inc., 1961–1963.

Palante, Georges. "L'Ironie: Étude psychologique." *Revue Philosophique* 41 (Feb. 1906): 147–163.

Paulhan, François. *La Morale de l'ironie*. Paris: Librairie Félix Alcan, 1925.

Paz, Octavio. *Children of the Mire: Modern Poetry from Romanticism to the Avant-Garde*. Trans. Rachel Phillips. Cambridge, Mass.: Harvard University Press, 1974.

Peirce, Charles S. *Selected Writings: Values in a Universe of Chance*. Ed. Philip P. Wiener. New York: Dover, 1958.

——. *Collected Papers of C. S. Peirce*. Ed. Charles Hartshorne and Paul Weiss, (vols. 7 and 8 ed. Arthur Burks). Cambridge, Mass.: Harvard University Press, 1931–58.

——. *The Philosophy of Peirce: Selected Writings*. Ed. Justus Buchler. London: Routledge and Kegan Paul, 1940.

Pelc̀, Jerzy. "On the Concept of Narration." *Semiotica* 1 (1971).

Peters, Friederich G. *Robert Musil: Master of the Hovering Life*. New York: Columbia University Press, 1978.

Piaget, Jean. *Epistémologie des sciences de l'homme*. Paris: Gallimard, 1970.

Pike, Burton. *Robert Musil: An Introduction to his Work*. New York: Cornell University Press, 1969.

Pirandello, Luigi. *Choix d'essais*. Ed. and trans. Georges Piroué. Paris: Denoel, 1960–1968.

Poétique: "Ironie," 36, (novembre 1978).

Poggioli, Renato. *The Theory of the Avant-Garde*. Trans. Gerald Fitzgerald. New York: Harper and Row, 1968–1971.

Price, W. C. and Seymour S. Chessick, eds. *The Uncertainty Principle and Foundations of Quantum Mechanics: A Fifty Year Survey*. New York: Wiley, 1977.

Rasch, Wolfdieter. *Ueber Musils Roman "DMoE."* Goettingen: Vandenhoeck u. Ruprecht, 1967.

——. "Zur Entstehung von Robert Musils Roman 'DMoE'." *Deutsche Vierteljahrsschrift* 39 (1965): 350–387.

Rastier, François. *Essais de sémiotique discursive*. Tours: Mame, 1974.

Reichenbach, Hans. *The Direction of Time*. Los Angeles: University of California Press, 1956.

——. *The Rise of Scientific Philosophy*. Berkeley: University of California Press, 1962.

Reiss, Timothy J. "Archéologie du discours et critique épistémique: Project pour une critique discursive." In *Philosophie et Littérature*. Ed. Pierre Gravel. Montréal: Bellarmin, 1979, pp. 143–189.

——. "Cartesian Discourse and Classical Ideology." *Diacritics* (Winter 1976): 19–27.

——. "The Environment of Literature and the Imperatives of Criticism." Manuscript.

——. "Peirce, Frege, la vérité, le tiers inclus et le champ pratiqué," *Langages* (1980): 103–127.

——. "Semiology and its Discontents: Saussure and Greimas." *The Canadian Journal of Research in Semiotics* 5, No. 1 (Fall 1977): 65–102.

——. "The Word/World Equation." *Yale French Studies* No. 49 (1973): 1ff.

Ricoeur, Paul. *La Métaphore vive*. Paris: Seuil, 1975.

Rismondo, Piero. "Chiffrirschluessel fuer Musil." *Wort und Wahrheit* I (1956): 292–294.

Robbe-Grillet, Alain. *Pour un nouveau roman*. Paris: Minuit, 1963.

Root, John J. "Stylistic Irony in Thomas Mann." *The Germanic Review* 35, No. 2 (April 1960): 93–103.

Roth, Marie-Louise. *Robert Musil, les oeuvres pré-posthumes*. Paris: Recherches, 1980. 2 vols.

Salm, Peter, "Faust and Irony." *The Germanic Review* 40, No. 3 (May 1965): 192–204.

Sarraute, Nathalie. *L'Ere du soupçon*. Paris: Gallimard, 1956.

de Saussure, Ferdinand. *Cours de linguistique générale*. Ed. T. de Mauro. Paris: Payot, 1975.

Savan, David. "An Introduction to C. S. Peirce's Semiotics." Toronto: The Toronto Semiotic Circle, 1976.

Schaerer, René. "Le Mécanisme de l'ironie dans ses rapports avec la dialectique." *Revue de Métaphysique et de Morale* 48 (1941): 181–209.

Schlegel, Friedrich, *Kritische Ausgabe*. Ed. Hans Eichner, Ernst Behler, and Jean-Jacques Anstett. Munich: F. Schoeninhg, 1958– , 18 vols.

———. *Literary Notebooks*. Ed. Hans Eichner. Toronto: University of Toronto Press, 1957.

———. *"Lucinde" and the "Fragments."* Trans. and intr. Peter Firchow. Minneapolis: University of Minnesota Press, 1971.

Schoene, Albrecht. "Zum Gebrauch des Konjunktivs bei Robert Musil." In *Deutsche Romane von Grimmelshausen bis Musil*. Ed. Jost Schillemeit. Frankfurt: Fischer Taschenbuch Verlag, 1966–74, pp. 290–318.

Scholes, Robert. *Structuralism in Literature: An Introduction*. New Haven: Yale University Press, 1974.

Schorske, Carl E. *Fin-de-siècle Vienna*. New York: Vintage Books, 1981.

Schramm, Ulf. *Fiktion und Reflexion; Ueberlegungen zu Musil und Becket*. Frankfurt: Suhrkamp, 1967.

Sedgewick, G. G. *Of Irony, Especially in Drama*. Toronto: Macmillan, 1948.

Seidler, Inge. "Das Nietzschebild Robert Musils." *Deutsche Vierteljahrsschrift* 39 (1965): 329–349.

Sera, Manfred. *Utopie und Parodie bei Musil, Broch, und Thomas Mann*. Bonn: Bouvier Verlag, 1969.

Serres, Michel. "Exact and Human." *Substance* 12 (1978): 10–19.

Shklovsky, Victor. "Sterne's 'Tristram Shandy': Stylistic Commentary." In *Russian Formalist Criticism: Four Essays*. Ed., trans. and intr. L. T. Lemon and M. J. Reis. Lincoln: University of Nebraska Press, 1965, pp. 25–60.

Silone, Ignazio. "Robert Musil und sein Werk fuer die Dichtung unsere Zeit." *Universitas* 7 (1965): 699–706.

Skeat, W. *Etymological Dictionary*. New York: Capricorn Books, 1973.

Sokel, Walter, H. "Robert Musils Narrenspiegel." *Neue deutsche Hefte* 7 (1960–61): 199–214.

Steger, Hugo. "Literatursprache und Wirklichkeit, Robert Musils Roman 'DMoE'." In *Zwischen Sprache und Literatur, drei Reden*. Goettingen: Grimm, 1967, vol. 9, pp. 70–108.

Stern, J. P. "Karl Kraus' Vision of Language." In *Modern Language Review* (January 1966): 73–74.

Strelka, Joseph. "Robert Musil, der Utopist eines anderen Lebens." In *Kafka, Musil, Broch und die Entwicklung des modernen Romans*. Vienna: Rowohlt, 1959, pp. 36–64.

Suleiman, Susan. "Interpreting Ironies." Review of *A Rhetoric of Irony*, by Wayne C. Booth. *Diacritics* (Summer 1976): 15–21.

Thoeming, Jürgen. *Robert Musil—Bibliographie*. Hamburg: Rowohlt, 1968.

Thompson, Alan R. *The Dry Mock: A Study of Irony in Drama*. Berkeley: University of California Press, 1948.

Todorov, Tzvetan, ed. and trans. *Théorie de la littérature: Textes des formalistes russes*. Paris: Seuil, 1965.

Tomashevsky, Boris. "Russian 'Thematics'." In *Russian Formalist Criticism: Four Essays*. Ed., trans. and intr. L. T. Lemon and M. J. Reis. Lincoln: University of Nebraska Press, 1965, pp. 61–95.

Trommler, Frank. *Roman und Wirklichkeit, Eine Ortsbestimmung am Beispiel vom Musil, Broch, Roth, Doderer und Gütersloh*. Stuttgart: Kohlhammer, 1966.

Wahl, Jean. *Etudes Kierkegaardiennes*. Paris: Librairie Philosophique J. Vrin, 1967.

Weinrich, Harald. *Linguistik der Luege (kann Sprache die Gedanken verbergen?)* Heidelberg: L. Schneider, 1966.

Wienbruch, Ulrich. "Das Universelle Experiment." Diss. Köln: 1964.

Wiener, P. and F. Young, eds. *Studies in the Philosophy of Charles Sanders Peirce*. Cambridge, Mass.: Harvard University Press, 1952.

Wilde, Alan. "Desire and Consciousness: The 'Anironic' Forster." *Novel* 14 (Winter 1976): 114–129.

Wittgenstein, Ludwig. *Philosophical Investigations*. Trans. G. E. M. Anscombe. Oxford: Blackwell, 1958–1974.

———. *Tractatus logico-philosophicus*. Frankfurt: Suhrkamp, 1921–1964.

Zumthor, Paul. *Langue, texte, énigme*. Paris: Seuil, 1975.

———. *Essai de poétique médiévale*. Paris: Seuil, 1972.

INDEX

MARIKE FINLAY is Director of the Comparative Literature program and Professor of English at McGill University. She is author of *Powermatics: A Discursive Critique of New Communications Technology* and *The Romantic Irony of Semiotics: Friedrich Schlegel and the Crisis of Representation.*